Disclaimer

This book is self-published by the author and is neither authorized nor endorsed by the Academy of Motion Picture Arts and Sciences®. Oscar® is a registered trademark of the Academy Awards.

All material in this book is provided for educational and informational purposes. All intellectual property that has not been credited in this book has believed to be in public domain. If your copyrighted material appears in this book and you do not agree with our assessment that it constitutes "fair use", please contact the author.

Although the author have made every effort to ensure that the information in this book was correct at press time and while this publication is designed to provide accurate information in regard to the subject matter covered, the author assumes no responsibility for errors, inaccuracies, omissions, or any other inconsistencies herein and hereby disclaim any liability to any party for any loss, damage, or disruption caused by errors or omissions, whether such errors or omissions result from negligence, accident, or any other cause.

Copyright © 2024 by Aygul Karlieva.
ISBN: [9798882992513]

All rights reserved. No portion of this book may be reproduced in any form without written permission from the author.

Author

Aya Karlieva is a Turkmen-British media producer and writer focused on exploring female-driven stories. After graduating from Emerson College in Boston with a Bachelor of Arts in Media, she worked as a development and production assistant for film companies in Hollywood. In addition, she has written blogs, hosted interviews and produced video series focused on the success stories of women in film, music, science, politics, technology and sports. Aya loves to research and bring to the forefront of public attention the notable accomplishments of women in all spheres of life.

Introduction

To inspire and motivate ourselves to do better for women and to do better as women, we can look back on the past that will, without a doubt, remind us of how talented, determined, resilient and downright influential women have always been in history, especially the history of film and TV. The past is full of positive changes championed by women — and so is the future.

When we progress through this book and come to understand the special stories of each actress, we will see that without hardships, failures and setbacks they would not have reached the level of fame and fortune they possess. Through the countless obstructions of seemingly limitless rejections, sexual harassment, life-threatening health problems, blacklisting, public humiliations, lower wages compared to their male counterparts, years of unemployment and public scrutiny to name a few that many of these women have gone through, we notice that the one thing that kept these women relentless at doing this job called acting was not necessity. It wasn't as if they had no other job or career path they could easily pursue, but it is that their passion lies in acting. It is their livelihood — they must act and nothing else. It is their purpose.

Despite the countless setbacks, we can also take note that some of these Oscar winners had to self-start the films they won for: Ellen Burstyn and Jessica Chastain, for example. They put on their own producer hats and self-started their films. It is not an easy thing to accomplish as a woman but it certainly put them as women in a position of power and leadership.

The mission of Oscar: Best Actress is not to focus on only the bad or only the good distinctions and accomplishments of these women but to examine what makes them so spectacular and what made them qualified to win Oscars.

Since the very first Academy Awards in 1929, the Best Actress award has been given to 79 different actresses, as of 2023. Within that list of 79, only two actresses are a woman of colour — and that is Halle Berry and Michelle Yeoh. This probability is shocking. The statistic looks slightly better for the Best Supporting Actress award, however, where out of 84 actresses who have received this Oscar, twelve women of colour have won so far. There is an obivous diversity problem at the Oscars, which reflects the film industry as a whole.

The film industry is by nature a business and it has profited off of gender inequality since the beginning of motion picture history. The number of women working in the film industry are growing and there are also more women taking leadership roles in production. It seems that gender bias is changing and the toxic male population is not profiting off of women's labour and misrepresentation as effectively as it did before. The more women work in film (especially in not so typical feminine positions like wardrobe, hair and makeup) and voice their ideas, the better quality and more diverse characters we will see on screen. Gender inequality is a system of oppression that is slowly changing.

Let's dive into the fascinating world of women in film!

Table of Contents

Janet Gaynor	8	Joanne Woodward	174
Mary Pickford	16	Susan Hayward	182
Norma Shearer	24	Simone Signoret	188
Marie Dressler	32	Elizabeth Taylor	196
Helen Hayes	38	Sophia Loren	204
Katharine Hepburn	44	Anne Bancroft	212
Claudette Colbert	52	Patricia Neal	220
Bette Davis	60	Julie Andrews	226
Luise Rainer	66	Julie Christie	232
Vivien Leigh	72	Barbra Streisand	238
Ginger Rogers	80	Maggie Smith	246
Joan Fontaine	86	Glenda Jackson	252
Greer Garson	92	Jane Fonda	258
Jennifer Jones	98	Liza Minnelli	266
Ingrid Bergman	104	Ellen Burstyn	272
Joan Crawford	112	Louise Fletcher	280
Olivia De Havilland	120	Faye Dunaway	288
Loretta Young	128	Diane Keaton	296
Jane Wyman	136	Sally Field	302
Judy Holliday	142	Sissy Spacek	308
Shirley Booth	148	Meryl Streep	316
Audrey Hepburn	154	Shirley MacLaine	324
Grace Kelly	162	Geraldine Page	332
Anna Magnani	168	Marlee Matlin	338

Cher	344
Jodie Foster	350
Jessica Tandy	358
Kathy Bates	364
Emma Thompson	370
Holly Hunter	378
Jessica Lange	384
Susan Sarandon	392
Frances McDormand	398
Helen Hunt	404
Gwyneth Paltrow	410
Hilary Swank	416
Julia Roberts	422
Halle Berry	430
Nicole Kidman	438
Charlize Theron	446
Reese Witherspoon	452
Helen Mirren	458
Marion Cotillard	464
Kate Winslet	470
Sandra Bullock	476
Natalie Portman	482
Jennifer Lawrence	490
Cate Blanchett	496
Julianne Moore	502
Brie Larson	508
Emma Stone	514
Olivia Colman	520
Renee Zellweger	526
Jessica Chastain	532
Michelle Yeoh	538

Janet Gaynor

Janet Gaynor was the first actress to ever win the Academy Award for Best Actress, and the circumstances were pretty interesting. In the early days of the Oscar ceremonies, actors and actresses would receive an Oscar for more than one film. Gaynor actually won for Street Angel (1928), 7th Heaven (1927), and Sunrise: A Song of Two Humans (1927). These first few Academy Awards were still figuring out how to organize the ceremony and three years later, the Academy prohibited the practice of awarding an acting Oscar for more than one performance at one ceremony. The 1920's in America were a revolutionary time for women. They could finally vote. Women could smoke, drink, wear shorter dresses and cut their hair short. The sense of freedom garnered from this change gave women the opportunity to lead the life they wanted.

1920's Hollywood was booming with young starlets like Ginger Rogers, Joan Crawford and Loretta Young, all of whom we will explore later on in the book. And one of these starlets had been a four-foot-nine Janet Gaynor, originally from a neighbourhood just outside of Philadelphia. After doing various film work in Hollywood as an extra, Janet rose to prominence quickly.

Hollywood became the fifth largest industry in the US by 1926 and Janet had landed her first leading role in Johnstown Flood that same year. It was obviously a silent film, as talking films were not yet being made. Janet was catapulted into stardom and within a few years had the honour of becoming the first female Oscar winner for the Best Actress Category. As Janet was known for her plain and unassuming sense of style, even her dress to the Oscars ceremony was plain. Yet she gave deep and powerful performances that led her to become, at one point, the highest paid actress under Fox's contract.

"I don't mind playing naive girls, but I will not play dumb

Janet Gaynor

For the sake of this book, we'll be focusing mainly on Street Angel. This silent film stars Gaynor as Angela, a young woman who starts turning tricks in order to pay for her sick mother's medications. When prostitution doesn't earn her enough money, she starts trying to steal instead. Eventually, she's caught and is sent to jail, but manages to escape ... only to find that her mother has died. The rest of the movie is tragedy after tragedy as Angela tries to hook up with the circus while on the run from the law. A romance strikes up between her and a painter named Gino (Charles Farrell), but her past is always following her.

It's a little odd to watch a film like this and try to gauge the acting abilities of its stars. These early silent films utilise a much more theatrical approach to acting, so Gaynor's performance

here is tough to compare with, say, a later Best Actress performance from Meryl Streep. Still, the film is an effective tear-jerker, and it works largely because of the charm emanating from Gaynor.

For a long time, Gaynor was the youngest woman to win a Best Actress award. She won the Oscar at age 22. She was dethroned as the youngest in 1987 when Marlee Matlin won for Children of a Lesser God at age 21. Then, in 2013, Jennifer Lawrence won for Silver Linings Playbook at age 22, making Gaynor the third youngest actress to win the award.

Interestingly enough, there's another strange duplication when it comes to the film and the Academy Award. Not only did Janet Gaynor win multiple Best Actress Awards, but Street Angel also has the distinction of being one of the only films to be nominated for an Academy Award two years in a row. While Gaynor's award and nomination for acting was in 1929, Street Angel ended up earning other nominations in 1930 for Best Art Direction and Cinematography.

The circumstances around this first Academy Awards were a bit strange. As mentioned, the categories weren't totally worked out, nor were the rules for nominations, hence why Gaynor was about to win for three different films in the first place. By the next year, many of the categories that appeared at the first ceremony were eliminated. This first awards show had twelve categories, and by the next year, they was narrowed down to seven. Some of the edits to the categories included the removal of the "Best Unique and Artistic Picture Award" and "Best Engineering Effects".

Gaynor herself said that, while she was excited to win the Academy Award that year, it didn't feel as prestigious as later Academy Awards. She commented that "being the first year, the Academy Awards had no background or tradition ... had I known what it would come to mean in the next few years, I'm sure I'd have been overwhelmed." She commented that at the ceremony, she was more excited to meet Douglas Fairbanks than she was to actually win the award.

When silent films became a thing of the past and "talkies" became revolutionary in film production, Janet found even more fame. Her fans finally could hear her voice. After her Oscar win, Janet went on to star in over 20 feature films throughout the 1930's. Though Street Angel was originally made as a silent film, it actually has the distinction of being the first "talkie" to be shown in New Zealand. The movie didn't actually have any dialogue for this release, but it did have a recorded music score added, which qualified it as a "talkie".

Janet Gaynor

Janet Gaynor

Gaynor did eventually get another Best Actress nomination in 1938. She starred in the first screen version of A Star Is Born, which was critically acclaimed and would go on to be remade three more times. This is one of twelve films that feature both Janet Gaynor and Charles Farrell. 7th Heaven is one that features the two of them. Both movies feature a scene where Gaynor's character is wrapping Farrell's character's coat around her. Gaynor and Farrell were actually known for being "America's favourite love birds".

After A Star Is Born reached so much acclaim, Gaynor would go on to star in one more film, a screwball comedy called The Young in Heart. After that film was released, she made the choice to retire, even though she was still considered to be one of the industry heavyweights. She went on to start a family with Adrian Greenberg (usually referred to only as Adrian).

Janet said this about her retirement from the big screen: "Making movies was really all I knew of life. I just wanted to have time to know other things. Most of all I wanted to fall in love. I wanted to get married. I wanted a child. And I knew that in order to have these things one had to make time for them. So I simply stopped making movies. Then as if by a miracle, everything I really wanted happened."
In 1957, Janet left retirement and returned to the big screen for her final bow in Bernadine.

Mary Pickford

The Second Academy Awards' Best Actress Academy Award went to Mary Pickford for her performance in the film Coquette. The film was actually Pickford's first ever "talkie" and was an interesting point in her career since she was considered one of the biggest stars of silent film. By this point in her career, she had her own production company, and was one of the producers of Coquette. She produced the film along with Sam Taylor, who also directed it. In addition to this, Mary was also instrumental in cementing Hollywood as a hub of innovation and artistry. She was one of the founding members of United Artists, part of the 36 founding members of the Academy Awards and a supporter of the first motion picture archive in the US located at the Museum Of Modern Art in LA. Mary's career began in Toronto as a theatre actress when she was seven years old. She was business-savvy and money-oriented from an early age. In 1909, at the age of 17, D. W. Griffith screen tested Pickford for the Biograph Company. She instantly caught his eye. She went on to star in 51 films by the end of 1909. Not to mention that she insisted on getting paid $10 a day compared to other Biograph actors who got paid $5.

From 1909 onwards, her rise to fame was quick. She was known to cinema goers as the "Girl with the Golden Locks". She firstly established herself as a silent film superstar. Then, after departing Biograph, Pickford collaborated with Adolph Zukor of Paramount Pictures. Not only did they form a contract where she would be paid $10,000 a week but Pickford would have full producing authority of the films she starred in.

"You may have a fresh start any moment you choose, for this thing that we call 'failure' is not the falling down, but the staying down."

In 1930 Pickford won the Oscar for the performance of a lifetime in her first ever "talkie" called Coquette. Coquette must have been a revolutionary film for Pickford and her fans, because not only was Pickford heard for the first time on film but her transition from being typecast as a waif, babydoll, Lolita-type character to a more womanly and sophisticated character happened in this film. She cut her famous curls into a flapper bob and trained her voice to be more stern. It was a major box office success. Pickford said this of the film: "I was forced to live far beyond my years when just a child, now I have reversed the order and I intend to remain young indefinitely."

Coquette is about a Southern gal, Norma, who loves to flirt. She has plenty of adoring men who fawn over her, and her father, a doctor, wants to marry her off to Stanley Wentworth due to his high social standing. Norma, however, falls in love with Michael, played by Johnny Mack Brown. The film is based on the successful stage play of the same name, which had opened in 1927 with Helen Hayes as the starring role.

Admittedly, this is one of the few films from the Academy Awards that really does not hold up. Usually, even the more dated movies that pop up in the Best Actress categories are at least worth watching for historical context or for the performances, but Coquette is a bit lacklustre. It's clunky and clearly suffers from technical limitations caused by inexperience with sound film. The Rotten Tomatoes for the film is pretty low, with a 44% critical score and a 24% audience score. One review calls it a "terrible,

overwrought early talkie" and one critic notes that the actors overact. Contemporary reviews of the film were a bit kinder, but even then, response was still mixed.

However, it can't be argued that Pickford didn't work quite hard for her nomination. In the beginning, a film could only qualify for an Academy Award if it reached a certain amount of commercial success, and Pickford made sure that Coquette qualified. She put together a contest to win the orchid dress she wears in the film for publicity. It definitely worked, too, because the film would end up being one of Pickford's biggest commercial successes.

Notably, Pickford was one of the first actors to ever campaign for her Oscar. That's a fairly common practice now, but it was unheard of at the time. The Academy Awards weren't quite as prestigious as they are today—which Janet Gaynor pointed out when she reflected on her win at the very first Academy Awards—so Pickford's campaigning was unprecedented. She went so far as to invite the Central Board of Judges for tea at the Pickfair mansion, where she lived with Fairbanks.

Mary Pickford was an accomplished actress, of course, and an icon in her own right. She was known as "America's Sweetheart" during the silent film era and was listed as the 24th greatest female stars of classic Hollywood in a 1999 list from the American Film Institute (AFI). This particular Oscar win was controversial, though, as many didn't feel that Pickford actually deserved it.

For context, Pickford had already garnered clout in the world of Hollywood. She founded United Artists with Charlie Chalin, D.W. Griffith, and Douglas Fairbanks (who was also her husband at the time). On top of that, she was a founding member of the Academy of Motion Picture Arts and Sciences, the organisation that oversees the Academy Awards. Because of her various connections, many felt that she won because of favouritism. Turner Classic Movies' article on the film quotes an newspaper column about the win, sharply writing that "the Academy is handing out its cups on a political or social basis."

To be fair, though, while Pickford's performance in Coquette truly does not feel like an Academy Award winning performance, her win could be seen as a sort of industry acknowledgement. She had starred in hundreds of films—she had been in over 150 short films by 1916—so she certainly deserved some type of Hollywood award. Seeing as how the Academy Awards didn't exist for most of her career, many now view Pickford's Oscar as more of a career-achievement as opposed to an award specifically for her performance as Norma.

By the time Coquette came out to the public and Mary was awarded an Oscar at the age of 38, her fame already hit an all-time high and this achievement was not celebrated as much as it should be by her fans, who had already started to obsess over new emerging actresses in the "talkies". It seemed that nobody wanted to see the modern, ladylike and serious Pickford but rather wanted the iconic, curly haired, clumsy ingénue the world cherished so much but one that Pickford kept trying to escape from well into her 30s. Pickford would retire from acting in 1933, just a few years after her Best Actress win. Her final film appearance was Frank Borzage's Secrets.

After the win, Pickford's personal and work life slowly began to deteriorate. She and Fairbanks divorced, she remarried and her popularity waned among the cinema goers. Pickford did, however, win an honorary award at the Academy Awards in 1976. She was recognized for "her unique contributions to the film industry and the development of film as an

Mary Pickford

artistic medium." Mary Pickford was not present at the awards ceremony. The presentation was made at her Pickfair estate and taped for inclusion in the broadcast.

Pickford's journey from being a moneyless, fatherless eldest child from Toronto, Canada, to becoming a major motion picture star and businesswoman is inspiring. The duality of Pickford representing a naive yet playful little girl character throughout her on screen career and representing an assertive and fierce woman behind the screen is telling of her multidimensional and talented persona.

Her troubled childhood pushed her to become the primary breadwinner in her family and ultimately made her one of the first women in Hollywood who sat at the executives table to make big decisions in film production. I think Pickford's influence behind the scenes of filmmaking is just as prominent as her acting. She truly paved the way for all women in film.

Norma Shearer

As silent films slowly went out of fashion upon the emergence of sound films, aka "talkies", new talent subsequently emerged. In the 1930's Hollywood did a total revamp to service the production of sound films. Now a new, fresh and modern set of requirements were needed for somebody to become a Hollywood star. And so, the beginning of 1930's cinema introduced a different type of female protagonist. Complicated, dynamic and individualistic women, with a feminist leaning agenda, were sure to keep everyone in the cinema on the edge of their seat.

Everybody loved Norma Shearer on the big screen as she was one of the first actresses to bring the femme fatale type character into fashion. And she was the third ever winner of the Oscar for Best Actress in 1931.

However, not everybody loved her off screen. The theme of nepotism and her lack of physical attractiveness (according to Hollywood execs) was ever present in her life. Her slightly cross-eyed bright blue eyes and strong legs were criticised by many. Nevertheless, she persisted for many years to secure a contract with the big companies.

"An actress must never lose her ego - without it she has no talent."

It was a long and difficult road for Norma to get her foot in the door. The native Canadian moved to New York City and first tried her hand on Broadway and modelling. But film was her calling and she eventually starred in a 1921 B movie called The Stealers. This earned her a contract offer from Louis B Mayer and Irving Thalberg of MGM. By 1925 Shearer's career had skyrocketed and she was getting first billing. That same year Shearer, then 23, and Irving Thalberg, the vice president of MGM, started their highly-criticized relationship. Two years later they married.

Not only was Shearer now married to a Hollywood heavyweight, but her brother, Douglas Shearer, was already the top sound designer and recording director not only at MGM but in all of Hollywood. In fact, he won seven Oscars in the span of his career. So, Norma had a one-up over other actresses once sound films began to be produced. However, she had to prove to everyone that she was capable of a transition from silent to sound.

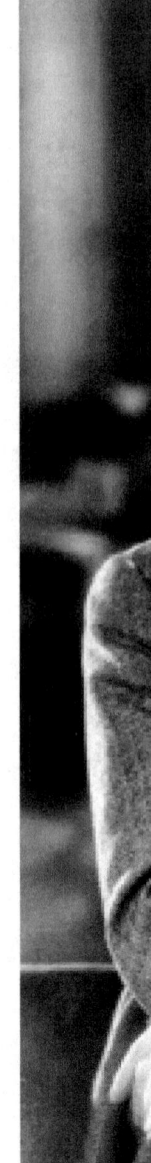

Norma Shearer

By the time The Divorcee came out in 1930, Shearer was a highly praised and imitated actress. Other actresses who competed for the Oscar that year voiced their agitation with Shearer being the wife of an MGM boss. Sherer said, "It is impossible to get anything major accomplished without stepping on some toes. Enemies are inevitable when one is a doer."

The Divorcee goes as so: socialites Jerry (Shearer) and Ted (Chester Morris) get married. After a few years of being married, the couple is visited by a group of socialite friends who bring along a woman named Janice, a catty and pushy woman. When Jerry catches Ted and Janice romantically embracing in the kitchen during the get-together, she grows distant and cold. Yet Ted tries to brush off his past affair with Janice. When the two part ways bitterly, Jerry, now a bachelorette, goes on a string of dates with a variety of affluent men. Yet after some time, she realises she cannot get Ted out of her head. He truly is her one and only love. When the two run into each other at a New Year's party, they reconnect and give each other another chance, realizing that they still love each other.

The timeless glamour of the 1930s which drapes Shearer throughout the movie frames her in her prime years as a movie star. Her rather natural acting for that time is quite refreshing and therefore has stood the test of time after over 90 years since the film came out. Her range of emotions proves her versatility on screen, and her promotion of how diverse a woman can be emotionally and experimentally was ahead of its time. In The Divorcee, when Ted finds out that Jerry actually has cheated on him too, his reaction is aggressive and far more distraught than hers was, yet when Jerry finds out about his affair, even though they are now on the same playing field, it shows how differently men and women react to the same wrongdoing they both make. The Divorcee simply gave a new perspective on gender roles and gave a very realistic account of how a woman is demonised for any bad decision and action, yet a man can get away with exactly the same bad behaviour.

Norma Shearer

Norma Shearer

Although Shearer wanted to play more liberated and complex characters. The Production Code at the time, also known as the Hays Code, forced her to resort to playing more classic and delicate female characters. Nevertheless, she continued her success as a leading lady in films like Romeo and Juliet in

1936, Marie Antoinette in 1938, and The Women in 1939 which was an all-female cast which co-starred Shearer's biggest acting opponent, Joan Crawford. Shearer was even considered to play Scarlett O'Hara in Gone With The Wind.

Norma Shearer was the first person to ever receive five Academy Award nominations as well as being the only sister-brother duo with her brother Douglas to win Oscars. Norma Shearer stands as one of the first leading ladies in Hollywood who pioneered female characters to be more provocative and liberated on film.

Marie Dressler

Marie Dressler's acting career spanned from her early teens until her death. The story of her rise to international success as unconventional, to say the least,. Dressler's ability to capitalise on her comedic talent early on made her stand out. When she moved to Hollywood, her comedic ability and distinct look stood out even more among the glamorous and youthful actresses. Dressler's collaborations with other Hollywood personalities like Charlie Chaplin, Mary Pickford, Greta Garbo, Jean Harlow and, of course, her frequent co-star Wallace Beery solidified her as an essential individual in filmmaking, particularly comedy films.

At the age of 14, the native Canadian who moved to the US with her family, started her career, hopping from different stock companies, to vaudeville, then to part of a chorus line before finally securing a role on Broadway in 1892 at the age of 24. Dressler's moment of fame came in 1896 when she was featured in a musical comedy Ladey Slavey. Dressler's first love was theatre before film, and she loved entertaining any audience with her big, broad slapstick humour and great singing voice. That was exactly the formula Hollywood was looking for in the early 1900s.

"It is not how old you are, but how you are old."

When Tillie's Nightmare, another major Broadway stage production, was first performed in 1910, it served as an unpredictable stepping stone for Dressler to enter Hollywood. Four years later Tillie's Nightmare was made into the very first feature length silent comedy named Tillie's Punctured Romance. It obviously featured Dressler as the lead and co-starred the then up-and-coming Charlie Chaplin.

In the book, Marie Dressler: The Unluckiest Star, Dressler said this of the casting: "Instantly there leaped into my mind the name of a young chap I had seen in London several years back. I knew that boy had genius, that he would someday be acclaimed a star. I had run across him a few days before in Hollywood. Now I started a great hue and cry: 'Where is Charlie Chaplin? I want Charlie Chaplin.' Everybody thought I was crazy. Maybe I was, but I knew what I knew. And I knew that Chaplin could act. He was an enormous success in Tillie. I'm proud to have had a part in giving him his first big chance."

We would expect Dressler's stardom to instantly skyrocket after this film premiered. She did star in a few more sequels to this popular film, but Broadway was something she ultimately tried to return to, only to be jeopardised by the US entering World War I. Just like Mary Pickford and Charlie Chaplin, Dressler, between 1917 and 1918, was part of the group of actors who put their allegiance into campaigning for Liberty Bonds as part of the war effort, as well as giving free performances to servicemen. Once the war was over, Dressler's plan to revive her stage career was luckless. She decided to retire from show business and was broke all the way into the mid 1920s.

Marie Dressler

However, in 1927, she returned to the big screen for smaller roles. The year 1930, as we all know, launched the era of sound films. Some silent stars were not able to persist into sound. But sound productions brought many treasures for Dressler. She secured a contract with MGM, starred as a more dramatic character in Anna Christie, a talkie with Greta Garbo, and of course played the main role in Min and Bill with Wallace Beery. And by the time the Academy Awards came around, the honour of winning the Best Actress award would go to none other than Marie Dressler.

In 1931, the previous years Oscar Winner, Norma Shearer, presented Dressler the award for best actress for her titular role in Min and Bill. She went on to star in even more hits, like the movie Emma, which nominated her for her second Oscar in 1932 but was awarded to Helen Hayes.

Dressler made many unsuccessful attempts to establish her own theaters groups, or stay relevant in her native environment which was Broadway or sell her scripts. But through all those ups and downs, Dressler's comeback to the big screen is uplifting and of course she was undoubtedly one of kind in Hollywood history. That is why she won the Oscar at the fourth academy awards and remained incredibly adored by audiences up until she her death.*

"Always aim for achievement, and forget about success."

Helen Hayes

After starring in her first feature film ever, Helen Hayes won the Oscar in 1932 for her performance. It is ironic how she swiftly won a Best Actress Award for her debut, yet she was never a fan of film acting or even her performance in films, especially as many actresses dedicate years of their life to film acting until they get that long-awaited Oscar. Nonetheless, Helen Hayes' career is a long standing one in which she earned many other distinctions.

These distinctions being that she is one of 15 people in entertainment history who has won an Academy Award, Emmy, Tony and Grammy award in their lifetime, making her an EGOT (Emmy, Grammy, Oscar and Tony). In fact, she was the first ever woman to do so!

From the age of five up until 85, Hayes was immersed in theatre. By her teens she was starring regularly on Broadway and by her early 20s her name was lit on major Broadway plays. She absolutely loved it!

Helen Hayes

When she married Charles MacArthur, a popular journalist and playwright, at the age of 28, they moved to Hollywood. Film acting was something Hayes didn't consider as a career, in fact she found the whole production process tedious and alien when compared to her life in theatre. Nonetheless, she gave it a go in 1931 when MacArthur co-wrote The Sin Of Madelon Claudet from a play called The Lullaby. It was an MGM production and Hayes actually shot Arrowsmith back-to-back with Madelon Claudet. Both films were financially and critically acclaimed and nominated for Oscars in 1932. And Hayes' dramatic and tear-jerking performance earned her the Oscar for Best Actress for her passionate and heart wrenching portrayal of Madelon Claudet in The Sin of Madelon Claudet.

The movie is chronicled as a flashback of the sorrowful and neglected fate of French Madelon who is wrongfully imprisoned for dating a crook, and then resorts to prostitution and stealing after being released 10 years later in order to support her son, whom she had out of wedlock from a previous lover many years ago. The story of Madelon is more so about her all-consuming love for her son who has never grown to know that she is his mother (she gave him up early in his life to be raised by friends and teachers a boarding school) and the measures, often illegal and scandalous, she'll go to in order to provide a better life for him.

A year later, A Farewell To Arms, another film Hayes starred in, won various Oscars. It might have looked like Hayes was at the peak of her career, but behind closed doors she was not satisfied in Hollywood. She said this regarding her departure from the big screen: "I'm leaving the screen because I don't think I am very good in the pictures and I have this beautiful dream that I'm elegant on the stage."

Helen Hayes

Deservedly so, Helen Hayes won the Best Actress Oscar for this film debut because of the range of emotional turmoil she projects on screen. Her character has been through so many hardships, heartbreaks and pain, it would seem that acting out the struggle might come off as melodramatic and forced, but Hayes manages to bring tears to our eyes with her scintillating portrayal of a self-sacrificing mother who goes through so many transitory chapters of life: from simple country girl, to abandoned pregnant girlfriend, to jewel thief fiancé, to ex-convict trying to survive in the real world and finally to helpless woman. With such a chronology we would think this film would drag, but with its 1h 15m runtime, it does a splendid job of being concise for such a moving tear jerker.

In a matter of a couple years, Helen returned to Broadway. Continuing her journey as a film star was not her passion, so she returned to her stomping ground – the theatre, her first love. She tirelessly and enthusiastically headlined in major productions like Mary of Scotland in 1933, Victoria Regina in 1935 and Happy Birthday in 1947. Happy Birthday earned her a Tony Award for Best Performance by a Leading Actress in a Play.

No wonder she is regarded as the "First Lady of American Cinema". She was devoted to the stage and stayed true to herself and went after what she wanted. She did occasional film appearances and in 1970, at the 43rd Academy Awards she won her second Academy Award for Best Supporting Actress for her role in Airport! 38 years after winning her first!

Hayes alternated by working on TV, radio, film and obviously theatre way into the 1980s. This woman was unstoppable! Furthermore she published four autobiographies between the 1960s and 1990s. During her lifetime she won more awards and distinctions for her work, including an Emmy, a Grammy, another Tony and the Medal of Freedom in 1988.

Helen Hayes career and life story is a phenomenon. She was able to weave in and out of film, tv, radio and theatre within the span of 80 years. Her acting talent was always rewarded, and to this day her name and story is incredibly influential.

Katharine Hepburn

Turns out that in early 1930's Hollywood, a name that would be very well known for decades to come, was actually incredibly rebellious. Katharine Hepburn's presence in Hollywood was very long-lasting and domineering. She is sometimes regarded as the first lady of cinema. Acting was no game for her. She did not come to play in Hollywood, she made everybody take her seriously, and for that she remains the reigning queen of being the only person to have won four academy awards.

Unlike most new actresses at that time, Hepburn grew up in a large, liberated and well-off family from Connecticut. That encouraging and privileged environment shaped Katharine into a formidable and active young woman. This same attitude carried on into her working life.

When she graduated college, she set out to attain Broadway success and in 1932, at the age of 25, was recruited to Hollywood to join RKO. Hepburn's alpha-female behaviour, which consisted of her dressing up in masculine pant suits, her condescending outspoken New England accent and her setting boundaries to keep her personal life private, rubbed almost everyone the wrong way. It was obviously a shock to the Hollywood executives' systems. Nonetheless, Hepburn pursued her career and had her screen debut in 1932's A Bill Of Divorcement.

A year later, Hepburn starred in Morning Glory which co-starred Douglas Fairbanks and Adolfe Menjou. The drama film was directed by Lowell Sherman. Hepburn rallied for this role of Eva Lovelace, a struggling actress in New York City. This was Katharine's third ever film role and she was only 26. But this ambitious, hopeful and fearless character helped solidify Hepburn as a serious actress.

"As one goes through life, one learns that if you don't paddle your own canoe, you don't move."

In Morning Glory, eager, talkative and open-natured budding actress, Eva Lovelace, finds herself swept up in the belief that Louis Easton, a theatre producer and agent played by Menjou, will help make her a star. Eva, pushy and assertive but in an endearing way, finds herself in a swanky New York party where she hangs out with Easton and his assistant Joseph Sheridan, played by Fairbanks Jr. Eva is charismatic not in a shy or reserved way but rather a charming, head-in-the-clouds kind of way. After a few glasses of champagne, with no food in her stomach for she is poor, Eve drunkenly showcases her acting chops to the party crowd, reciting Shakespeare's Romeo and Juliet

and Hamlet. After impressing Easton and Sheridan, Eva stays the night at Easton's home. The morning after, Easton insinuates that the two spent the night together. But it is something that he regrets for he feels that he took advantage of her when she was inebriated. Quite naive in her belief that Easton may have feelings for her and believing that he is her only ticket to success, Eva becomes unsure of her potential when Easton becomes distant from her after their boozy night together.

Eva's lack of close family or friends make her emotionally attached to Easton who is far older than her and also serves as father figure in her life. She is also blind to Joseph Sheridan who becomes attracted to her. Joseph always has her back and wants the best for her. In fact when her big stage debut happens she says, "You've always seemed to be the only one to understand through it all. You've always been awfully good to me." Joseph confesses his love promptly but she only sees him as a friend. She has tunnel vision and the aim is only success in acting.

The meaning of this film lies in its very title: Morning Glory. This defines the fleeting moment of fame for a starlet. Eva does not know if she will succeed in acting but she is present and does not mind if she makes mistakes; she is here to accept her fate and become an actress even if it does make her a morning glory. At the final moments of the film she yells, "I'm not afraid ... to be a morning glory. I am not afraid!"

Katharine Hepburn

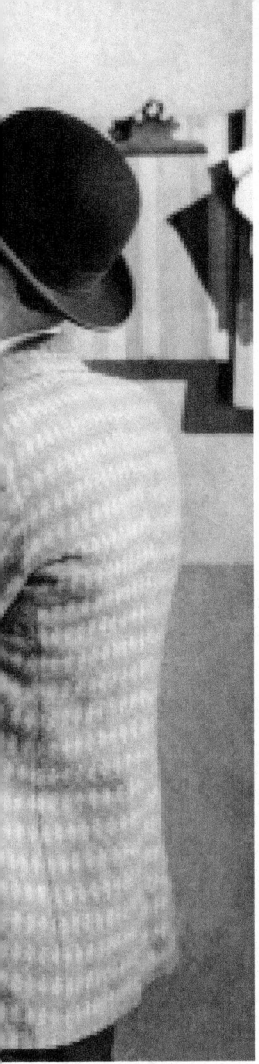

Katharine continued to star in more successful films like Little Women and Bringing Up Baby. But she starred in even more flops, and she began to be labelled as "box office poison". And with her refusal to play the "Hollywood Game", it looked like her Hollywood chapter was coming to an end and so she returned to Broadway.

In 1938, Hepburn made a major career and business move after the play she acted in called Philadelphia Story got a lot of praise on Broadway. Without hesitation, she bought the film rights and returned to Hollywood to finally make her mark as a power figure. Her roster of films grew rapidly. Along the way, Spencer Tracy and Katharine began to co-star in many films together and ultimately had a secret relationship behind the screen.

Hepburn's Oscar success did not stop at Morning Glory. She won three more Best Actress Oscar for her roles in Guess Who's Coming To Dinner in 1968, The Lion In Winter in 1969 and On Golden Pond in 1982. And on top of her four Oscar wins, Hepburn has been nominated for best actress 8 more times for a variety of memorable roles like in The African Queen, Philadelphia Story

and The Rainmaker, to name a few. Hepburn's rebellious nature also made headlines at the Oscars as she would never attend to accept her awards—for any of the four times she won! Nor did she give interviews. A large part of people's fascination with her was obviously her unique acting style, but also her unique attitude on screen. Her behaviour showed her unconventionality and rule-breaking nature. You either loved Katharine or you hated her. There was no in between.

I think Katharine is also a fashion icon. Her reprimanding demeanour was highlighted further with her love of pant suits. Her masculine personal style consisted of blazers, leather shoes and slicked-back hair. This style clearly influenced later actresses, particularly Oscar-winning actresses like Diane Keaton and Jodie Foster, whom we will later explore in this book.

When asked what star quality is, Hepburn replied, "It's either some kind of electricity or some kind of energy. I don't know what it is, but whatever it is, I've got it." I think this gives a definitive clue of who she truly was. Hepburn's career was a long one that spanned for over 60 years. She is deemed as an absolute legend by many these days. Her attitude was unstoppable and her legacy will inspire many for years to come.

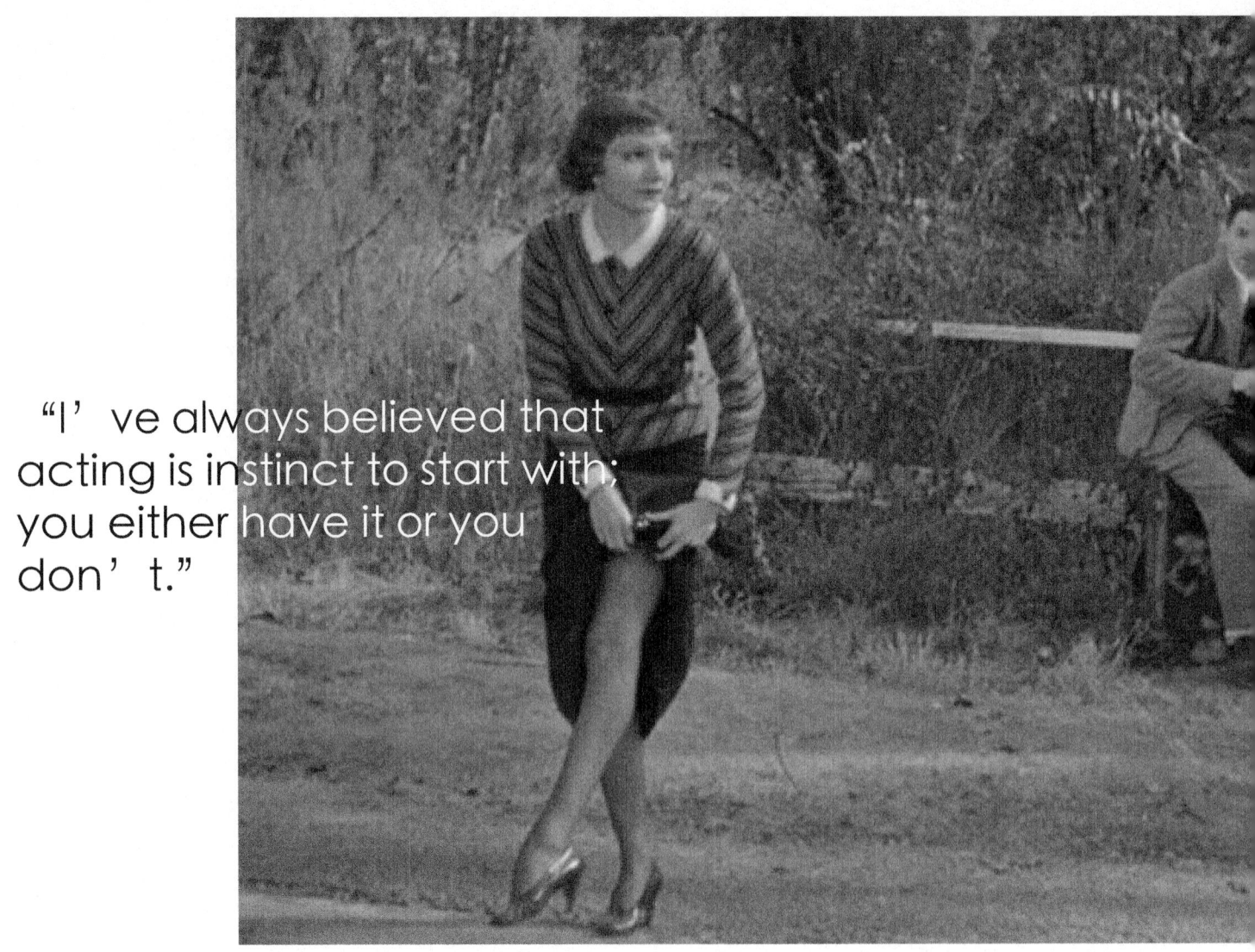

"I've always believed that acting is instinct to start with; you either have it or you don't."

Claudette Colbert

The French-born ingénue from New York City did not expect to catch the acting bug. Since childhood she was enthralled by Broadway and decided to pursue an acting career instead of her original dream of fashion design in her early 20s. Colbert's breakout role was in the stage production called The Barker in 1927, during which she met her first husband. She became a Broadway regular and eventually caught the eye of Frank Capra, a Hollywood director.

Colbert went on to star in a line-up of successful films: The Sign Of The Cross in 1932 and Cleopatra in 1934, both directed by Cecil B De Mille. Actually, the year of 1934 was the most successful for Claudette as it also featured her in The Imitation Of Life and It Happened One Night.

The latter film, the screwball romantic comedy It Happened One Night, swept at the 7th Academy Awards. The film was the first romantic comedy to win Best Picture (then technically called the "Outstanding Production" category). The movie chronicles the budding romance between the rich heiress Ellie Andrews and reporter Peter Warne. In 1993, the film was selected for preservation in the U.S. National Film Registry by the Library of Congress for being "culturally, historically, or aesthetically significant."

It Happened One Night is also one of only three films to win an award in all five awards—Best Picture, Best Director, Best Actor, Best Actress, and Best Adapted Screenplay. The other two films are The Silence of the Lambs and One Flew Over The Cuckoo's Nest. It Happened One Night is still considered one of the greatest ever made, and for good reason. It deserves every one of the illustrious awards it received.

In the case of Claudette Colbert in particular, her performance is whimsical and her comedic timing is on point. She has great chemistry with co-star Clark Gable, who would also win the Oscar that year. Her flapper style in the film would become an iconic look, and her performance would go down in history as one of her best.

Despite the praise Colbert received for her performance, she was initially unimpressed with the film. In fact, she didn't even want to work on it in the first place. Colbert had worked with Frank Capra previously on the lost film For the Love of Mike, and had such a bad experience that she never wanted to work with him again. She refused to take the role of Ellie until finally the studio rearranged the shooting schedule of the film so Colbert could go on vacation and doubled her salary.

Colbert wasn't the first choice for Ellie, either. Myrna Loy and Miriam Hopkins had both turned

down the role first. Bette Davis was also in the running for the part, but due to her contract with RKO, she was unable to commit. Davis would actually end up a write-in nominee for Best Actress that year for her performance in Of Human Bondage.

When Colbert was finally chosen for the role, both her and Gable were openly dissatisfied with the script. But after Capra brought on Robert Riskin to write the script, Gable and the majority of the studio started to have a little more faith in the project. In fact, the script changed so much that Myrna Loy later commented that the final film looked nothing like the script she initially turned down.

Despite the marked improvements, though, Colbert still wasn't too happy with the production. She really, really did not like Frank Capra. According to Capra's later autobiography, Colbert threw "many little tantrums" due to her thorough dislike of him. She was notoriously difficult on set, and the famous hitchhiking scene where Ellie lifts up her skirt was a notable point of contention. Colbert didn't want to show too much of her body for the

film—despite having disrobed in previous films—which actually resulted in a rewrite for the "walls of Jericho" scene. For the hitchhiking scene, Capra brought in a chorus girl to shoot the scene instead, intending to film a quick close-up of the skirt going up, but Colbert interrupted him before he could film. Capra later wrote, "We waited until the casting director sent us a chorus girl with shapely underpinnings to 'double' for Colbert's. When she saw the double's leg, she said: 'Get her out of here. I'll do it. That's not my leg!'"

In fact, Colbert was very strict about lighting and camera angles (she wanted to be shot her from her left side only) and was very particular about her wardrobe, her hair and makeup. Her demands went as far as having sound stages built especially to her demands. She said this, "I know what's best for me, after all I have been in the Claudette Colbert business longer than anybody."

Though she was difficult on set, Capra still maintained that Colbert was "wonderful in the part". Colbert herself, however, was not convinced. She still felt the film was awful, and reportedly told one of her friends afterwards that she had just finished filming "the worst picture in the world". In fact, she was so convinced that she wouldn't win the Best Actress award that she hadn't even planned to attend the ceremony at all. She was about to head off on a train to go on vacation when she was informed of her win. Columbia Pictures chief Harry Cohn sent someone after her to bring her over to accept the award. She showed up in a suit, accepted the award, gave a brief thanks, and then headed back to the train.

In the end, Colbert did eventually thank Capra for her win. Upon winning the Academy Award, she said, "I owe Frank Capra for this." In a later interview with the American Film Association, she expanded upon her thoughts on Capra, stating that he was "that rare artist, a storyteller who makes you believe every word." Still, up until her death, she was still perplexed at how enduring the film's legacy ended up being—considering the fact that neither her nor Gable actually wanted to do it.

Colbert loved pushing the boundaries onscreen with risqué outfits, erotic double entendres and even nude scenes, like her ones in The Sign of The Cross, Cleopatra and even in It Happened One Night. Unfortunately this kind of cinema did not last long once the Production Code was enforced in 1934. However, Colbert truly was a money-making, movie-making machine. Most of her films through the 30s and 40s kept becoming hits, like The Gilded Lily, Midnight, It's A Wonderful World, Boom Town, Arise My Love and Since You Went Away. Eventually she was earning around $150,000 per picture. And in 1938, she was the second highest paid person in Hollywood that year.

As her career flourished and she entered middle age, it was difficult for her to transition from a young comedienne image to a more mature image on

screen. By the 1950s she retired from the big screen but made a few appearances on film, TV appearances and Broadway. She even won a Golden Globe near the end of her career for the 1987 television series The Two Mrs. Grenvilles.

Claudette Colbert's resume is very impressive. Facing crises like the Great Depression, the Production Code and other Hollywood female competition, Colbert still established herself as a world-renowned actress who always impressed audiences with her talent whilst holding her own behind the screen.

"I will never be below the title."

Bette Davis

Not only did Bette Davis stand out with her unconventional looks but also did so with her strong-willed attitude. She did not settle for second best and never stood for mediocrity.

After taking on acting classes and hitting Broadway, Bette was recruited from the stage to the screen during Hollywood's revamping of film productions in the early 1930s. Universal Studios did not know what to do with the 22-year-old, so they cast her in a few minor roles. In a sea of alluring blondes, Bette stood out but very much felt like the odd one out. She knew that her acting had to be top notch.

In 1932 Warner Brothers signed a contract with Davis. She starred in Of Human Bondage in 1934 for RKO. When that movie came out, it put Davis on the map. The following year, at the 1935 Academy Awards, she was nominated for the Best Actress Award but she lost to Claudette Colbert. It was a big deal that Davis didn't win because her performance was deemed by many, even Norma Shearer who had won four years earlier, as the best in Oscar history. The problem was that Hollywood executives were going around telling people not to vote for Davis. That year, the awards had a write-in ballot voting technique. It was used only that one time. This loss infuriated Davis, but nonetheless she moved on. She had to prove herself more.

But it seemed that it was not Davis's time yet, because she actually won the Oscar for Best Actress the following year in 1936! Her win was for her performance in Dangerous. Dangerous is a two-hander drama following the tumultuous romantic relationship between washed up, alcoholic Joyce Heath (Davis) and wealthy architect and theatre investor Don Bellows (Franchot Tone). We follow the journey of Bellows trying to revive Heath's stage career that has long been forgotten and in the midst of this project, Heath seduces the engaged Bellows. Heath is a dangerous woman, in fact she herself is aware of her conniving ways of using men for their fortune as she openly remarks that she is a minx. Not only does Joyce seduce and steal Don away from his fiancée who is a better match for him but she also lies to him that she herself is married to a man she used for money and left.

Bette Davis plays a mostly-convincing seductress but not in a sensual way, a la Marylin Monroe, but rather a pushy, overly dramatic and conniving way. She doesn't use her sexuality but rather she relies on the idea of being helpless and dangerous which plays on the reverse psychology of Don. Bette Davis' acting at times comes off as natural and convincing but at times melodramatic, and therefore does not stand the test of time and wouldn't be considered a timeless performance, in my opinion. But if we consider the style of acting Bette Davis represents, which has always leaned towards overly dramatic and pronounced, then it is not as jarring to watch.

Apparently Davis didn't want to even attend the ceremony to accept her award for Dangerous. But she was forced to by Jack Warner of Warner Brothers. Her first ever Oscar was actually considered a consolation prize for her snub the year before. Her act of rebellion triggered executives even though she was great on screen. The studios resisted casting Davis in more major roles after Dangerous and she kept getting pigeonholed into roles. This moment really was the last straw for Davis with Hollywood and its manipulations.

Her whole diva act did not fly. So she fled to England while still on contract with Warner Bros in 1937. Once Warner Bros found out the breach of contract, they took Davis to court. They sued her and terminated her contract. Funnily enough, this feud did not last long and Davis miraculously got offered a new contract, a salary raise and starring roles in a bunch of fabulous films. This milestone finally made Bette Davis a household name.
Another turning point in her career was of course her second Oscar win in 1939 for her leading role in Jezebel. This time she accepted the award. This film definitely pushed the envelope of gender norms and female liberation.

Two years later, Davis, now a truly admired and business savvy woman, became the first ever president of the Academy of Motion Pictures and Sciences. Davis was switching up the status quo in Hollywood. She knew that being under contract with Warner Brother would provide security, a safety net, primarily in terms of money and career. The eccentric actress kept making headlines with her dramatic and intense films and ultimately, throughout the entirety of her career, she was nominated for 10 Oscars. The list of honours goes on for Bette Davis and she goes down in history as a cinematic idol.

But Davis's career was also a rollercoaster ride full of ups and downs. It is clear just how passionate she was about the film industry and acting. She went through great lengths to sustain her career. The 1930s and 1940s were most productive for Davis. A line-up of more box office hits like Dark Victory, Elizabeth The First and The Letter to name a few cemented Davis as a star. After ending her contract with Warner Brothers, Davis, in 1950, made more cinematic successes like All About Eve and The Virgin Queen. Every single thing she starred in made big waves.

After a lifetime of successful, award-winning motion pictures, Davis eventually received the American Film Institute Life Achievement Award. She was the first woman ever to get it. And many more distinctions like an Emmy and the Kennedy Honor. It sounds outrageous just how much this woman had achieved in her lifetime. Her work was her life. She retired only a year before her death. Bette Davis' tireless and self-disciplined work ethic and her exceptional acting puts her down in history as a very powerful woman in cinematic history.

Luise Rainer

Luise Rainer's self-determination and desire for freedom pushed her to become one of the best actresses in her time. Her enigmatic yet boundary-setting attitude upon her arrival in Hollywood set her up as somewhat as an outcast. Fellow actors respected her and producers wanted to exploit her. This woman's career in Hollywood was fleeting, and she may be well known today for her role in a controversial film, but nonetheless there are many major achievements under her belt.

The German-Jewish born actress's career took off in German theatre. She then starred in a few German films in her teenage years and was scouted by MGM. At the age of 25, in 1935, Luise was optimistic about performing in Hollywood movies under her long-term contract with MGM. With William Powell, she starred in The Escapade that same year.

"I always considered myself the world's worst actress."

Her first movie success prompted her to be cast in That Great Ziegfeld opposite Powell again. This film's popularity skyrocketed and Rainer's performance was not left forgotten. At the 1936 Academy Awards, the category of Best Supporting Actress was introduced. Rainer's role in Ziegfeld should have been considered for this category in the 1937 ceremony due to the smaller role she had. But MGM managed to place Rainer to run for the Best Actress spot. And just like that, she won it!

This was controversial among the Hollywood community. Rainer was brand new to the scene, she was a foreigner among the collection of the seasoned actresses and, of course, her clearly smaller role in the film warranted this controversy. Some claimed that her infamous crying scene defined her performance in the film. For Luise it was never about the glamour, the fame and awards. She did not even want to come accept her Oscar but MGM forced her to. All she wanted was to master the art of performance.

This determination led to her headlining in the film The Good Earth, which nominated her for her second consecutive Oscar in 1938. She played an ethnically Chinese woman in the film. This incident of a white woman being cast instead of an Asian woman for the role has remained a controversy. To this day, the story of how Anna May Wong, an Asian-American actress, who fought for a chance to play O-Lan in The Good Earth and was denied, is famous. But let's keep in mind the unfortunate and blatantly racist production code at that time. The anti-miscegenation code concluded that Asian actors and actresses could not perform with white ones. Simply put, at that time a white woman playing another race or ethnicity was a matter of a fact. Rainer was not the first and only one to do so at that time. I mean, this still happens to this day, with white actors playing non-white roles. Why?
This role earned Rainer her second-in-a-row Oscar. She was the first ever to win two consecutive Oscars. The "Viennese

teardrop", as some nicknamed her, said this regarding her wins: "When I received this Academy Award I did not feel any great thing about it. It wasn't something I had coveted because I hardly knew what it was."

By this point in her life, Rainer was butting heads with Louis B Mayer. Irving Thalberg, who was head of MGM, passed away during the filming of Good Earth. He was Rainer's anchor and guardian who pushed her to her successful roles. Once he passed away, Mayer pushed her roles she did not want. She did not want to win anything, she lived to immerse herself in acting. She became unhappy with her roles through the 1930s and ended her long winded and troublesome MGM contract.

By 1939, Rainer left Hollywood. She said this about her Hollywood career: "I was very young. There were a lot of things I was unprepared for. I was too honest, I talked seriously instead of with my eyelashes and Hollywood thought I was cuckoo. I worked on seven big pictures in three years. I have to be inspired to give a good performance. I complained to a studio executive that the source was dried up. The executive told me, 'Why worry about the source. Let the director worry about that.' I didn't run away from anybody in Hollywood. I ran away from myself."
It is clear just how dignified and strict to her integrities Rainer was, as her career flourished her personal life went downhill. Maybe her European mentality on acting and artistry influenced her departure from the big screen. She still remained in show-business, in both theatre and TV shows.

Rainer lived to be almost 105 years old and spent her final years in England. She lived for the art of acting and Hollywood did not come out the way she expected it to be. She carved her own happiness in Europe. She started a family, travelled and acted on stage mostly. But her short Hollywood story is most famous as her presence on film was incredible and powerful.

"I'm a Scorpio, and Scorpios eat themselves out and burn themselves up like me."

Vivien Leigh

Two of Vivien Leigh's most successful films are still talked about as cinematic and acting masterpieces. In addition, they are both highly historically and culturally significant. And for these films, she holds the title of being a two-time Oscar winner.

Not many know of the personal life of Vivien Leigh. Her mental and physical health deteriorated as her career took off. Her turbulent romances with other film and theatre stars made headlines. And her long-suffering life ended suddenly at 53.

Turns out that the actress known for her southern belle roles was British. She was educated all around Europe and spoke French and Italian fluently. It was easy for Vivien to do different types of accents and she enrolled at the Royal Academy of Dramatic Art. She made her stage and screen debut at the age of 22 in 1935 and fell in love with Shakespeare's work. She began performing at the Old Vic in London. And there she met Lawrence Olivier, a well-known actor. Although Leigh was already married and had a daughter by the time they met, she began an affair with Olivier.

Their whirlwind of a relationship began just as George Cukor and David O. Selznick started their nationwide search for the infamous, unforgettable role of Scarlett O'Hara for Gone With The Wind, directed by Victor Fleming. The hunt for the perfect Scarlett was a frenzy. Everybody wanted to play her. 1,400 women were tested for this role. Previous Oscar winners like Katharine Hepburn, Norma Shearer and Bette Davis rallied for the role. And it seemed like somebody established and well-connected, like them, would get the part. But no—after Leigh put her name in to be considered through her American agent, Cukor gave her a screen test. He instantly knew she was the one.

As of that moment, the everlasting legacy of Gone With The Wind began, with Vivien Leigh and Clark Gable as the major stars of the film. Vivien Leigh was unknown in Hollywood upon getting cast in the film and Clark Gable was well, you know, he was Clark Gable! As such, she was paid $25,000 and Gable $120,000. Such a gender pay gap still exists today, unfortunately. In fact Leigh had a gruelling time working on Gone With The Wind. She was shooting day-in and day-out from start to finish of production. Clark, on the other hand, worked for only 71 days.

One of the memorable female characters in film history is without a doubt Scarlett O'Hara. She is a strong woman because her actions prove her endurance and relentlessness. The almost 4-hour epic follows the life of Scarlett O'Hara, the eldest of three daughters to a rich Georgia plantation owner. The film intertwines Scarlett's life from the age of 16 to 28 with the events of the American Civil war and the destruction it brought to the lives of Southerners.

Scarlett is determined and hard-headed. These qualities help her power through the tough times when her family is not there for her. Even though she is a spoiled, entitled and outspoken brat. Rhett Butler (Gable), a wealthy but not so virtuous bachelor who is attracted to Scarlett and eventually her third husband, sees himself in Scarlett. He says to Scarlett, "because we're alike. Bad lots, both of us. Selfish and shrewd. But able to look things in the eyes as we call them by their right names," before they finally kiss.

Scarlett is creative (her eclectic fashion sense says so), she believes in self-preservation and finds no problem stepping over others, even loved ones to get what she wants. She doesn't care what other people think about her and this fearlessness also helps her achieve her goals. Scarlett's capriciousness leads to her downfall, though. She will never be happy. Even when things come to her favour and she gets what she wants, she remains egotistical and this ultimately pushes everybody away from her. Blinded by unrequited love, Scarlett forgets about being a good human.

We loath Scarlett and her life choices and how she treats others. But we can't help but feel her pain after so many losses in her life: her parents, her daughter, her first two husbands and her closest friend. Scarlett O'Hara goes down in history as one of the most complex female characters. And Vivien Leigh's performance really made an emotional response from the audience.

Vivien Leigh

To prove how powerful this film was, it is to this day is the highest grossing film ever. Not Avatar, Titanic or Star Wars. But Gone With The Wind—with adjustment of inflation. And of course it made Vivien an overnight success. Funnily enough, she loved the stage far more than film and throughout the duration of her life she starred in only 19 films.

The legacy of Gone With The Wind stands strong. However, today, we can't ignore the white supremacy undertone of the film with its glorification of slavery. Once the 1940 Academy Awards arrived, Gone With The Wind won 8 awards and Vivien's performance won her the Best Actress award. On top of this, she and Lawrence divorced from their spouses and married each other. They started co-starring in stage productions and in films like That Hamilton Woman.

Leigh continued her career on stage and on screen throughout the 1940s sporadically due to her health problems. The second pinnacle of Leigh's career happened in 1951, when the film adaptation of The Streetcar Named Desire came out. This film is also a highly regarded film for its performances, especially in film history. The combination of Marlon Brando and Leigh was unstoppable. And for this emotionally draining performance, Leigh received her second Academy Award in 1952 for Best Actress. Kim Hunter, who starred in the movie too, won Best Supporting Actress. Leigh was not able to attend this time due to her tour of the play Cleopatra, theatre remaining her true love. She said this,

"When I come into the theatre I get a sense of security. I love an audience. I love people, and I act because I like trying to give pleasure to people."

Despite her major achievements, Leigh battled bipolar disorder, tuberculosis, miscarriages while working. As a result this made her stage and screen appearances infrequent. But what actually distinguished Leigh was her commitment to her work and her ability to transform into flawed and deeply complicated women. It made her magnetic. Her performances were powerful and the two films she won Oscars for made huge waves in the movie industry. On top of that, she has been considered to be one of the most beautiful women to have ever lived. I hold a lot of respect and sympathy towards Vivien Leigh. It was not easy being her and she will forever be remembered in this eternal image of Scarlett and Blanche.

Ginger Rogers

Ginger Rogers and her frequent on-screen film partner Fred Astaire put musicals on the map. They brought a sense of light and happiness in a seemingly drama-fuelled Hollywood. It was always Ginger's dream to be on the stage and on the screen. She started in vaudeville, then Broadway and then finally landed in Hollywood. By 1930 she was very popular on Broadway and acted in a few short films for Paramount at Astoria Studios. After being in three Pathe films, Ginger decided to move to Hollywood and begin her Hollywood dream. By that point, she was in her early 20s and had a great resume of being a wonderful dancer and singer.

From 1933 to 1939, Ginger and Fred Astaire united to make nine major musical films: Roberta, Swing Time and Shall We Dance to name a few. Watching them float so elegantly in sync is a pleasure to watch. Ginger was a natural. Her ability to act, dance, sing made her a hot commodity. On top of that, she was beautiful. And you know what happens when you're the full package, you get pigeonholed into playing the parts you're best at. And on top of that, she kept getting underpaid! She was the star of all her films, yet she was not top billing. Unlike other previous Oscar winners like Mary Pickford or Katharine Hepburn who asserted their expectations early on, Ginger fought for higher pay and better scripts for a very long time.

"I do everything the man does, only backwards and in high heels!"

Musicals really died out by the late 1930s. They were more expensive to produce and so production companies instead invested in non-musical features. This was actually really good for Roger's career track, as it was a portal for her to dive into serious roles. She terminated her long contract with RKO and that gave Ginger lots of freedom. Kitty Foyle, a 1940 film, directed by Sam Wood and based on Christopher Morley's 1939 bestseller, also titled Kitty Foyle starred Rogers as the title character of Kitty Foyle, a young working class woman carving her way through the bustling New York City.

Kitty is friendly, sensible and down to earth. However she is troubled by the thought of having to choose one man to be with. She must choose between her affluent ex-boyfriend who comes back to her asking to run away together or a New York City doctor who promises to take their relationship seriously. Kitty needs to pack her bags and decide now, before it is too late. As she begins to pack her bag to run away with Wyn Strafford (the rich ex-boyfriend) Kitty's thoughts begin to flow into memories and she will find her reasons to leave with Wyn there.

We follow Kitty's humble beginnings, where as a teenager in Philadelphia she is introduced to the rich Wynwood Strafford the 6th (VI) who instantly becomes attracted to her. He later hires Kitty as his secretary. And consequently the two begin a romance. As the two take this relationship seriously and eventually marry Kitty meets Wyn's family: an uptight upper-class family who instantly disapproves of Kitty and their decision to marry. The class disparity between Wyn and Kitty leads to Kitty standing up to the family and their snarky comments on her identity and she leaves Wyn and sets off to New York City to start her independent life from scratch.

While working at a department store for women, Kitty meets doctor Dr. Mark Eisen. Mark instantly takes a liking to Kitty and tries to date her. His lack of financial stability and pushiness makes Kitty aloof to his flirtations. Although the two do not instantly hit it off, they slowly begin to form a relationship. Kitty flows back to reality and realises that Wyn is no good for her, for he is already remarried with a son. And Mark, he is more on her level and Kitty decides to stay with Mark and end things once and for all with Wyn.

Ginger Rogers

Kitty Foyle is about female independence, class disparity, the struggles of forming meaningful relationships and the idea that following your heart is most important. It's a beautiful story about a woman claiming what is right for her.

Ginger Rogers really brought a lot of truth and reliability to the character of Kitty. Ginger's natural and aloof approach to acting has held up to this day as a wonderful female performance; it's not in the slightest melodramatic and corny. And the story as a whole certainly is still relevant. The outfit worn by Ginger in the film even sparked a fashion trend in womenswear: the Kitty Foyle dress it was called, so aptly. It was a classic black or navy 40s dress but accented with a white collar and cuff.

Ginger Rogers lived a long and fruitful life, the cherry on top is that she had the chance to direct an off-Broadway musical called Babes In Arms. She was 74 years old. Ginger Roger's innate sophistication and multi-talent kept her career going for a very long time. Her professionalism, clean living lifestyle and artistic streak made her very likeable and admired. She was definitely the Golden Girl of Hollywood's Golden Age.

"Marriage, as an institution, is as dead as the dodo bird."

Joan Fontaine

While her older sister was already making a name for herself in Hollywood, it did not take long for Joan Fontaine to join the army of actresses trying to secure their moment of shine. On the contrary, to the majority of budding actresses, Joan's shine lasted for decades all the way into the 90s. In fact, she and her sister Olivia De Havilland are the only sister duo to win the Best Actress Oscar.

Joan, the fair-haired and delicate-looking of the two sisters, got signed by Warner Brothers in 1934. Initially she was in her sister's shadow, but quickly got a few films and stage appearances under her belt. Then she moved on to RKO where she starred in a chain of movies like A Million To One, The Musical Damsel In Distress, which also starred Ginger Rogers, and of course The Women opposite Norma Shearer and Joan Crawford.

When it was clear that Joan had great on-screen presence, she was cast in Alfred Hitchcock's Rebecca in 1940. She was nominated for the Best Actress Oscar in 1941 for her performance but lost to Ginger Rogers. In fact, 1941 was a huge year, because Joan teamed up once again with Hitchcock to bring Suspicion to the screen, co-starring Cary Grant. The movie brought a lot of attention and was a huge hit.

In the film, Joan plays Lina McLaidlaw, a quiet, modest young woman from an affluent English family. On a train ride she meets Johnnie Aysgarth, played by Cary Grant, a sharp-tongued, suave playboy who takes Lina's breath away. Although they part ways, Johnnie certainly leaves a potent impression on Lina.

After arriving back to her hometown, Lina attends a horse racing event where she runs into playboy Johnnie. It seems too good to be true. He instantly tries to court her, but Lina's reserved and hesitant temperament stops her from dating him. But after overhearing her father remark about her never being marriage material, Lina makes a sudden decision to kiss Johnnie and elope with him, much to her father's disapproval. Lina makes this rebellious decision and with Johnnie's romantic appeal, she feels confident as ever.

When the newly married couple move to a new estate, Lina finds out that Johnnie may not be who he seems to be. His mysterious past leads her

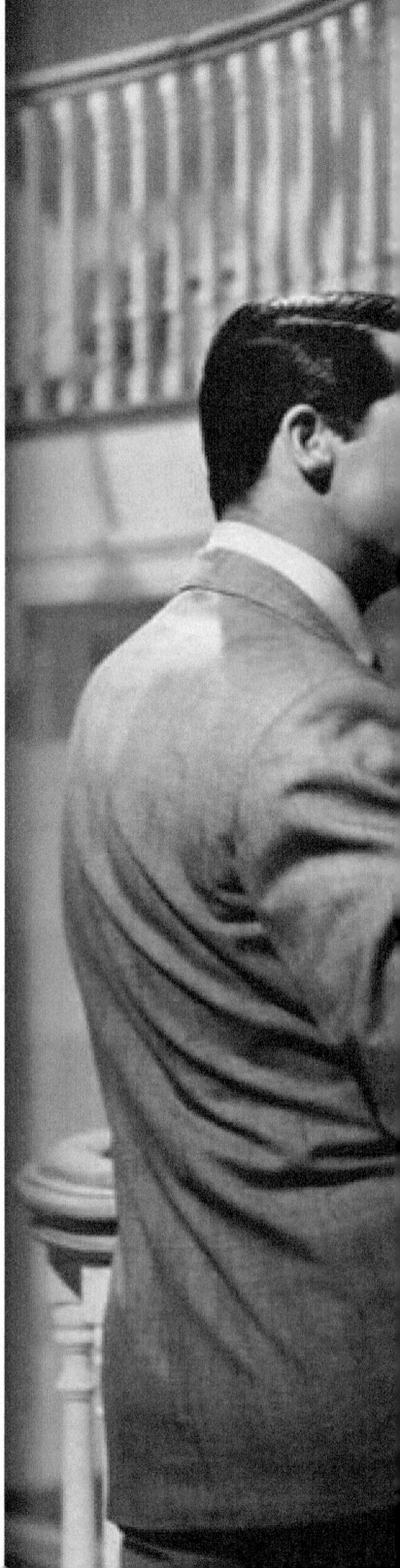

to suspect that Johnnie is certainly not a clean-cut man with a steady job and good resources. Her suspicions become a truth when she finds out that Johnnie has not a penny to his name and his only hope financially is to live off of the coattails of Lina's trust fund given to her by her now deceased father. Although Johnnie's gambling past comes to light where he is in debt, Lina still is so wrapped up in love with him that she forgives all of his lies and mistakes. But after the sudden mysterious death of his close friend, Lina's suspicion extends to paranoia for she now believes that Johnnie is a killer. But once again Johnnie's talent in manipulation leads her to feel silly for even thinking that he is a murderer.

Time and time again, Lina becomes certain that Johnnie is a villain who is now out to get her. In the final moments of the film, we believe that Lina will finally come to her senses, divorce Johnnie and get rid of any connection to him—but once again, Lina's naivety tests positive and Johnnie once again has the upper hand in the relationship as they drive home together.

The ending is ambiguous, a la Hitchcock, as to whether Johnnie is a murdering crook or not at all. Whether Lina's suspicions were mere fantasies created in her head is uncertain. As the couple drives away into the distance, we wonder will Johnnie kill Lina too or will they live happily ever after? That is the appeal of the film—it is up to the audience to decide. Hitchcock truly is the master of tension and mystery that leaves the endings on a bittersweet note.

In this thriller, Joan truly embodies a good girl who has no backbone and as a viewer we only want the best for her, for she does not have a bad bone in her body, however this very quality makes her quite boring and mousy in a way. The ending especially adds the final nail in the coffin of making Joan as Lina a fool. Nonetheless, Joan was perfect for the part.

The 1942 Oscar's were incredibly competitive in the Best Actress category. Bette Davis, Greer Garson, Barbra Stanwick were nominated along with Joan. Olivia was also nominated for Best Actress that year for Hold Back the Dawn. The two sisters who always competed and quarrelled faced another big moment in their relationship.

Joan Fontaine

A moment that set off a lifelong feud between them. Because it was not Olivia, the older one and the more experienced one who won the Oscar that year, it was Joan. She said this about Olivia: "Olivia has always said I was first at everything. If I die, she'll be furious because, again, I'll have got there first." And Joan did.

And on top of this, she was more than her career, she had an amazingly long life. Her romantic, family and child relationships were always rocky, but she was always self-assured and was proud of her achievements. She ended up being the only Oscar winner for all of the Hitchcock films. She said this about her life: "You know, I've had a helluva life. Not just the acting part. I've flown in an international balloon race. I've piloted my own plane. I've ridden to the hounds. I've done a lot of exciting things."

Greer Garson

When the US intervened in World War II upon the bombing of Pearl Harbour on December 7th, 1941, Hollywood came up with a new genre of films that would attract public interest: war movies. Therefore, a new female protagonist had to be created for the screen: a noble, assertive and brave type of woman would be best for these war films. Greer Garson may have played a set of similar roles throughout her acting career, but her impact on cinema goers made headlines, and her contributions in and out of cinema during war added to her appeal. On top of that she received a well-deserved Academy Award in 1943 and was nominated 6 other times for the Best Actress Award.

Greer Garson's career went into orbit when she was 33 years old. That's quite late for somebody, especially a woman, to start her acting career. The reason behind this is very much understandable. Prior to stepping into Hollywood, Greer was not sure what to pursue career wise and opted to attend University of London. This made sense as she was English and very intelligent. Throughout the duration of her literature studies she had the desire to be an actress. After finishing her degree with honours, Greer worked as a secretary briefly and eventually took on acting.

At the age of 27, Greer appeared on stage, notably playing in the Twelfth Night. Garson got really lucky in 1937 when she was 32, because Louis B Mayer, head of MGM was scouting for London talent. And he saw talent, beauty and strength in Garson which was perfect for Hollywood. Garson was immediately signed to MGM.

"When you can't wait for your ship to come in, you've got to row out to it."

Greer Garson

Here's a really cool thing: Greer starred in her first ever movie called Goodbye Mr Chips in late 1938 and was already nominated for Best Actress at the 1940 Academy Awards for her role in this film, but obviously lost to Vivien Leigh. I guess the saying "good things come to those who wait" is fitting here. Greer consequently was hit with a wave of similar Hollywood roles of loyal and nurturing women like those in Pride & Prejudice, Blossoms In The Dust and Random Harvest. But Greer's next gig was a huge hit since it was a commentary on World War II: Mrs. Miniver (1942).

Mrs. Miniver, a war drama directed by William Wyler, was inspired by the 1940 novel Mrs. Miniver by Jan Struther starred Garson as the lead as Kay Miniver, an upper middle class wife, mother and shopaholic who lives in a quaint village called Belham outside of London. Walter Pidgeon plays Clem, her husband, Richard Ney, her eldest son as Vin, and two more young children.

At the onset of WW2 we see Kay and her family deal with the hardships of Nazi bombings on England, their village struggles and her eldest son going to war as a pilot. Kay is even confronted by a wounded Nazi soldier who she stumbles upon outside her home and in this scene she acts on survival, but also on motherly instinct, where she gives him food and a cool cloth.

Greer inhabits the role of a mother figure throughout the script. She is noble, sweet natured, yet simultaneously is fearless, for she is the glue that keeps this family together. The film as a whole is a story of endurance, class struggles, loss of a loved one and British patriotism. Even though this film was pure Hollywood production, it was still incredibly well received for its gut-wrenching plot lines and character arcs. From scenes of Clem shipping off to Dunkirk, to Vin falling in love with Teresa Wright, the granddaughter of a snobby old money townswoman to the final sermon at the end of the film, Mrs Miniver is an emotional story about the English folk during WW2.

This female-driven story solidified Garson as an effective actress. And for her performance she was awarded the Best Actress Academy Award in 1943. Her Oscar speech is the longest in Oscar history. It was 5.5 minutes. Much like later Oscar Winner's Meryl Streep and Kate Winslet, Greer specialised in only playing the motherly, noble and mature women who face hardships with dignity and maturity. But unlike Streep and Winslet who have a sprinkling of a few unconventional roles, Greer Garson remained to play the same type of woman in her films following her Oscar win. On top of her fame, Greer's marriage to Mrs Miniver co-star, Richard Ney, who was a lot younger than her, received a lot of public scrutiny. They eventually divorced and Greer remarried to a Texas millionaire.

Greer continued her career and starred in Madame Curie, The Valley Of Decision, Adventure and Mrs Parkington. Greer stayed with MGM until 1954, even though it is clear that they disregarded her longing to expand into play different roles. Even at the beginning of her Hollywood career, they tried to put Greer on a strict diet for her to starve herself to be a smaller size. MGM had full autonomy over Greer's career moves and her looks. Nonetheless she was getting Oscar nominations year in and year out for her performances throughout the 1940s.

But when the war ended, so did Greer's fame. Her films were becoming box office failures by the end of the 1950s, even though she got nominated one more final time in 1961 for her role in Sunrise at Campobello. It was difficult for her to reignite her popularity, even after a few random TV and film appearances. But we know that Garson had brains that matched her beauty and that she was more than just an actress. She moved on to philanthropic ventures, which solidifies her as a noble and giving woman on and off screen.

Greer was nominated for an Academy Award five years in a row: 1941, 1942, 1943, 1944 and 1945. She holds the record for most consecutive nominations with Bette Davis. She was the third ever British winner of the Academy Award for Best Actress. The previous Brits were Vivien Leigh and Joan Fontaine. Greer said this about work: "Starting out to make money is the greatest mistake in life. Do what you feel you have a flair for doing, and if you are good enough at it, the money will come."

Greer Garson goes down in history as a very loved figure of female strength and resilience through the 1940s era of war cinema. Upon her arrival to Hollywood, the tall Englishwoman struggled to fit into the typical girly, skinny and bubbly mould and found herself to be typecast as a female war figure in films. Her effective voice, mature look and intellect secured her many distinctions, including the Oscar which puts her down in history as an icon of female driven films.

Greer Garson

Jennifer Jones

In a Hollywood career that had spanned for over five decades, and having receiving five Oscar nominations and one Best Actress Oscar at the age of 25, Jennifer Jones garnered fame and fortune very suddenly with the help of producers and publicists to stir media attention. Even since the 1940s, the media in America has been centred on actresses' lives. This created the image of Hollywood actresses as celebrities. Even since early Hollywood days, executives knew how to mastermind simple actresses and actors into celebrity status. This was certainly the case for Jennifer Jones. Her career and life has been compared to Vivien Leigh, who also had a tumultuous life.

Jennifer Jones found herself in David O Selznick's casting studio in NYC to audition for the role of Scarlett O'Hara, which ultimately went to Vivien Leigh. Jennifer Jones and her first husband, an actor too, were about to quit acting after unsuccessful attempts to succeed in the movie industry, but were saved by Selznick's attraction to Jennifer in this audition. Her naivety and youthful look pushed Selznick to pursue Jones to sign a seven-year contract with him. On the contrary to Selnick's beliefs, Jennifer had very little confidence in her acting abilities. But from this moment, Selznick served as her lord and saviour, who transformed and groomed Jones into the star that the world would soon be introduced to. Jones signed the contract in 1941, at the age of 22.

Two years later, she starred in her headlining role of Bernadette Soubirous in A Song For Bernadette. It is to this day one of the highest grossing films of all time. Jones wowed director Henry King during the screen test for Bernadette and won out over hundreds of applicants. Among the other actresses auditioning for the role were Anne Baxter and Linda Darnell.

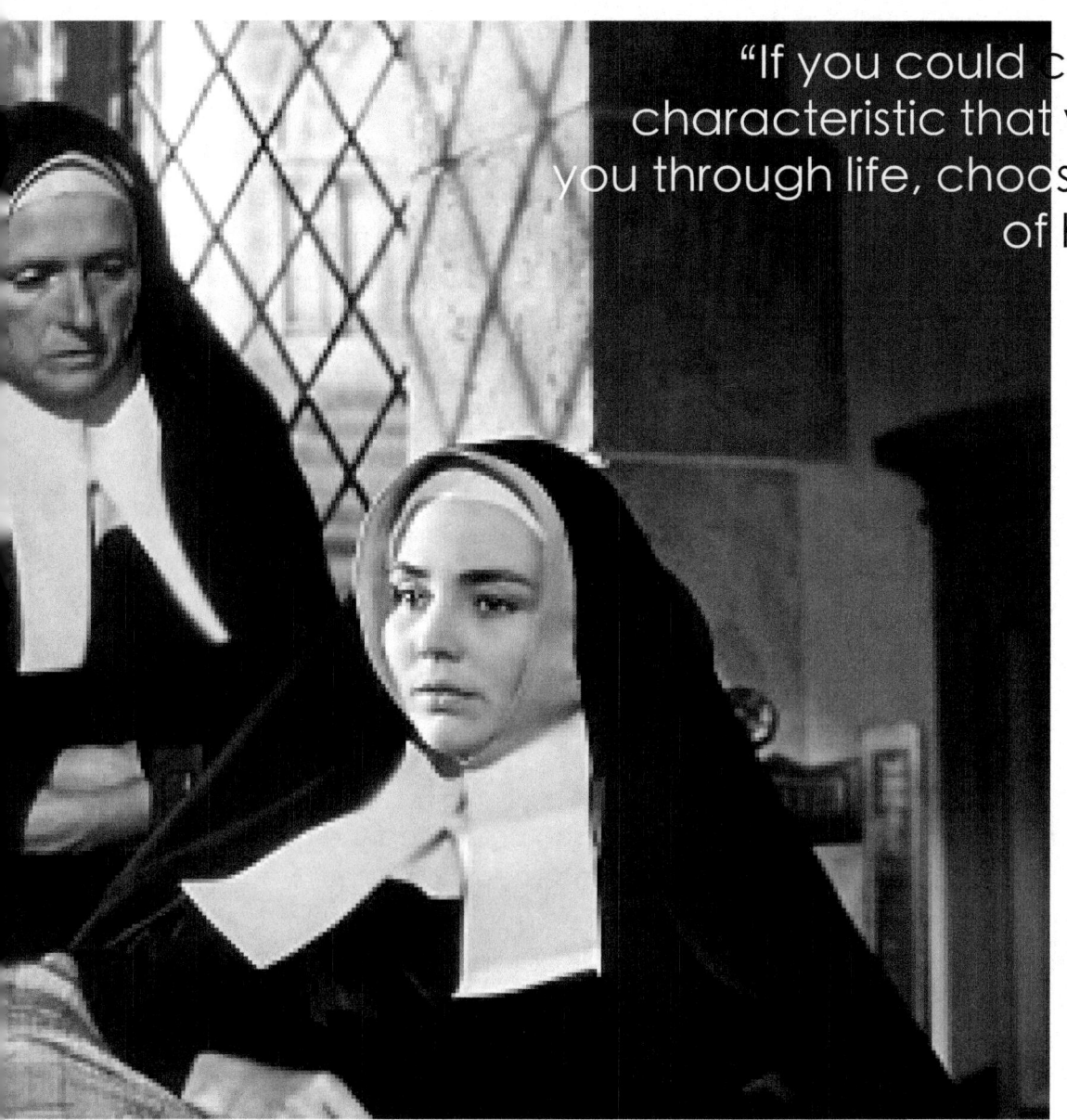

"If you could choose one characteristic that would get you through life, choose a sense of humour."

The Song For Bernadette is based on the biography of the same name and follows the canonised Bernadette Soubirous. Bernadette saw visions of a divine woman, presumably the Virgin Mary. Of course, those around her didn't always believe her and vilified her for her visions. Jones ended up becoming known for playing these saintly roles early on in career. A few years later, though, she played against the type as the more lustful Pearl Chaves in 1946's Duel in the Sun.

The marketing campaign pushed the narrative that the producers had discovered Jennifer Jones and that this was her first ever role. The credits even read: "... and introducing Jennifer Jones as Bernadette." In reality, though, she had been in two films prior: New Frontier and Dick Tracy's G-Men. Eventually, the public would catch on to the fact that this was not actually her first role. According to Turner Classic Movies' review of the film, gossip columnist Louella Parsons was particularly miffed about the narrative that this was Jones's first film.

A critical and financial success, the 1943 biographical film The Song of Bernadette earned many awards at the 16th Academy Awards. Not only did it snag the awards for Best Art Direction (Black-and-White), Best Cinematography (Black-and-White), and Best Music Scoring of a Dramatic Picture, it was also nominated for eight other categories. And, of course, it earned star Jennifer Jones her first Academy Award for Best Actress.

English actress and previous year's winner Greer Garson presented the Best Actress trophy to her at the 16th Academy Awards, and Jones made her acceptance speech quick—she was apparently very nervous, and started crying soon after she stepped down from the stage. Apparently, she was so overwhelmed by the event that she actually forgot her Oscar statue in the cab on the way home!

She beat Joan Fontaine and Greer Garson who won in previous years and Ingrid Bergman who would win the following year. To Jennifer, this win was a shock. She said this later in life about her sudden rise to fame: "When you're young, you're full of hope and dreams. Later you begin to wonder. I did 'The Song of Bernadette' without knowing what was going on half the time." Jones also won the Golden Globe for Best Motion Picture Actress at the very first Gold Globes ceremony. This made her the first actress to win both the Best Actress Oscar and Golden Globe!

It was obvious that Jennifer was a right fit for other great productions, so her impressive performances in films like Since You Went Away, Love Letter and Duel In The Sun were justified with consecutive Oscar nominations in 1945, 1946 and 1947. All were diverse roles which showed Jones ability to be a chameleon on screen.

It's true that David O Selznick and Jones had a special relationship, because he really invested and nurtured Jones' career. Furthermore, behind closed doors they were having an affair which resulted in them getting married in 1949 after divorcing their previous spouses. By this point Jones was already divorced and had two children. This marriage reminds me of Norma Shearer, who I previously covered, and her hypergamous marriage to Irving Thalberg. Both Oscar-winning actresses knew that their marriages would give them lots of security and elevation. In Selznick's biography called Showman, David L. Robbins states that Jennifer was "so meek, so young, so lovely, so entirely ready to be David's creation that she left all the responsibility with him."

Jennifer Jones

Selznick and Jones continued to cultivate successful and also unsuccessful films throughout the 1950s: Carrie, Ruby Gentry, Madame Bovary, Terminal Station and Love Is A Splendored Thing, for which she got nominated her final time for the best actress Oscar. Selznick eventually retired from show business and eventually passed away in 1965 and as a result Jones career went downhill. In 1967, she attempted to kill herself. A few years later in 1971 Jones remarried and rarely appeared on screen. Nonetheless, she was nominated for a Golden Globe for her performance in Towering Inferno in 1974.

This slow departure from the big screen and Hollywood gossip was good for Jones because she was never a fan of being in the centre of public attention. Her long career of being under the microscope came to an end when she focused on other things like establishing the Norton Simon Museum in the name of her multimillionaire businessman husband. She spent her time collecting art. Jones once said this: "Most interviewers probe and pry into your personal life, and I just don't like it … I respect everyone's right to privacy, and I feel mine should be respected, too." This eventually gave way to a lack of publicity, and resulted in her star power waning over the years.

Although her name cannot be uttered without having David O. Selznick come to mind, Jones still was arguably a diverse talent on screen. Her reserved attitude in real life was contrasted on screen as she would dominate all of her films. That being said, she's still a phenomenal actress. Hardcore film fans will likely recognize her ethereal charms and beauty, even if her name isn't as well-known. She continued to receive accolades after her retirement and death. The American Film Institute Life Achievement Award ceremony in 1989 and would appear at a few more Academy Awards ceremonies for various tribute specials. In September 2017, she was named Turner Classic Movies' Star of the Month. There is even a minor planet, 9249 Jennifer, named after her.

"Be yourself. The world worships the original."

Ingrid Bergman

The legendary Ingrid Bergman is no stranger to the Academy Awards. Her first Best Actress win was for Gaslight, but prior to that she had already been nominated for the award for her performance in 1944's Whom the Bell Tolls. She would later go on to win Best Actress in 1957 for Anastasia and Best Supporting Actress in 1975 for Murder on the Orient Express. On top of that, she would get three more Oscar acting nods.

After starring in the Swedish film Intermezzo in 1936, Bergman was recruited by David O. Selznick to re-enact an English version of Intermezzo. When she arrived in Hollywood, they wanted to change her whole image. She was too tall, her nose and eyebrows were too big, her teeth crooked and to top it all off, she did not speak English. But this image gave off a regal and sophisticated vibe amidst all the peroxide blondes with fluttery eyelashes and manicured eyebrows. Selznick cultivated the careers of Vivien Leigh and Jennifer Jones who were previous year's winners of the Oscars. His new project was Bergman. After the Hollywood version of Intermezzo: A Love Story came out in 1939, everybody was drawn to Bergman and the film became a success.

Bergman was then cast in more cinematic successes like Rage in Heaven and Adam Had Four Sons in which she would blow everybody away not only by her performances but her dedication and professionalism on set. But she was always getting cast as these noble and proper women and she wanted to try something new. So she persuaded producers to cast her in a villainous role in Dr Jekyll and Mr Hyde. This was in 1941.

1942 brought Casablanca to the screen which starred Bergman and Humphrey Bogart. Just as he did with Jennifer Jones, Selznick, a master manipulator, got Bergman roles that showed off her talent. And this steady boosting got Bergman her first Oscar nom in 1944 for her role in For Whom The Bell Tolls. She lost to Jennifer Jones.

Her first Oscar win was for Gaslight. George Cukor's Gaslight is a psychological drama about a husband who, well, gaslights his wife Paula and manipulates her into thinking she is going insane. It is a remake of a 1940 British film with the same name—Cukor had originally wanted to change the name to The Murder in Thorton Square to avoid confusion. The film is often credited with bringing the term "gaslight" into popular lexicon.

Gaslight made an impression on the Academy Awards beyond just Bergman's performance. It was nominated for a total of seven Oscars, including Best Picture, and ended up winning Best Production Design alongside the Best Actress win. Notably, in 2019, the film was selected for preservation by the National Film Registry for being "culturally historically or aesthetically significant".

Bergman's performance as a woman wrought with psychological distress is fantastic. Her downward spiral is utterly believable and her despair is palpable. In fact, in order to prepare for the role, Bergman had actually gone to various mental hospitals to see what it was like to suffer a nervous breakdown. She was openly proud of her performance in the film (as she should be!) and considered it one of her greatest acting challenges.

Ingrid Bergman

Funnily enough, Bergman was initially reluctant to take on the role. She was used to playing strong and independent women, and this was against this type for her. Of course, in the end, she did take on the role of Paula and absolutely nailed it. Ironically, after she had finally agreed to take the role, there was an issue with MGM Studios and David O. Selznick, who had Bergman under contract. MGM Studios had promised Charles Boyer top billing as part of his contract, and Selznick was not happy with Bergman's demotion. He threatened to pull Bergman from the film, but Bergman was so determined to play Paula alongside Boyer that Selznick relented. Supposedly, if Selznick had not allowed her to be loaned for the film, she would have been replaced with Greer Garson.

Bergman finally met Boyer on her very first day of shooting—the day they filmed their passionate trainside kiss. Boyer was actually much shorter than Bergman, so they had to arrange for him to stand on a box for the scene. In fact, for the entirety of the film's shoot, Boyer would wear two-inch heels. Bergman was incredibly uncomfortable with the scene—after all, she had just met the man and subsequently refused to do another love scene on the first day of shooting again. This didn't totally work out for her, though because in 1961's Goodbye Again, she would have to kiss Anthony Perkins early on in the shoot. Bergman actually asked him to kiss her privately in another room so that she could prepare, and not get too flustered when kissing him in front of the camera.

Ingrid Bergman

Despite their awkward beginnings, Bergman and Boyer got along quite well on set. In fact, in her autobiography, Bergman said that Boyer was one of the kindest actors she had ever worked with. She also said he was possibly the smartest actor that she ever worked with. According to her, "he was widely read and well educated, and so different."

In 1946, she was Oscar-nominated again for The Bells of St Mary's and again in 1949 for Joan Of Arc. In between these two nominations she starred in two of Alfred Hitchcock's films, Spellbound and Notorious. But by the end of the 1940's, her films were not well received and she made a move to Italy. Her dream was to work with Roberto Rossellini. When they got the chance to work together in Italy after her break from Hollywood, they fell in love and started an affair. They both had spouses and children and this whole ordeal was scrutinised by the media on a whole other level. Suddenly, everyone was on their moral high horse in America and made this affair that resulted in children out of wedlock a headlining scandal. But we know Ingrid did as she pleased. She got a divorce from her husband, remarried to Rossellini and had her children in Italy. One of these children is Isabella Rossellini who is a famous and seasoned actress in her own right.

Bergman shocked the whole Hollywood system because suddenly she was not that angelic and righteous girl that everyone believed she was. Now suddenly she was evil and a disgrace to womanhood. Oh how times have changed! Or have they really? Double Standards. Bergman in fact had already had previous affairs with other famous individuals like Spencer Tracy, Gregory Peck and Victor Fleming.

But when it was time for Bergman to return to the place that made her a worldwide icon, what was Hollywood to do? Exile her because her personal life was apparently a disgrace? Oh no, Bergman's undeniable elegance and emotional intelligence on screen was irreplaceable. And Bergman exhibited one of the coolest comebacks to Hollywood in 1956, when she starred in Anastasia, a film that co-starred Helen Hayes who had received the Oscar too. For this Bergman won her second Oscar in 1947. Bergman simultaneously starred in Swedish and other European films. In 1975 Bergman won her third and final Oscar for her performance in Murder On The Orient Express. Both she and Meryl Streep have won three Oscars.

On top of her film career, Bergman succeeded in stage productions mainly on Broadway. But her film career is more iconic. Overall Bergman won Oscars, a Tony, and Emmy, a BAFTA and Golden Globe in her career spanning over 50 movies.

What makes Ingrid Bergman's power different from other powerhouses of women like Bette Davis or Katharine Hepburn is that she was assertive in a softer, friendlier and feminine way. That is why everyone in the film industry was obsessed with her. She complimented all of her male and female co-stars and fit into all types of female characters. All of her achievements indicate her natural talent, beauty, strength and hard work.

Joan Crawford

Joan Crawford snagged her first (and only) Academy Award for her role in the 1945 Michael Curtiz crime drama Mildred Pierce. Infamously, Crawford did not attend the ceremony—she reportedly pretended to be sick. However, when she won, she ushered the press into her home to accept her Oscar. Crawford was dramatic like that. Her antics off-screen are practically as iconic as her performances. If there were to be a face attached to the term "iron woman", it would have to be, hands-down, Joan Crawford. She is regarded as one the greatest actresses in Hollywood history, and she believed so herself. She was dramatic on screen but off screen the drama was on a whole other level! Crawford was a loved and despised woman in her time and we will delve into her on- and off-screen achievements to see what made her that way. There was certainly something spectacular about Joan Crawford.

Just like Ginger Rogers, Joan found out her talent in dancing early on. Although coming from a south-west, harsh background with a constantly remarrying mother, the fatherless Joan, who would meet her biological father well into her adulthood once and never again, knew that she would be a star. She threw away her boring menial jobs and college studies and set out to win a dancing competition, then join a chorus line and finally packed her bags to Hollywoodland in her late teens. In a matter of three years, from 1925, when she was 19, to 1928, Joan started carving out her acting career in silent films. Our Dancing Daughters that came out in 1928 was Crawford's ticket to fame. Once talkies came into fashion, so did Crawford, who had signed with MGM to star in such films as Untamed, Grand Hotel, Sadie McKee, No More Ladies and Love On The Run—all throughout the 1930's.

However, Crawford ran into a hurdle by early 1940s. A new wave of actresses came to Hollywood, Vivien Leigh and Ingrid Bergman included. Not only that, but Crawford was not as fresh-faced and youthful as the others were and she realised something must change in order for her to remain a priority and a hot box office commodity. So she left MGM for Warner Brothers and was cast in her biggest role yet, Mildred Pierce in 1945. This

"I never go outside unless I look like Joan Crawford the movie star. If you want to see the girl next door, go next door."

performance challenged Crawford's acting abilities. And she loved a challenge. Bette Davis actually turned down this role.

The film tells the story of Mildred, a hard-working divorcee who will do anything for her daughter, Veda. Unfortunately for Mildred, Veda (Ann Blyth) is an absolutely terrible person. The film begins with the murder of Mildred's second husband, Monte (Zachary Scott), and then explores Mildred's tragic life via flashback. Mildred works hard and opens a restaurant so that she can support Veda and her second daughter, Kay. When Kay tragically dies, Mildred throws herself fully into making her

Mildred Pierce is an especially entertaining film to revisit so many years later. Many of the performances in the film are rather campy. These days, actors don't deliver ridiculously boastful lines like, "You'll never be anything but a common frump, whose father lived over a grocery store and whose mother took in washing." Wally, played by Jack Carson, is deliciously smug and over-the-top, and it's a treat to see those types of old-timey put-ons. These actors compliment the admittedly hacky and melodramatic story incredibly well.

Contemporary critics were quick to point out that the film's story lacks believability. It's true, Veda is so detestable that it's hard to believe a seemingly level-headed woman like Mildred would go to such lengths to please her. Still, the ridiculousness of it all is part of the fun, right? It's what brings audiences back after all these years!

Of course, Joan Crawford's performance is a selling point as well. In fact, it was Crawford's acting that likely kept the film from being critically panned. As mentioned, critics had mixed reception to the film's actual narrative and writing. A contemporary New York Times review noted that the film "lacks the driving force of stimulating drama", and Harrison Reports points out that Mildred's affection for her daughter has "no logical basis". Just about everyone had glowing words for Crawford, though! Her portrayal of Mildred Pierce helps ground the film. While other actors in the film bask in the melodramatic campiness, Crawford dials it back a bit and lends some believability to the role. The script might not do much to establish character connections, but

Crawford's paradoxical doe-eyed hardness does a lot of the heavy lifting.
That isn't to say that Crawford's performance isn't completely grounded. She dips into some over-the-top territory. There are plenty of moments where the camera is lingering on some big wet tears welling up in Mildred's eyes. One scene in particular has Veda slapping her mother in the face, and Crawford goes down with a delightfully corny look of shock on her face. She knew exactly when to keep her performance reigned in and when to play it up for maximum drama.

It's incredible how watchable the movie is after all these years. I would say that it "aged well" but that's not entirely true. There is a rather unfortunate stereotype character with Lottie, played by Butterfly McQueen. McQueen was often typecast as dim-witted maid characters. Her iconic high-pitched voice is easily recognizable. As soon as Lottie utters her first line, you'll probably recognize her as Prissy from Gone With The Wind, who gives the iconic line, "I don't know nothin' bout birthin' no babies!" McQueen is a delightful actress who deserved a much more nuanced career. Her character in the film serves as a harsh reminder of the racism present in early Hollywood. It's a shame that her role was so utterly devoid of any real character development. Nevertheless, the film has an enduring legacy and has continued to be referenced after all these years.

The Carol Burnett Show had an episode with "Mildred Fierce", the Sonic Youth album Goo has a track named "Mildred Pierce" and there's even a restaurant in Florida called Mildred's Big City Food that's a reference to the film. Most notably, the film has been selected for preservation by the Library of Congress for being "culturally, historically, or aesthetically significant".

Mildred Pierce is an especially entertaining film to revisit so many years later. Many of the performances in the film are rather campy. These days, actors don't deliver ridiculously boastful lines like, "You'll never be anything but a common frump, whose father lived over a grocery store and whose mother took in washing." Wally, played by Jack Carson, is deliciously smug and over-the-top, and it's a treat to see those types of old-timey put-ons. These actors compliment the admittedly hacky and melodramatic story incredibly well.

Contemporary critics were quick to point out that the film's story lacks believability. It's true, Veda is so detestable that it's hard to believe a seemingly level-headed woman like Mildred would go to such lengths to please her. Still, the ridiculousness of it all is part of the fun, right? It's what brings audiences back after all these years!

Of course, Joan Crawford's performance is a selling point as well. In fact, it was Crawford's acting that likely kept the film from being critically panned. As mentioned, critics had mixed reception to the film's actual narrative and writing. A contemporary New York Times review noted that the film "lacks the driving force of stimulating drama", and Harrison Reports points out that Mildred's affection for her daughter has "no logical basis". Just about everyone had glowing words for Crawford, though! Her portrayal of Mildred Pierce helps ground the film. While other actors in the film bask

in the melodramatic campiness, Crawford dials it back a bit and lends some believability to the role. The script might not do much to establish character connections, but Crawford's paradoxical doe-eyed hardness does a lot of the heavy lifting.

That isn't to say that Crawford's performance isn't completely grounded. She dips into some over-the-top territory. There are plenty of moments where the camera is lingering on some big wet tears welling up in Mildred's eyes. One scene in particular has Veda slapping her mother in the face, and Crawford goes down with a delightfully corny look of shock on her face. She knew exactly when to keep her performance reigned in and when to play it up for maximum drama.

It's incredible how watchable the movie is after all these years. I would say that it "aged well" but that's not entirely true. There is a rather unfortunate stereotype character with Lottie, played by Butterfly McQueen. McQueen was often typecast as dim-witted maid characters. Her iconic high-pitched voice is easily recognizable. As soon as Lottie utters her first line, you'll probably recognize her as Prissy from Gone With The Wind, who gives the iconic line, "I don't know nothin' bout birthin' no babies!" McQueen is a delightful actress who deserved a much more nuanced career. Her character in the film serves as a harsh reminder of the racism present in early Hollywood. It's a shame that her role was so utterly devoid of any real character development.

Nevertheless, the film has an enduring legacy and has continued to be referenced after all these years. The Carol Burnett Show had an episode with "Mildred Fierce", the Sonic Youth album Goo has a track named "Mildred Pierce" and there's even a restaurant in Florida called Mildred's Big City Food that's a reference to the film. Most notably, the film has been selected for preservation by the Library of Congress for being "culturally, historically, or aesthetically significant".

To quote from the will: "In October 1976, Joan had made a will leaving a trust fund of $77,500 to Cathy and Cynthia (her other adoptive daughters), $35,000 to her long-time friend and secretary, Betty Barker, and smaller bequests to a few other people." However, "A court settlement was reached on July 13, 1979, awarding Christina and Christopher $55,000 from their mother's estate." As you can see, these highly praised, almost worshipped actresses were neither wicked nor virtuous. Often, behind their incredible performances and achievements in and out of the acting realm, these women had drama even more shocking than the films they starred in.

But let's not disregard Crawford's talent, beauty and strong will that gave every major actress in Hollywood a run for their money. As MGM screenwriter Frederica Sagor Maas said, "No one decided to make Joan Crawford a star. Joan Crawford became a star because Joan Crawford decided to become a star."

Olivia De Havilland

Olivia De Havilland lived to be 104 years old. Her legacy in cinema is a lengthy one with lots of stories to tell since her emergence to the Hollywood scene in mid 1930s. But it was not an easy climb to success in Hollywood. Olivia had to prove herself as an irreplaceable woman on the scene which was flooded by other talent. Olivia De Havilland's younger sister was Joan Fontaine, who won the Best Actress Oscar a few years earlier, making the sisters the only sibling duo to win the Best Actress awards.

Olivia was immersed in acting since her teenage years and acted in Shakespeare's A Midsummer Night's Dream in high school. As a result, she caught the attention of Max Reinhardt who cast her in his production of Midsummer and subsequently Olivia reprised her role in the movie version in 1935 for Warner Brothers, who put Olivia under a 7-year contract, which later she would sue them for. Since this moment, Olivia was cast in a series of roles that did not necessarily display her acting power, but nonetheless put her on the map. She starred in eight films overall with her constant co-star and heartthrob Errol Flynn. In 1939, Olivia got her second big break since her Warner Bros contract: it was her portrayal of Melanie Hamilton in Gone With The Wind, opposite Vivien Leigh. For this role, De Havilland was nominated for Best Supporting Actress at the 1940 Academy Awards, but lost to Hattie McDaniel, who was in Gone With The Wind too, making her the first ever African American woman to win an Oscar.

"I don't need a fantasy life as I once did. That is the life of the imagination that I had a great need for. Films were the perfect means for satisfying that need."

After this role, the following year, Olivia was considered for the Best Actress Oscar for her role in Hold Back The Dawn but lost to her younger sister Joan. This situation made Olivia angry, not only with her sister, but with the whole Hollywood system. She decided to stop getting shoved "sweet young thing" roles and demanded more substantial roles from Warner Brothers. She said, "I wanted to do complex roles, like Melanie for example, and Jack Warner saw me as an ingénue. I was really restless to portray more developed human beings. Jack never understood this, and he would give me roles that really had no character or quality in them. I knew I wouldn't even be effective." The studio did not like that their contracted actress, or a mere property that they treated her as, had a voice. So they suspended her for 6 months and forced her to take a break from acting. When the 6 months was up and her 7-year contract was coming to an end, Olivia sued Warner Bros for their claim that she was to make up for the 6 months she was suspended from. This story proves just how manipulative, unfair and unprofessional Hollywood was, especially to women.

As a woman, if you were outspoken and stood your ground, you would be considered box office poison and nobody would work with you again, yet on the flip side if you were submissive and passive you would get exploited and pigeonholed. Olivia stood her ground and throughout the duration of her battle with Warner Bros she did not appear in any film. But it worked out in the end because ultimately she won the trial and on top of this success, the court made it a law that "all performers were to be limited to a seven-year contract that would include any suspensions handed down. This became known as the "De Havilland Decision".

In 1946, she returned to the big screen in a succession of successful films, one of them was To Each His Own. Directed by Mitchell Leisen, To Each His Own is a drama about Josephine 'Jody' Norris played by De Havilland who has a

child out of wedlock during WW1 in London. With a line-up of worthy suitors, Jody, a coffee shop owner and the daughter of a lonely pharmacist, is swept off her feet by an American pilot who in a matter of days of getting acquainted gets her pregnant right before going back to war. When Jody finds out she is with child, she also is broken by the news that her pilot lover was killed in action.

Jody faces a problem, which at that time was a big deal: she was to have a baby, not only alone without any support but also out of wedlock. She makes the decision to hide her pregnancy. When she gives birth she is forced to give away her new-born son to an acquaintance who herself lost a child. This woman adopts Jody's biological son.

As the story progresses, we follow Jody trying to have some sort of connection with the boy who resides nearby at his new home. Jody becomes a business woman who eventually makes a lot of money. But money can't buy happiness and the only desire of hers is to live and love her son. Remaining unmarried and focused on work and making meet ups with her estranged son, she is eventually shut out of his life and never to see him again until many years later.

After so many years, Jody, now withered and lonely, meets her now twenty-something-year-old son who has forgotten her. After the two connect once again, the final scene finally gives closure to Jody and her son when he finally realises that Jody is his true biological mother—a secret that was always kept from him. Jody finally feels the mother and son love she always longed for.

This heartfelt drama about a woman trying to essentially fix her past mistakes and resolve them is realistic. At first Jody seems almost stupid, air headed and foolish for letting go of her son and hiding the truth in order to save face but as the story progresses and she takes matters into her own hands, we see her blossom into a much more resilient, hard-headed and smart woman. This character arc is very evident and truly gives Olivia De Havilland a round of applause for her ability to not only physically age but also embody a woman at different stages of her life: from foolish young barista to driven woman.

Olivia De Havilland

For her role in this film she won the long awaited and very much desired Oscar for Best Actress at the 1947 ceremony. She indelicately brushed past her sister at the ceremony when passing to accept her statuette, as if to state, "now it's my turn, I too can win the Oscar". Olivia, being just a year older than Joan, always had a competition going on. Olivia felt like Joan had a one up over her in all aspects of life. The fact of the matter is that Olivia did have a one up over Joan, because she won her second Best Actress Oscar three years later at the 1950 Academy Awards, for her role in The Heiress, which was a feminist infused film. Her dream to play darker and stronger roles came true by the late 40s, as she starred in films like in The Snake Pit. However, after her second Oscar win, Olivia pretty much departed Hollywood and starred in a few film, TV and Broadway appearances. She ultimately retired and moved to her beloved Paris in the 1950's.

On top of Olivia's achievements, she was the first woman to be the Cannes Film Festival Jury President in 1965. She was considered for some film roles that went to other actresses who won the Best Actress Oscar for these roles like Blanche Du Bois in Streetcar Named Desire which went to Vivien Leigh and Mildred Pierce which went to Joan Crawford.

Olivia ruled Hollywood with her diverse characters and her outspoken attitude that attracted masses. She said this about women characters in film: "I think the lack of women's roles is due to the fact that everyone, men and women, have some idea of creating a 'new' kind of 'modern' woman. They aren't interested in the fantasy of women anymore. Personally, I think women ruled from the first, and that we were better off not to let the men know about it. Movies should return to mystiques."

Olivia De Havilland was most proud of her work in Gone With The Wind. She left Hollywood when TV started to take over; she disliked TV and knew that she had already secured her success and saw no need to continue her work. Some stars like her left and some transitioned to dabble in TV. She dedicated all of her time and focus on developing her characters. She looks back on her acting past with relish and that is what makes Olivia one the great actresses of old Hollywood.

Olivia De Havilland

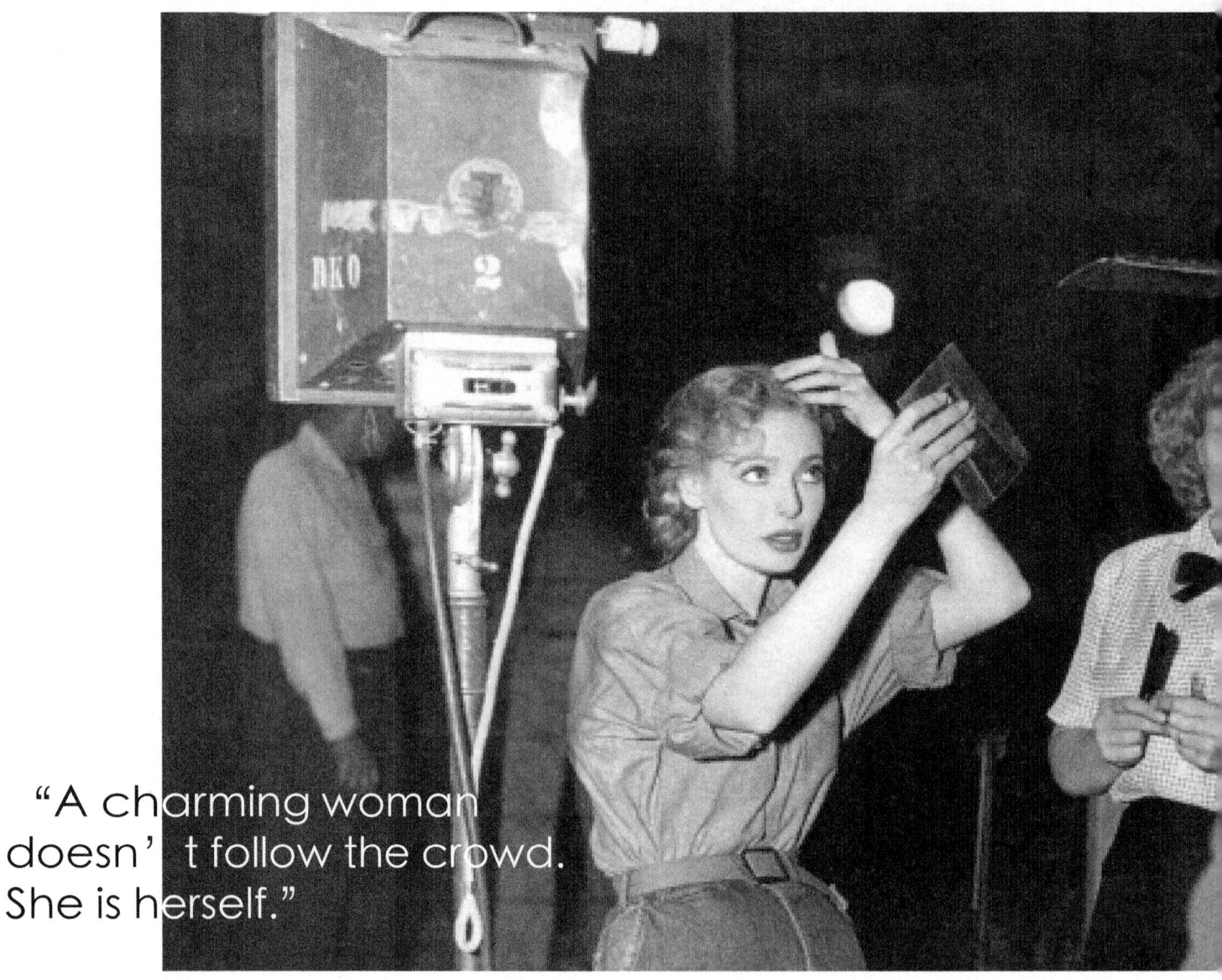

"A charming woman doesn't follow the crowd. She is herself."

Loretta Young

Loretta Young wanted to transition to TV when it started booming in Hollywood at the end of the 1940s. A new decade started which meant a new film formula was created. Just as it did from the 1920s transitioning to the 1930s with sound films, new actresses were introduced. It was not her time yet to transition and she decided to continue her success in film rather than TV. Loretta Young's rise to become an Oscar winner was strategic and committed. She did not fall into acting by mistake, but worked on projects she deemed worth her time since the 1920s. But that doesn't mean that she experienced a series of stumbles in her life. Her tireless and intricate work ethic indicated her passion towards acting and her meaningful Oscar win for a controversial film makes her a film icon.

Loretta, formerly Gretchen, began appearing as an extra when she was four years old because her two older sisters were small actresses and her brother-in-law an assistant director. She began to take acting seriously early on and scored minor yet effective roles in The Only Way and The Primrose Ring. By her teens, she knew that acting was for calling. She changed her name to Loretta and started learning everything about film production: from lighting to camera angles to learning her lines incessantly. Her small yet strong frame, big green eyes and fair complexion made her the perfect ingénue for the films. She starred in numerous films through her teens and was second billing in The Head Man in 1928.

By her 20s, Young was part of the Fox team after leaving First National Studios, thus making her a major Hollywood staple. She had to transition from ingénue to leading lady at this time. But an unfortunate incident happened in 1935, which startled Young's career and public image. Her co-star in 1935's Call Of The Wind, the infamous Clark Gable, who was married at that time, sexually assaulted Young when she was 22, and she consequently got pregnant. She hid from the media and public to not taint her wholesome and strictly Catholic image. Filming of movies that Loretta had lined up were cancelled and Loretta and her mother disappeared from the public eye.

There are a few other reasons why Young's win was so shocking to many. For one, a comedy performance hadn't won Best Actress since Claudette Colbert won for It Happened One Night over ten years prior. Plus, the Katie Holstrom character actually wasn't on-screen that often—she's absent from a large part of the last half, though the character itself remains important throughout the whole story. In fact, Young had been in another movie that year called The Bishop's Wife, and some contended that that was the performance she should have been nominated for. After all, Young has more screen-time in that movie.

Loretta Young

Young herself didn't think she stood a chance against Russell or the others in the running. In fact, she had actually told her loved ones not to bother coming because she assumed there was no way she'd win. Reportedly, when the Oscar award was being announced, Rosalind Russell had already started to stand up—that's how confident she and everyone else were that the award would go to her.

But it was for the major character that Loretta played in The Farmers Daughter that she won her first nomination for the Best Actress Oscar in 1948. Shocked yet jubilant, Young flowed to the stage in an emerald, green taffeta dress to accept her statuette. At the end of her speech she said to her golden statue, "as for you, at long last". There apparently wasn't any bad blood between the two actresses over the controversy, though. Russell and Young were good friends. Russell would end up being nominated for Best Actress three more times in her career, but never won. Young, on the other hand, was only nominated for one more Oscar, for 1949's Come to the Stable.

Once she had her baby daughter, she kept the whole situation a mystery and pretended that she had in fact adopted her daughter. Judith, Loretta's daughter, found out later in life that her father was in fact Gable. Gable did not take any accountability for his heinous actions. Loretta Young later married a second time to Tom Lewis and had two sons with him, and gave Judith, now Judy, the last name Lewis. Despite this drama, Young was a sought-after actress and went on to work on more projects, even when she was pregnant with her children.

She went on to star in Kentucky, in 1938 which was a huge success. In 1939, she decided to reject the 5-year, $2 million contract with 20th Century Fox and work freelance instead. Young wanted important and powerful roles and disagreed with Hollywood execs too much. She wanted respect, recognition and an Oscar. During WW2 she starred in Ladies Courageous and in 1947 she starred in a massively popular comedy: The Farmer's Daughter. This film challenged the status quo in American society, because although it was considered a "bright comedy" it discussed topics of immigration and politics in the US.

In The Farmers Daughter, Loretta plays the character Katie Holstrom, a farmgirl who heads out to the city to follow her dreams of going to nursing school. It's a classic set-up about a country gal who heads out and immediately realises that things are tougher in the city than she expected. Katie quickly runs out of money, and has to take on a job as a maid for a Congressman (played by Joseph Cotten) and

Loretta Young

his mother. Before she knows it, she's swept up into a world of romance and politics.

The Farmer's Daughter really gave Young a chance to shine and show off her chops with comedy. However, Young was initially hesitant to take on the role. Not only did it differ from the usual roles she played, it required a Swedish accent. At first, Young tried to convince the higher ups that she would be better off doing a Southern accent, but her request was denied. Instead, producer Dore Schary insisted that she was right for the part and just needed a little more direction. So, he assigned her to the famous accent coach, Ruth Roberts. Roberts had actually been assigned to help actress Ingrid Bergman lose her Swedish accent when she came over to holiday. Young jokingly recalled that, "Ruth took away Ingrid's accent and gave it to me."

Speaking of Ingrid Bergman, she was actually the first choice for the lead role in The Farmer's Daughter. However, she declined the role—supposedly because of rumours that she and Joseph Cotten were having an affair. In the end, it likely benefited the film that Bergman turned it down, not just to avoid gossip columns but because Young's performance ultimately received high praise. While her performance was highly acclaimed, though, her win still came as a huge surprise. The other actresses in the running for Best Lead Actress that year were Joan Crawford (Possessed), Dorothy McGuire (Gentleman's Agreement), Susan Hayward (Smash-Up, the Story of a Woman), and Rosalind Russell (Mourning Becomes Electra). Russel was considered to have the award in the bag, especially since she had already won the Golden Globe for her performance in the drama.

It's also worth noting that the other performances in The Farmer's Daughter were equally stellar. Though she was not nominated for an Oscar, Ethel Barrymore churns out an impressive performance as the powerful mother of Congressman Morley. She apparently was incredibly kind on set, going above and beyond to help Loretta Young feel better after she had a miscarriage during shooting. Meanwhile, Charles Bickford earned himself a nomination for Best Supporting Actor for his role as the butler Joseph Clancey. He would go on to be nominated for the award two more times for The Song of Bernadette and Johnny Belinda.

However as the 40s came to an end, Young's filmography tapered although her films were still successful. Instead, she would go on to become a formidable television actress, winning three Emmy awards and garnering five more nominations. Thousands, and eventually millions by 1953, of households had television sets. Now Loretta's fans could watch her on the regular in the comfort of their own home. She had her own anthology series, The Loretta Young Show, from 1953 to 1961. Loretta hosted a half hour drama anthology series in which she regularly acted in too. Everybody loves her dazzling entrances in beautiful gowns. She'd also win a Golden Globe in 1986 for her performance in the TV film Christmas Eve. Lady In The Corner was her final TV film appearance in 1989.

Now we know just how hard working and passionate Loretta Young was about acting. She knew the business inside and out and fascinated audiences for many years. She once said, "A charming woman. Don't follow the crowd. She is herself." She always appeared in interviews, photoshoots and got talked about in gossip columns at the height of her career. She worked throughout the silent, sound, Technicolor, TV and radio eras of Hollywood making list of performances very extensive. And by the time she retired, she had a tight knit loving family, grandchildren and time to sleep in and travel. Loretta Young embarked on a journey of a lifetime to become one of the best actresses in mainly 1930s and 1940s cinema. For her hard work, professionalism and beauty she was awarded an Oscar.

Jane Wyman

Jane Wyman's life was like a kaleidoscope. The diverse list of a multitude of film and TV performances proves her longstanding and stable career in Hollywood. The little girl she once was always had tricks up her sleeve, like lying about her age and name in order to pass as an older girl in order to get acting jobs. The young, ambitious and energetic Jane Wyman, formerly Sarah Jane Mayfield or Sarah Jane Faulks, eventually ascended to star status in a matter of no time and eventually had the honour of becoming the Best Actress Oscar recipient in 1949.

Jane grew up between Missouri and California, worked at random and insubstantial jobs and was raised by her neighbours, since her biological father passed away early and her mother would visit her once in a while from Cleveland. Jane, the only child, was left to her own devices, despite her strict "adoptive" parents. Jane enrolled in dance classes and eventually tried her hand in radio singing. By the time she turned 16, she was already married for the first time—the first of her five marriages.

She made the executive decision to move to Hollywood at the age of 15 after dropping out of high school. She joined a chorus line, of course, due to her talent in dance. Her transformation into a Hollywood star had begun as she plucked her eyebrows pencil thin, bleached her hair and made a connection with a successful dance director for Hollywood films, his name was LeRoy Prinz. This connection got Sarah Jane her first set of minor film roles. All of this happened in the early 1930s during the Great Depression. Her pay checks for the roles in films like The Kid From Spain, College Rhythm and Anything Goes were very much needed for her and her family back in Missouri during these tough times.

"The opportunity for brotherhood presents itself every time you meet a human being."

Soon enough, in 1936, when she was 19 years old, Jane was signed to Warner Brothers for a $60 a week acting contract for the time being. In addition, Jane officially took on the stage name of Jane Wyman. But roles most suitable to her did not come flooding in magically and it took a solid few years for Jane to blossom into a mature and serious young woman capable of playing serious and mature characters. But before that happened, she got typecast in dumb blonde roles in B movies. But we know Jane was no dumb blonde, she was street smart and naturally intelligent and talented. These qualities were of course noticed, only by the mid 1940s.

By 1945, Wyman was ready to be the leading lady of her films. No longer blonde, but brunette and age 28, Wyman appeared in The Lost Weekend. This film won four major Oscars at the 1946 Academy Awards. It was clear that Wyman's career was going to go full steam ahead. The following year, in 1947, Wyman headlined in The Yearling the film for which she received an Oscar nomination for Best Actress. This achievement we can call the appetiser, just a preparation as to what would

happen at the Academy awards two years later.
Wyman, who already had a strong fascination with the Broadway production of Johnny Belinda by Elmer Blaney Harris, was cast as the main role of a deaf-mute woman named Belinda. The incredibly dark, emotionally and visually intense film was very successful. Jane Wyman underwent intensive preparation to play such a powerful role in a controversial film at that time.

Johnny Belinda is about the horrors of rape, trauma and growing up deaf in a narrow-minded community. Jane Wyman plays the young Melinda McDonald, the daughter of farmer Black McDonald played by Charles Bickford. In the small fishing community of Cape Breton Island on the east coast of Canada, Belinda is the only deaf person. Everyone believes she stupid and cannot make her own decisions only due to the fact that she is deaf. When a doctor comes to town, Dr. Robert Richardson, played by Lew Ayres, to start his new job, he befriends the MacDonald family and makes a strong connection with Belinda. He teaches her to lip read and sign language.

One night Belinda finds herself working in the barn and is greeted by a dark and scary figure, Locky McCormick, a local man. He is drunk and throws himself on Belinda and rapes her. Unable to escape, she suffers his abuse. Unable to tell anyone or even identify who raped her she locks away the incident even though traumatised. When the news comes out that she is pregnant, her father and aunt try to find out who took advantage of Belinda, even questioning the truthfulness of Dr Robert. Belinda has her child but more horrible things face the family: the murder of her father by Locky, them becoming penniless and the townsfolk trying to take away the child from Belinda.

This harrowing story, truly, is about the unfair treatment of people with disabilities, the rotten nature of rapists and the power of opinion narrow minded and prejudiced people hold over those different from them. Johnny Belinda is a shocking story that keeps the viewer on edge. Without a single word or even sound coming from Jane Wyman, she still managed to evoke the emotion of a lost, scared and confused child. Although 31 when the film came out, Jane has a talent of evoking innocence and airiness to her rendition of Belinda.

Jane Wyman

Judy Holliday

Judy Holliday's successful career in film and theatre, specifically in Hollywood and on Broadway, developed from a few career moves in her early 20s. Without knowing where she would end up, Judy, unlike other actresses who knew what they wanted to do from an early age, like Katharine Hepburn or Joan Crawford, Judy somehow went with the flow and came out on the other end as a unique feminine icon of natural intelligence, charisma and individuality. Before the emergence of the typical "dumb blonde" icons like Marylin Monroe, Jayne Mansfield, Goldie Hawn and Reese Witherspoon, Judy Holliday proved that this archetype is not so dopey and ditzy as they may seem. That is why she won an Oscar for best actress in 1951 for this type of role.

Judy Holliday was born Judith Tuvim to a Jewish family in New York City. The thought of having Jewish women act in Hollywood was considered taboo, and were always represented as loud, obnoxious and squeaky voiced women—caricatures, really. Yet, we all know that Hollywood was a Jewish-male-run industry since the beginning. The double standards were clear. When Judy did not get into Yale university, even though she was incredibly intelligent, her interest in media production and stage performance was the immediate course of action upon finishing school. As a native New Yorker, it was easy for Judy to make connections in the arts world in New York City. Her first job was as a switchboard operator at Orson Welles Mercury Theatre, and from there Judy transitioned to performing on stage. At the age of 17, in 1938, she toured the east coast as part of a nightclub act called "The Revuers". Once the group disbanded in 1944, Judy went on to act in small roles, but a year later, she was cast in her first Broadway play called Kiss Them For Me. This career turn was successful for Judy, and it opened a portal for her to discover a role that would attract Hollywood.

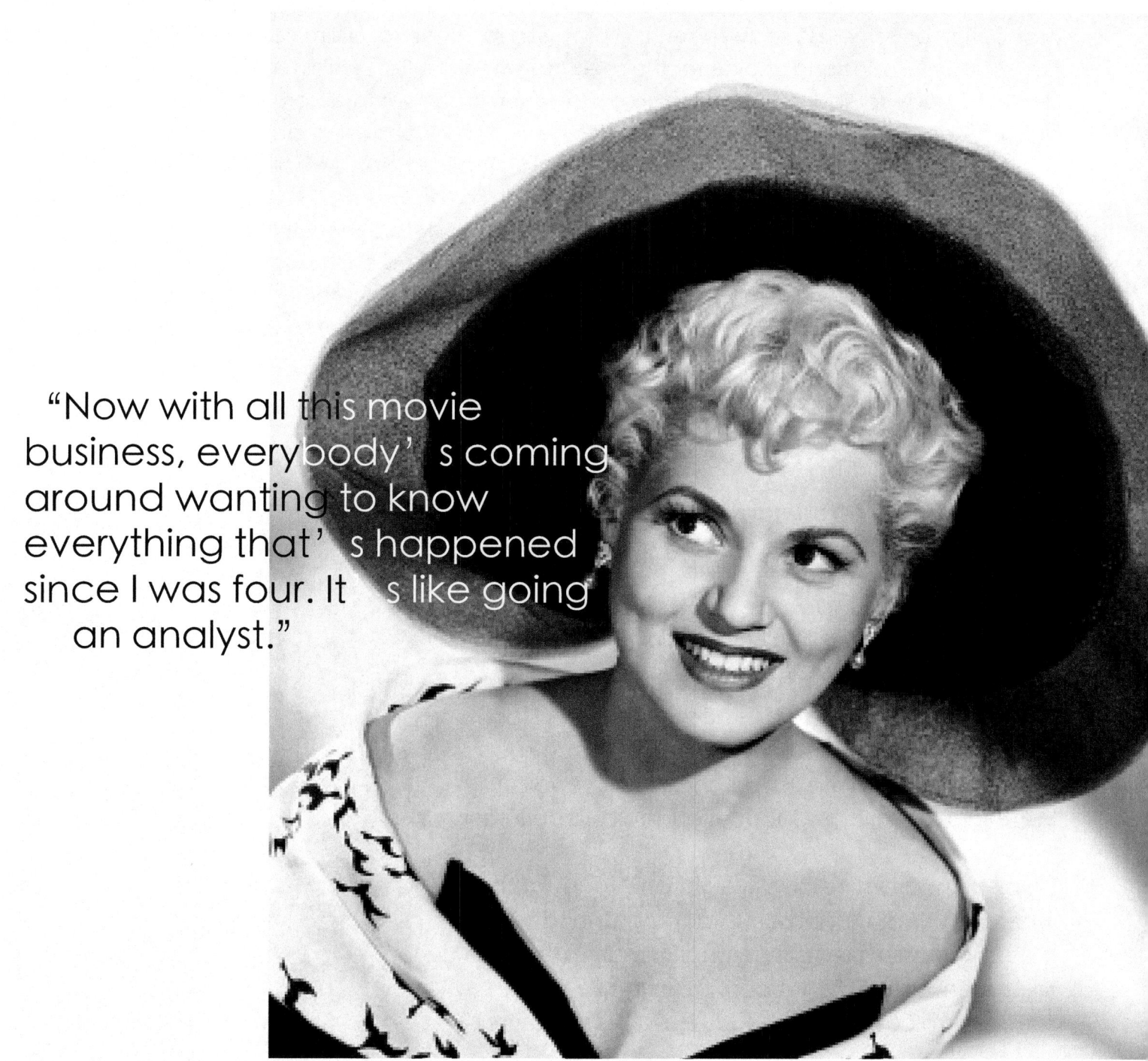

"Now with all this movie business, everybody's coming around wanting to know everything that's happened since I was four. It's like going an analyst."

In 1946, Judy was cast in the titular role of the scatter-brained Billie Dawn in the Broadway production of Born Yesterday. When the play was rewritten for a film version by Garson Kanin, Judy was second choice for the role and when the first actress up for the role declined, Judy sealed her ticket to fame. However, Judy, being a completely unknown actress then, made Columbia Picture studio head Harry Cohn reluctant to cast her. As a result, Kanin, George Cukor, Spencer Tracy and Katharine Hepburn, rallied to have Judy do something substantial to get her in the spotlight. So she was cast in Adam's Rib in 1949 which co-starred Tracy and Hepburn. The two Hollywood stars knew that this opportunity to act in Adam's Rib would give enough reason for Judy to be cast in Born Yesterday. Judy still had to do a screen test and wait until Cohn was sure she was the right fit in comparison to other actresses' screen tests. But Judy finally secured the coveted role and starred in the 1950 film version.

Judy Holliday

Billie Dawn in Born Yesterday is basically owned by Brock, a millionaire. He dresses her up, keeps her guarded and provides a lavish yet empty life. He loves her regardless of her lack of social etiquette and wit, an ex-vaudeville without any culture or social skills, Billie finds herself out of her element when in the company of Brock's acquaintances. Her childish voice, lack of manners or any intelligence worries Brock and so he hires a local DC reporter, Verrall, to teach Billie about etiquette and culture.

Brock is unattractive, overweight and foul mouthed whereas Verrall is handsome, put together and witty. It becomes obvious that he and Billie are attracted to one another. Billie is a peroxide blonde, ditsy, squeaky-voiced woman (Judy Holidays signature)

who is down to earth. The two fall in love and start a romance behind Brock's rough and rude back. Brock treats Billie with a lot of disrespect. Regardless of his wealth, it is clear that this man comes from rags to riches and holds no affection to Billie, despite constantly stating that he loves. No, he loves to possess her. He shouts at her, shoves her and tells her to shut up. She brushes of his abuse and remains cool calm and collected with sprinklings of womanly retaliation like screeching back at him and playing difficult to be around.

After reading, visiting museums, having educated conversation about politics and looking up words in the dictionary she realises that her whole life she has been played, especially by Brock. She realises she won't let him manipulate and control her. After a very physical quarrel where he beats her and forces her to co-sign contracts for his businesses she refuses to sign, Brock realises he must fire Verall because he doesn't like the influence he has on Billie. He keeps saying that he "loves that girl" a mere moment after beating her up.

Billie confronts Brock and tells him she's leaving after almost a decade of dating. She finally understands what kind of relationship and life she wants. Brock begs for her forgiveness and hand in marriage. He once again has a temper tantrum and threatens her, she is fearless and stands on her own. Without surprise it is uncovered that Brock is a crook. Verrall and Billie hold the facts against Brock and threaten to publicise his past. With this ultimatum Brock lets Billie go. And as the ending scene, a few months later, we see Billie and Verrall newly married and starting a new life.

Judy Holliday

Judy Holliday's performance was highly praised: her emotional range, comical effect and vulnerability on screen proved her worthy of getting nominated for the Best Actress Oscar at the 1951 Academy Awards. And she won! She was up against Bette Davis who was nominated for her role in All About Eve. Now that was an achievement on Judy's side, to say the least. She also won a Golden Globe that year, too.

We would expect Holliday to go on and move to LA, film maybe 5 movies a year and feature on magazine covers every month, in typical Hollywood star fashion. But that was not the case. She remained in her dearest New York, got married, had a son and kept her friend group and connections tight. Holliday only appeared in six more films after Born Yesterday. The Marrying Kind, The Solid Golden Cadillac and Bells Are Ringing were well received. She was nominated for BAFTAs and Golden Globes too. Her last film was in 1960. She also did a few stage productions. For her stage performance of Bells Are Ringing in 1956, she won a Tony Award for best performance by a leading actress in a musical.

I am sure that Holliday would have gone on to make other great productions, whether they were film, stage or music albums. But she battled cancer in the early 1960s and unfortunately passed away in 1965 a couple weeks before her 44th birthday.

Judy Holliday was a fascinating personality on and off screen. She was super smart about the ways she went about life, she immersed in various aspects of arts and culture and always stood up for herself. An interesting dichotomy when she was always cast and treated as a silly little blonde. Holliday said, "You have to be smart to play a dumb blonde over and over and keep the audience's attention without extraordinary physical equipment." She was the icon of the urban working girl character. She definitely left her mark on the history of Hollywood, Broadway and the Oscars.

"Actors should be overheard, not listened to, and the audience is 50 percent of the performance."

Shirley Booth

A theatre actress by trade, Shirley Booth found herself accepting a Best Actress Oscar in 1953 at the age of 55 for her well received acting in Come Back, Little Sheba. An unpredictable moment for sure, since this was her film debut. Shirley Booth's repertoire consisted mainly of plays, a few films and a sprinkling of TV shows. She was known to play unglamorous, raw and emotionally repressed women who gave a closer look into the experience of real women in America, rather than that glamorous and colourful life often depicted on screen. It is interesting that Booth won an Oscar because in the congregation of glamorous, glittering stars, Shirley was an older woman with no intention of becoming a Hollywood siren. Much like Marie Dressler, Booth was different and so was her story.

Booth dropped out of high school against her father's will; he detested the idea of her pursuing acting. She acted in stock companies since her teenage years but professional journey started in 1925 when she debuted on Broadway at the age of 27 in Hells Bells opposite Humphrey Bogart. Booth used to lie about how old she was and knocked off around 8 or 9 years off of her real age to appear younger. She would spend all of the 1930s and 1940s on stage in plays and in musicals. By the early 1930s she was already very popular in the theatre community because she did a variety of comedies, dramas and musicals. The Philadelphia Story and My Sister Eileen to name a few. Booth co-starred with Katharine Hepburn in the former.

Booth began to win Tony awards for Best Actress for her performances in Goodbye, My Fancy and in the drama called Come Back, Little Sheba. And when it was time for Come Back, Little Sheba to be cast for the screen, directed by Daniel Mann, it took a lot of convincing for Paramount Pictures to cast Booth. She had never starred in a film, she was an older actress and it was difficult for her to switch her stage acting habits to adapt to film acting. Nonetheless, Booth knew the material and characters inside and out and casting her as the lead role of Lola Delaney should have been a no-brainer. And Booth's reputation as a highly talented and professional actress was very desirable for Hollywood. Even Bette Davis was a huge fan of Booth.

And in the 1953 Academy Awards, Booth managed to get nominated for best actress for her film debut. And better yet, she won it. That same year she won her third and final Tony for her stage role in The Time Of the Cuckoo. Also that year, the Awards were televised for the first time. The surge of about 25 million tv sets through American households was an opportunity for Hollywood to expand the Oscars on TV.

Shirley Booth really knocked it out of the park with Come Back, Little Sheba. Not only did she originate the role of the lead character Lola on Broadway, she also won a Tony Award for it. This made her the first actress to ever win both the Tony and Oscar for the same role. Then she went on to win at the New York Film Critics Circle Awards, and the Golden Globes. She later became one of only a few performers to achieve the Triple Crown of Acting—an Academy Award, an Emmy Award, and a Tony Award. As if all that wasn't impressive enough, she also won an award at the Cannes Film—once again clearing an Academy Award "first" by becoming the first actress to win an Oscar and a Cannes award for the same performance.

Come Back, Little Sheba is a drama about the loveless marriage between "Doc" Delaney (Burt Lancaster) and Lola. It has a similar vibe to movies like Who's Afraid of Virginia Woolf? in that it focuses on a middle-aged housewife who is intentionally made to look frumpy. It also features an outsider character who comes in and shakes the relationship up a bit when Marie, a beautiful young college student, moves into the household. Marie is played by Terry Moore, who ended up receiving a Supporting Actress nod for her performance. "Sheba" refers to the name of Doc and Lola's old pet dog who ran away prior to the events of the story. Lola openly mourns this dog throughout the film.

The dynamic between the three characters is fascinating. This claustrophobic drama has Doc falling head over heels for Marie, who is fully aware of her charms and the effects she has on him. Meanwhile, Lola is oblivious to Doc's feelings and adopts Terry as a sort of surrogate daughter. Doc and Lola had lost their baby previously, and Lola is hardcore projecting onto the college student. As the film goes on, emotions begin to rise and Doc's true feelings bubble to the service.

Lancaster and Booth play off of one another incredibly well in the movie. Lancaster gave the role of Doc a whole new perspective, playing him more boisterously than his stage counterpart. Meanwhile, Booth's meek and pathetic performance complimented him very well. They really make it feel like the audience can sense the decades of turmoil the two have put each other through, and every one of their interactions with the other is cringe-worthy, in a good way. The two worked with one another very closely, and Booth commented that Lancaster would call her up late at night to discuss the part and how to approach it. Reportedly, Lancaster was actually quite nervous around Booth and was slightly intimidated by her experience compared to his.

Critics initially felt Lancaster wasn't right for the role, but Booth defended him, saying that he would be a great actor in due time. Lancaster would later go on to say that Booth was the greatest actress he ever worked with. The two would stay in touch later in life.

Interestingly, Booth almost did not take on the role due to other theatre commitments. Mann reached out to Bette Davis to star in the film instead, but Davis turned it down. Obviously, things worked out and Booth was able to step into the role after all. She made her film debut at age 54 … though her publicists decided to pretend she was about a decade younger than that! Another fun tidbit about the film is that Booth's character actually mentions Jennifer Jones's performance in The Song of Bernadette during the film. Jennifer Jones had won the Best Actress Award for that film. This marks the first time an Oscar-winning performance referenced another previous Oscar-winner.

The film adaptation of the play received rave reviews, and Booth in particular was lauded for the depth she brought to Lola. The Pittsburgh-Gazette wrote that, "Miss Booth is the real force behind the overwhelming tug and the blistering realism of Come Back, Little Sheba," and critic James Monaco wrote decades later that her "brilliant work … remains etched forever in the memory of anyone who has seen the film."

We would expect Booth's filmography to go off. But that was not the case, because she starred in only four more films after that. The last being in 1958. But as we know, TV shows were becoming hits. Some actors refused to try TV acting and others like Booth transitioned. She still also appeared in theatre sporadically. Booth said this about her co-star from Come Back Little Sheba: "Burt Lancaster advised me against doing Hazel. 'Don't do television,' he warned. 'It'll ruin you!' Burt is a doll and a heck of an actor, but I'm glad I didn't follow his advice. Everybody under 40 knows me better from Hazel, not from my movies!" Indeed, she ended up winning the Emmy for Outstanding Lead Actress in a Comedy Series for it!

Shirley Booth

Booth then headlined in a very popular show called Hazel from 1961 to 1966. It was Booth's favourite gig because she said, "I liked playing Hazel the first time I read one of the scripts, and I could see all the possibilities of the character—the comedy would take care of itself. My job was to give her heart. Hazel never bores me. Besides, she's my insurance policy." She later worked on other stage productions and TV shows that were also quite favourable like The Glass Menagerie on CBS and Hay Fever. Booth's final project was providing the voice for Mrs Claus in the animated TV special called The Year Without A Santa Claus in 1974.

Shirley Booth's Hollywood dream in film productions may have been fleeting, but nonetheless her entrance and exit from the scene was memorable. She came to do what she needed to do and got an Oscar for it. Shirley Booth's theatre success did not happen overnight. Her tireless and dedicated effort to keep an audience entertained kept her stage career long lasting and earning her lots of respect.

Audrey Hepburn

I cannot think of a more influential and universally loved figure for fashion, femininity and films than Audrey Hepburn. To this day, women try to emulate her radiant chic look. Her films, her timeless elegance and her achievements other than acting will be remembered forever. Let's find out how this fresh-faced beauty ended up winning an Oscar for best actress at the age of 24.

Audrey Hepburn's regal nature was already ingrained in her DNA. She was born to a Dutch baroness and an English father who believed he was descended from the English aristocracy. Audrey was born in Belgium, grew up in England and moved to the Netherlands at the onset of World War II with her now single mother. Believing that they would be safe in the seemingly neutral country, Audrey, who was six, and her mother faced hardships in Nazi-occupied Holland. This time in her life Audrey remembered so vividly. She said, "We saw young men put against the wall and shot, and they'd close the street and then open it, and you could pass by again … Don't discount anything awful you hear or read about the Nazis. It's worse than you could ever imagine."

When the war ended and Holland was liberated, Audrey went to ballet school and modelled on the side. Her privileged upbringing gave her poise, erudition and the ability to speak Dutch, English, French, Spanish and Italian. Audrey also was a chorus girl and took elocution lessons before she was scouted and cast in small parts in European films. This was her first taste of film acting.

When she was 22, she was cast in her first major role on Broadway stage in the play called Gigi in 1951. French novelist Colette spotted Hepburn during the filming of the movie called Monte Carlo Baby and immediately cast Audrey for the title role of Gigi. The success of this play made Hollywood executives notice the young and fresh-faced Hepburn. They had no choice but to get Hepburn a role that would change her life forever. William Wyler, the film director, was looking for the perfect princess Anne for his film called Roman Holiday. Once he saw Hepburn's screen test he said, "She had everything I was looking for: charm, innocence, and talent. She also was very funny. She was absolutely enchanting, and we said, 'That's the girl!'"

"As you grow older, you will discover that you have two hands, one for helping yourself, the other for helping others."

Audrey stunned audiences with her natural girly beauty and acting. She starred opposite Gregory Peck, who actually insisted that Hepburn got equal pay as him and equal headlining of her name by his in this film. This movie made Hepburn a star. The world was at her feet.

1953's Roman Holiday was one of the first major Hollywood performances for the exquisite Audrey Hepburn. It was then followed by exceptional and key roles in Breakfast at Tiffany's (1961) and My Fair Lady (1964) among others. But it is the romantic Roman Holiday that placed Hepburn's talent on the film industry map. Until then, she was rather unknown in the Hollywood of the 1950s but this forever changed after her Oscar win for her portrayal of the noble Princess Ann.

Yes, Audrey Hepburn won an Academy Award at the fragile age of 24 for playing a runaway princess who spends a free day of amusements and adventures in the city of Rome to then return to her royal duties in the most diplomatic and admirable way. Princess Ann escapes her responsibilities after experiencing their continuous frustration and enters a lovely fairy tale. Alongside a sincere role by Peck, her on-screen partner and fictional love interest, the young actress combines in her performance a beautiful symbiosis of a child's pure joy and liberty, and a young woman's romantic dreams of navigating big cities and lit streets. Hepburn provoked a smile and a positive reaction with everything she did—from eating gelato to riding a motorcycle. As an 'ordinary' girl instead of Princess Ann, albeit for a moment, she exudes the happiness of

Audrey Hepburn

freedom. This, of course, is contagious for the film's viewers, too! There was something contagious indeed—something special and undeniably unique about the star-quality, charisma and talent of Audrey Hepburn. Both in acting in Roman Holiday and when she received her Oscar statuette at the ceremony—her eyes are full of light. This is why millions of people have fallen in love with her through her performances and her life. She often seems to be able to effortlessly create an elegant, graceful and sophisticated character. And, furthermore, more than once or twice she has been called a 'fashion icon' as through her films and memorable performances, she has set concrete fashion standards. This began with Roman Holiday where alongside the Oscar for Best Actress, another award was won by Edith Head for Costume Design. From beautiful princess dresses to summertime-in-Rome white shirts and long skirts for a day of fun and romance, the fashion in the film left an impression. What is more, Audrey Hepburn was in the process of establishing new styles and a new ideal of female beauty, distinct from the voluptuous hour-glass figures and wavy hairs of Marilyn Monroe or Elizabeth Taylor. Audrey Hepburn had short hair, a confident posture and an inviting and warm smile.

In Roman Holiday, the main character Princess Ann goes on a journey of self-accepting her own path after having a taste of care-free fun and liberty. She makes a wise and diplomatic choice, performed with a quiet dignity and a wonderful charm by Audrey Hepburn, at the time only beginning her own career and life as a young woman. This was recognised with an Academy Award and with multiple well-deserved gestures of love from fans to follow, even today.

1954 was Hepburn's year. She won the BAFTA Award for Best British Actress in a Leading Role, a Globe Award for Best Actress Motion Picture Drama and of course the Academy Award for Best Actress. Hepburn rushed to the Oscar ceremony straight after her Broadway performance in Ondine. Still with her dramatic stage makeup but now in her lucky dress from Roman Holiday, Audrey had just made it on time to accept her statuette. Audrey won a Tony for her work in Ondine too in 1954. She did not

appear on stage after this.
Audrey, obviously, went on to headline more major motion pictures after signing with Paramount for a 7-year contract. Unlike other Oscar winning actresses like Olivia De Havilland, Bette Davis or Ginger Rogers, who battled their studios for breach of contract or other unfair treatment. Audrey's studio gave her 12 months between film shoots to focus on her stage career too. Hepburn illuminated the screens in movies like Sabrina, War and Peace, Funny Face, Love In The Afternoon and Nuns Story. This was all throughout the 1950's.

When the 1960's arrived, so did new stars, new films and of course new fashion. Fashion houses like Givenchy were making huge waves in the cinema. Audrey's success was not backing down either. In fact she appeared in probably her most famous film role of Holly Golightly in Breakfast at Tiffany's in 1961. It's one of the most famous films in the history of cinema, fashion and high society life. Givenchy designed the famous little black dress for Audrey to wear in the film among other looks. Audrey stated that the role was "the jazziest of her career" and added, "I'm an introvert. Playing the extroverted girl was the hardest thing I ever did."

After Breakfast at Tiffany's, Audrey, now in her 30s, played more extravagant and mature roles in diverse genre films like The Children's Hour, Charade, My Fair Lady, Two For the Road and Wait Until Dark. Audrey won three BAFTA's overall, for her role in Roman Holiday, Nuns Story and Charade.
When the 1960's were wrapping up, so did Audrey's acting career. Although she starred in a handful of lesser-known films and projects, she focused on family

and humanitarian work instead. Since her rise to fame, Hepburn had worked with UNICEF. In the 1980s Hepburn became a UNICEF ambassador and travelled extensively to help various emergency operations all over the world. She said, "I can testify to what UNICEF means to children, because I was among those who received food and medical relief right after World War II. I have a long-lasting gratitude and trust for what UNICEF does."

Hepburn won the Jean Hersholt Humanitarian Award at the 1993 Oscars for Outstanding Contributions to Humanitarian Causes. Her son accepted the award on her behalf since she passed away a few months before. In addition AFI has listed her as the third most greatest female film star, after Katharine Hepburn and Bette Davis. Audrey was such a fascinating person on and off screen, to say the least. Her humble, noble and gentle nature made her very special in the glamour and gossip filled Hollywood. As time goes by, her image and work keeps getting more and more valued. Something only a leading lady can do.

Grace Kelly

When the previous year's winner was the legendary Audrey Hepburn, someone incredibly special had to be next to receive the honour of the Best Actress Oscar. Someone who not only mesmerised people on screen, but also off screen with a high level of sophistication and natural beauty. The Oscar had to go to Grace Kelly at the 1955 Academy Awards for a role so different to what she was used to playing.

Grace Kelly, just like Hepburn, came from a privileged background, but in Pennsylvania. She had the best education, home, and clothing. There was nothing that Grace could not have. When it was time to decide her career, Grace, who was influenced by earlier Oscar winning actresses like Katharine Hepburn, Ingrid Bergman and Joan Crawford, decided to pursue acting. These actresses paved the way for aspiring actresses like Grace, so to speak. Grace had a one up over other aspiring actresses though, because she had connections in the world of film. Her uncles Walter C. Kelly, a vaudevillian, and George Kelly, a Pulitzer prize winning playwright, managed to help Kelly get a head start in the industry.

Grace quickly moved to New York City to attend the American Academy of Dramatic Arts and model on the sides. For her final graduation performance, Kelly played the role of Tracy Lord in the production of The Philadelphia Story. She would reprise this role in a remake later. Grace then went on to debut on Broadway stage and in TV series. Her performances in The Father, The Rockingham Tea Set and The Apple Tree were not left unnoticed because she was noticed by Hollywood director Henry Hathaway, who would offer Kelly her first film role.

"I don't want to be married to someone who feels inferior to my success or because I make more money than he does."

It was in the 1951 movie, Fourteen Hours, that Kelly proved to audiences that she could carry a scene. This film debut was followed by another film role in High Noon in 1952. Her tranquil and poised demeanour was just what Hollywood needed. But these two films did not truly prove Kelly's star quality. Believing that her career success was in film, Kelly took on private acting lessons in order to be taken seriously. She also signed with MGM. And in 1953, she appeared in Mogambo. The success of this film led to Kelly getting nominated for her first Golden Globe and Academy Award. From this point onwards,

Grace Kelly

Grace Kelly was getting closer and closer to becoming a worldwide star. Just like Audrey Hepburn, Kelly became a style icon. Her fashion on and off screen, to this day, is considered timeless and elegant.
In Grace, Alfred Hitchcock seemed to have found his next blonde for his movies. He cast Grace in his 1954 movies Dial M For Murder and Rear Window. The following year she starred in their third collaboration called To Catch A Thief in 1955. But this was after starring in her most successful film yet—Country Girl, a film that follows the career and personal life struggles of a washed up, alcoholic actor, Frank Elgin played by Bing Crosby.

Elgin's much younger wife, Georgie, played by Kelly, is demure and supportive of his talents in music and acting on Broadway but his older age, alcoholic tendencies and lack of self-confidence makes him lose out on stage roles. When he gets a coveted stage role given to him by a stage director Bernie Dodd, played by William Holden, Georgie begins to micromanage Frank.

She becomes defensive over him so that he does not get used by the director. Although wanting nothing but the best for her husband she comes off as clingy. Bernie and Georgie butt heads over Frank, who is weak minded and is slowly spiralling into alcoholism. As the story progresses we come to find out that the alcoholic past of Georgie too, who now is recovered. The couple lost their toddler son years ago when he got hit by a car. And ever since Frank has been ridden with guilt. The untimely and random blossoming romance between Georgie and Bernie makes matters worse in this love triangle. Frank manages to give a good performance and is not on the road to recovery yet the romance between Georgie and Bernie brings him truly back to his senses. Ultimately Georgie returns to Frank after her quick fling with Bernie. The two reunite and continue their lives with Frank's newfound fame and success.

Grace Kelly's subdued, soft performance as a sad, lonely and troubled wife of an artist was realistic. Sometimes someone suffering is silent and that is what Grace brought to the screen with her soft voice, intense stares and sullen eyes. Grace Kelly's performance was highly praised. And in the 1955 Academy Awards, she won the Best Actress Oscar, along with a Golden Globe.

That same year, Kelly met Prince Rainier the third at the Cannes film festival. The Prince of Monaco and Kelly eventually started a courtship and in 1956, around a year later, got married. and began her duties as a princess. Becoming a mother and philanthropist were her two new missions. The greatly publicised wedding between Grace and Rainer was a worldwide celebration. In fact, the royal wedding was probably the second biggest media sensation of its day, after the coronation of Queen Elizabeth the Second, because it was watched by 30 million viewers on live television and was described as "the first modern event to generate media overkill". While Grace had become a princess, her union brought a sudden end to her acting career at the age of 26. Her final film appearance was in the movie High Society, a remake of The Philadelphia Story, which originally starred Katharine Hepburn as the lead. Despite such an iconic career, Grace Kelly was quite vocal about her contempt of Hollywood. She said, "Hollywood amuses me. Holier-than-thou for the public and unholier-than-the-devil in reality."

Grace Kelly

But there cannot be light without the dark. Grace Kelly's life ended too soon at the age of 52 in a car crash. She suffered a stroke while driving and unfortunately lost control and rolled down an embankment with her daughter, who survived the crash. Grace Kelly will go down in history not only as a great actress, but a timeless beauty and style icon. She was a sought-after actress in her time and her Hollywood dream was short lived but she will always be remembered as the icon of elegance and class.

"Please don't retouch my wrinkles. It took me so long to earn them."

Anna Magnani

Grace Kelly, the previous year's Oscar winner, was an icon of elegance, class and soft femininity. But this time, a more rugged, fiery and foreign woman won the Oscar for Best Actress. In 1956, Anna Magnani, the first ever Italian actress to win the award, accepted her Oscar for a provocative role. These two women could not be more opposite.

Anna Magnani's legendary performances in Italian cinema lead up to her entrance into Hollywood. She was born to an Egyptian father and Italian Jewish mother. Growing up in Italy, learning French and studying acting at the Royal Academy of Dramatic Art in Rome for two years were the stepping stones to Magnani's introduction to film acting. From an early age, Anna was able to captivate audiences with her boisterous laugh, her uncontrollable cry and ability to sing on stage. This raw, uninhibited array of emotions in her performance got her the first of her acting jobs in Italy.

She spent her early 20s acting in a variety of experimental plays in Rome and in 1933, at the age of 25, she was noticed by filmmaker Goffredo Allesandrini, who she would then marry that same year. They shot Anna's first major film role called The Blind Woman Of Sorrento. From this moment onward, Magnani collaborated with other major filmmakers like Vittorio De Sica, Roberto Rossellini, Pasolini, Visconti, Fellini, Jean Renoir, Sidney Lumet, and Tennessee Williams. For another 20 years, Magnani chiselled a solid European filmography and eventually became a household name. This earthy, loud mouthed, dishevelled archetype that Magnani evoked on screen and off was her signature that would make her a worldwide acting legend. She became the icon of neorealism Italian cinema, a new movement that had emerged post World War II.

In the late 1950s Magnani and Roberto Rossellini started a romance, but upon Ingrid Bergman's emergence on the Italian scene, Rossellini switched course and fell in love with Bergman. Subsequently casting Bergman as the lead in Stromboli, the film that he planned to cast Magnani as the lead. But at least Magnani got something out of this relationship with Rossellini, and that was her powerful performance in the movie Rome, Open City directed by Rossellini in 1945. In fact, she created one of the most incredible scenes in film history—Pina's death scene.

So, Bergman went to Italy, but Magnani went to Hollywood at the beginning the 1950s, where Tennessee Williams was dying to work with her. Tennessee Williams, the playwright of earlier wonders like Streetcar Named Desire, wrote a play called The Rose Tattoo. He had Magnani in mind to play the lead of Serafina in the stage version, but she backed out due to her lack of English proficiency. Magnani's work was quite well known in the New York scene, due to the more eclectic crowd there, that followed less commercial work, and that focused more on the neo-realist cinema.

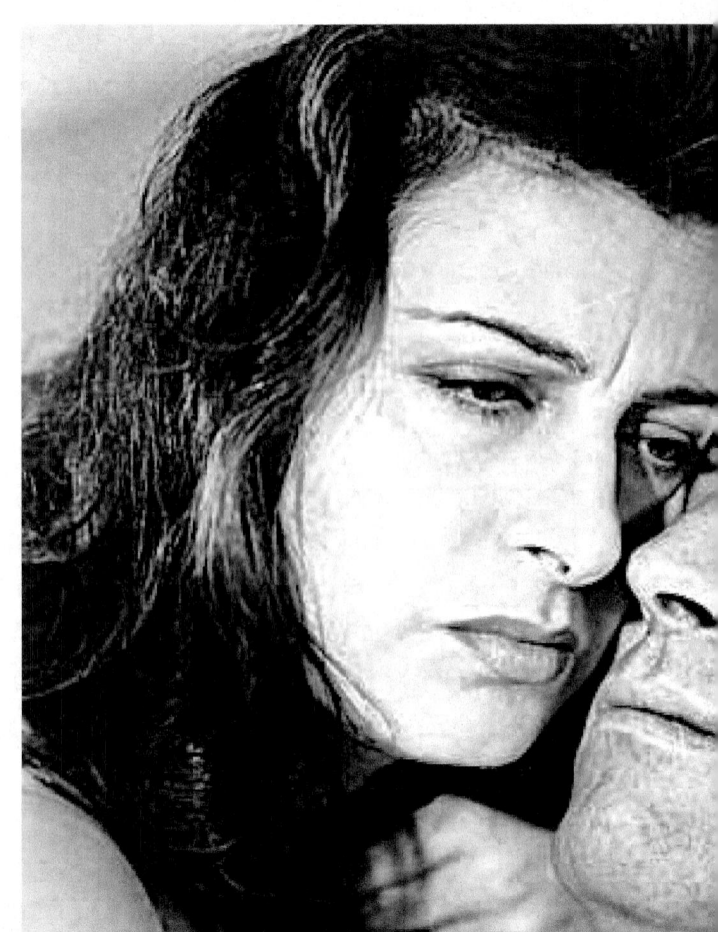

When the play was adapted to the screen in 1955, Magnani was ready to amaze the western world of cinema in her first ever English-speaking role. The union of Williams and Magnani, two unconventional legends in the arts world, made headlines. The provocative, envelope-pushing content of the film that paired with Magnani's and Burt Lancaster's erotically charged performances challenged the production code of Hollywood and pulled audiences out of their TV filled homes and back into the cinema.

Tennessee Williams said this about his choice of casting Magnani, which is quote telling of who she was as a person: "Anna Magnani was magnificent as Serafina in the movie version of Tattoo ... She was as unconventional a woman as I have known in or out of my professional world, and if you understand me at all, you must know that in this statement I am making my personal estimate of her honesty, which I feel was complete. She never exhibited any lack of self-assurance, any timidity in her relations with that society outside of whose conventions she quite publicly existed ... [s]he looked absolutely straight into the eyes of whomever she confronted and during that golden time in which we were dear friends, I never heard a false word from her mouth."

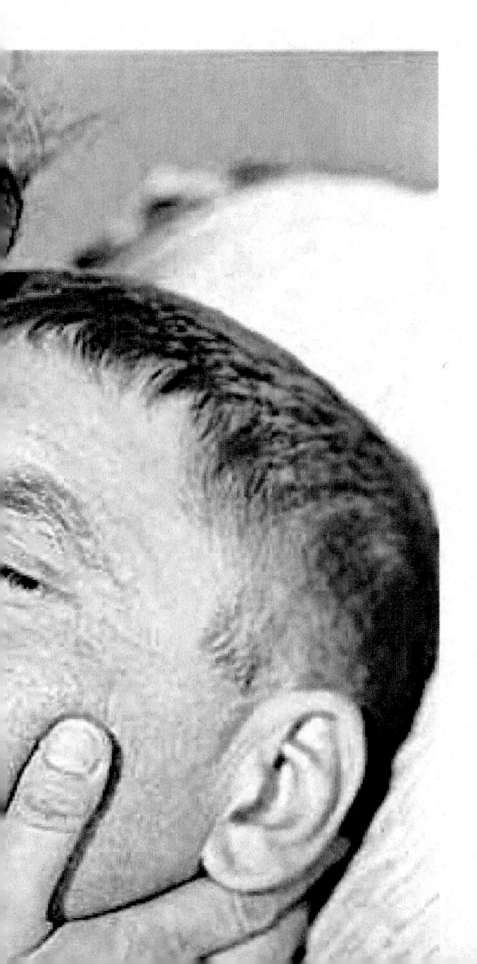

The Rose Tattoo centres on the tough life of Serafina Delle Rose, a southern Italian seamstress whose crook of a cheating husband is killed in a car crash suddenly. Now the widow Serafina is left to survive with her teenage daughter Rosa. Serafina mourns the loss of her husband for a long time. She misses him and takes pride in being the wife of his, even after years of him dying. Serafina embarks on a not so romantic relationship with the seemingly dim yet outgoing Alvaro Mangiacavallo played by Burt Lancaster. His boyish tendencies and lack of social skills enamour Serafina and his big and strong physique reminds Serafina of her late husband. Alvaro, now obsessed with Serafina, gets a rose tattoo on his chest, as a surprise to Serafina, whose late husband had a rose tattoo on his chest too. Serafina juggles the struggles of raising a rebellious teenage daughter who tries to live more like the white American teenagers who date, go on dances and trips. Ultimately, Serafina decides to move on with life and not mourn her husband anymore, she accepts Alvaro into her life and they rejoice together after a hot and cold relationship.

When awards season came, Magnani doubted that she would win anything so she went back to her home in Rome. But she was wrong. At the 1956 Academy Awards, her name was uttered as the winner of the Best Actress for her performance in The Rose Tattoo. Her co-star Marisa Pavan accepted the award on her behalf. In addition Magnani won the BAFTA and Golden Globe for this role too.

Magnani, who was known for her makeup free face, heavy under-eye bags and dishevelled hair continued her work with Tennessee Williams writing in their second film called The Fugitive Kind directed by Sidney Lumet. She starred in Passolini's Mamma Roma, Fellini's Roma and of course George Cukor's Wild Is the Wind.

Magnani's knack for dramatic performance and good taste in films that she chose to be in carved a beautiful filmography that truly revealed her passionate and unapologetically Roman essence. A type of leading lady nobody can emulate, some can try, but none can truly have the irresistible intensity as Magnani on film.

Anna Magnani

Joanne Woodward

In many cases, when two amazing actors get into a relationship, one of them prevails. This might have been the case for Joanne Woodward and her husband of 50 years, Paul Newman. The spotlight was always on him, even though they collaborated on numerous films together. But I think Joanne held her own without her husband attached to her success. With a filmography of diverse and deep characters, she won many awards like a BAFTA, 3 Emmys, 3 Golden Globes and of course the Best Actress Oscar.

Joanne came from a movie-loving family, hence her name, given to her by her mother in honour of Joan Crawford. It all started off with Joanne's participation in beauty pageants and local theatre productions in South Carolina. She went on to study drama at Louisiana State University and moved to NYC after graduating.

She studied at the Actors Studio, secured an agent, understudied some Broadway gigs and starred in TV productions in the early 1950s. That is when she met her future love of her life. Her partner to whom she would be married until his death. And that was Paul Newman, who was also a starting actor in the early 1950s.

After receiving some attention from Hollywood while sculpting her resume in NYC, Joanne signed to 20th Century Fox and starred in her film debut in 1955, Count Three And Pray. The following years she played a different type of role in A Kiss Before Dying. It was soon after that Joanne secured a role that promoted her to a Hollywood Star. Paul Newman was on the same trajectory as Woodward. We can say they rose to prominence together. Only three years after Joanne's film debut, she was cast in a role that made headlines. She portrayed a woman suffering from multiple personality disorder in the film The Three Faces Of Eve. Joanne proved to the audiences her diverse acting range in such a complex undertaking.

Playing one character on screen well is difficult enough, but how about playing three? In Nunnally Johnson's The Three Faces of Eve, Joanne Woodward plays a character with three different personalities: Eve White, Eve Black, and Jane. Woodward's performance(s) earned her the Academy Award for Best Actress, making her the first to ever win for portraying three different characters on-screen.

"Intensity is so much more becoming in the young."

The film tells the story of Eve, a woman who finds herself mysteriously getting severe headaches and blacking out, losing hours of her day. After visiting a psychiatrist, she discovers that she actually has dissociative identity disorder, then known as multiple personality disorder. The film then follows her quest to discover the source of her trauma.

Judy Garland was actually originally cast for the main part in this film, but she was notoriously unreliable by this point in her career. Garland was dealing with various addictions and mental health troubles by the 1950s, and ended up backing out of the film at the last minute. In fact, casting Eve proved incredibly difficult for Johnson, because in addition to Garland backing out, multiple actresses actually turned

the role down. They include names like June Allyson and Jennifer Jones, both of which feared the role for different reasons. So, Johnson chose to cast Woodward instead, though at that point, she was not a very well-known name. It was a risk to pick her, but it clearly paid off! The Three Faces of Eve was only the third film Woodward had been in at that point.

The screenplay was actually written with the help of real-life psychiatrists Hervey M. Cleckley and Corbett H. Thigpen. The film was also based on an autobiography by Christine Costner Sizemore, though her identity was unknown at the time as she had published the book under a pseudonym. Later, in 1999, a documentary would be made about Sizemore's life called Multiple Personality: Reality and Illusion. Supposedly, in order to get Sizemore's contractual approval for the film, she came in and signed three

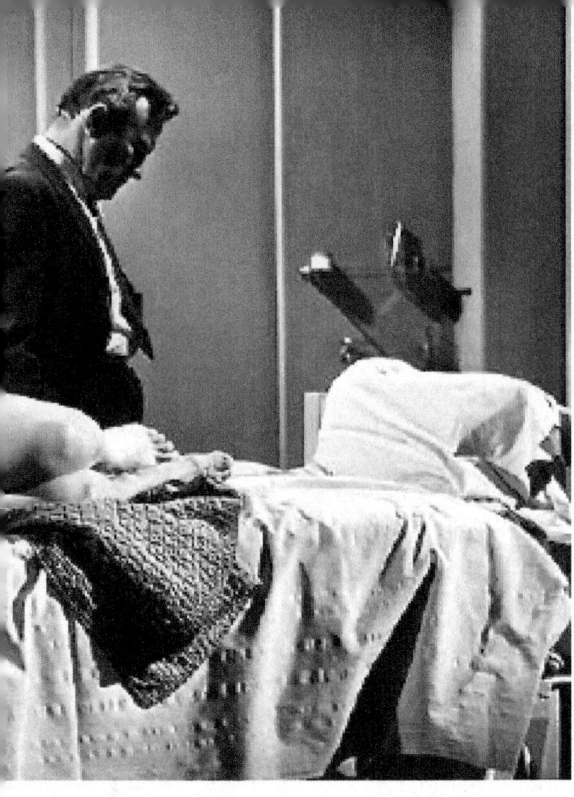

different contracts as each personality. Funnily enough, the film itself wasn't particularly well-received. The general consensus was that it was hokey and melodramatic. It is, after all, a very exploitative, almost B movie premise. The movie suffers from tonal whiplash and doesn't quite blend all the personalities' stories together as seamlessly as it should. All that being said, Woodward's performance was unanimously praised. The Three Faces of Eve actually became one of the few films to win Best Actress without getting nominated in any other category. The first to do this was 1935's Dangerous. Later, 1990's Misery would do the same.

Indeed, Woodward plays each character incredibly well. Eve White is the more neurotic of the three, while Eve Black is oversexed and over-confident. Finally, Jane is the "normal" one, who ultimately becomes the personality who wins out and takes control. Eve Black is perhaps the most entertaining to watch on-screen—Woodward plays her magnetically, with a bewitching sense of seduction. Joanne Woodward actually went on to appear in another film about dissociative identity disorder called Sybil in 1976. This time, however, she played the psychiatrist who treats a patient with DID as opposed to playing the character with DID.

Woodward's attitude about the Oscar win is pretty interesting. She herself didn't actually campaign for the Oscar at all. She was actually overall a bit cynical about Hollywood, at least at that time. She actually reportedly said that she didn't like her performance in The Three Faces of Eve that much and thought Deborah Kerr (nominated for Heaven Knows, Mr. Allison) should win.

"If I had an infinite amount of respect for the people who think I gave the greatest performance, then it would matter to me," she said. In fact, executives were starting to worry about her outspoken ways …but when she won the Oscar, that worry eased up. Woodward ended up being pretty excited about the Oscar win, and later said,

"I remember when I first won the Academy Award, and how much I loved it. I just wish there was an award around that you could really believe in again" Woodward famously attended the Awards in a homemade dress that only cost about $100. This ticked off a few people in the crowd, including Joan Crawford, who took it upon herself to make a statement about the dress. "Joanne Woodward is setting the cause of Hollywood glamour back twenty years by making her own clothes," Crawford had said. This amused Woodward, who actually shouted Crawford out when she returned to the Academy Awards in 1966, this time wearing a more couture gown from Travilla.

The Three Faces of Eve was Woodward's only Oscar win, though she did end up nominated for Best Actress a few more times. One nomination was for Rachel, Rachel, which was actually directed by her husband, Paul Newman. In addition to this major success, Joanne and Paul had married a few months earlier. Paul divorced his wife and married Woodward two weeks later. The couple three children together, in addition to the three children from Newman's previous marriage. Furthermore the newlywed couple co-starred in the first of many collaborations together. That same year of 1958, they starred in The Long Hot Summer.

Joanne Woodward

This union on screen was a winning recipe, so they continued to work together on more films like Rally 'Round the Boys (1958), From the Terrace (1960), Paris Blues (1961), and A New Kind of Love (1963). Nonetheless, Woodward still worked on films without her husband, like in The Fugitive Kind in 1960, opposite Marlon Brando and Anna Magnani, who won the Best Actress Oscar the year prior Joanne did. Let's not forget that Joanne was nominated two more times for the Oscar for her roles in Summer Wishes, Winter Dreams (1973) and Mr. & Mrs. Bridge (1990) which co-starred Newman again.

The couple worked together in another highly praised Newman directorial called The Effect of Gamma Rays on Man-in-the-Moon Marigolds (1972). The 1970s brought more gems to Woodward's career. She worked on films made for TV. She starred in Sybil in 1976 opposite Sally Field, she won an Emmy for her role in See How She Runs in 1978 and even directed a few series at the end of the 1970s and into early 1980s. Once the 1980s rolled in, Joanne won one more Emmy for her role in Do You Remember Love in 1985. The screen adaptation of The Glass Menagerie in 1987 brought Woodward and Newman together once again.

It is so evident just how bulletproof Joanne Woodward was. In the midst of her career that spanned for over 5 decades, she found a lifelong partner who also worked with her on many successful projects, she raised three children and contributed to philanthropic causes. She worked on Philadelphia opposite Tom Hanks as well as Age Of Innocence both in 1993.

By the end of her career, Joanne Woodward did not back down from participating in acting projects. She focused more so on stage productions and eventually directed plays for a local playhouse in Connecticut. She said this later in life looking back: "Initially, I probably had a real movie-star dream. It faded somewhere in my mid-30s, when I realised I wasn't going to be that kind of actor. It was painful. Also, I curtailed my career because of my children. Quite a bit. I resented it at the time, which was not a good way to be around the children. Paul was away on location a lot. I wouldn't go on location because of the children. I did once, and felt overwhelmed with guilt."

Joanne Woodward will go down in history as a naturally beautiful, sophisticated and strong woman. I think the success to such a high degree is because she was fearless and devoted to her craft. She said, "I'm a risk-taker. I like to test myself." With lots of films, TV shows and theatre performances, Joanne will always be remembered as a major influence in cinema through her compelling and bright performances.

Susan Hayward

The end of the 1950s brought more provocative, gritty and significant films in the US as a way to make a statement in the patriarchal, corrupt and sexist country. Only a handful of actresses had the opportunity, and really the talent and strength, to play intense and robust characters in such films. With this explosion of coquettish, fake-fragile actresses like Marylin Monroe, and even Grace Kelly with her angel like image, some actresses refused to follow this trend and went their own way. Just as Joanne Woodward won an Oscar for such a layered role the year before, so did Susan Hayward for a gritty role in an equally influential film.

Susan Hayward, a native Brooklynite, started her career as a pinup model. George Cukor and David O. Selznick, who were looking to cast the role of Scarlett O'Hara for Gone With The Wind, spotted Hayward's pinup images in a magazine. They called out the redhead to Hollywood to screen test for this role. The 20-year-old Susan had a feeling of hope and ambition instilled in her after this invitation to audition for a film and pursue Hollywood. Although Vivien Leigh was cast instead, and Hayward was told to go back to New York, she refused and had her return ticket refunded. This one decision changed her life.

Her lack of training, strong Brooklyn accent and subtle limp made her work even harder and pay her dues before securing something concrete in Hollywood. She signed with Warner Bros and then moved to 20th Century Fox. People saw lots of potential in Hayward, to a point where she was compared to a youthful Bette Davis.

Hayward did not want to play bimbos, ingenues or roles that were there to back the male counterparts. Throughout the 1940s she carved her career in films such as Hollywood Hotel, which was her debut, Beau Geste, Among The Living, Reap The Wild Wind and The Forest Ranger to name a few.

"I never thought of myself as a movie star. I'm just a working girl. A working girl who worked her way to the top –and never fell off."

Susan Hayward

1947 brought Hayward her first Oscar nomination for her role in Smash-Up: The Story of a Woman. In 1949 she was nominated again for My Foolish Heart. Her third nomination was in 1952 for With A Song In My Heart. Susan was now in her 30s, she was getting taken seriously as an actress and had the power to choose roles she deemed worthy. This reputation as a professional and individual woman was valuable to Hayward's appeal in Hollywood. She was nominated the fourth time in 1955 for I'll Cry Tomorrow.

It was not long until Susan Hayward was able to carry that golden statue home for her role as Barbara Graham in the 1958 film I Want To Live! The film is notable for depicting capital punishment, and the rather gruesome death scene towards the end of the film shocked audiences ... and impressed the Academy. It was the first film to depict a complete execution on screen. It was real, raw and disturbing compared to unusual films at that time.

The film is based on the life of Barbara Graham, a convicted murderer who was executed via poison gas at San Quentin Prison in 1955. The movie chronicles her rise from petty criminal to murderer. Of course, the film took quite a few liberties with the storytelling—the film posits that Graham didn't actually commit murder, but a taped confession from Graham that surfaced later said otherwise. In fact, Hayward herself later admitted that she believed Graham had, in fact, actually committed the murder. This wasn't something she actually admitted to until long after the film came out, though, as the story angle of Graham being innocent was key to the marketing of the film.

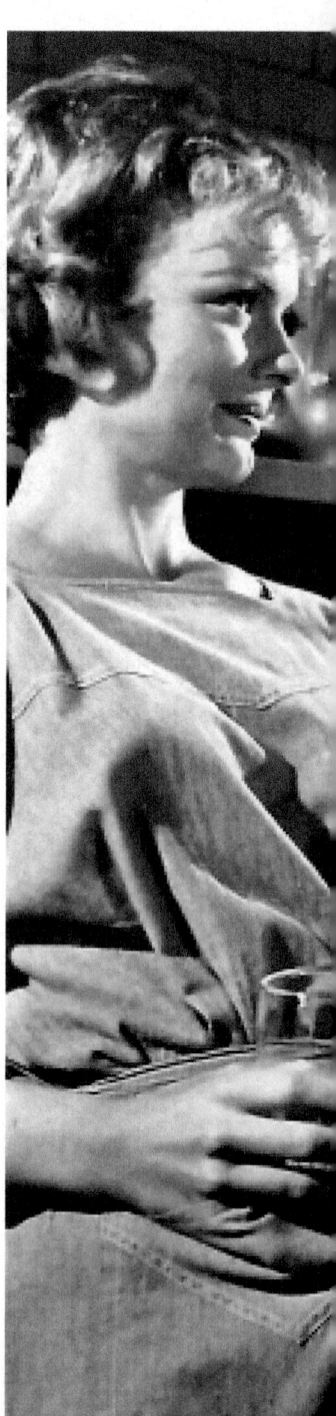

Hayward does an excellent job turning Barbara Graham into a character worthy of sympathy. She flashes her innocent eyes even when her character is being busted for a misdemeanour. She also has a glamorous and mischievous air about her that really helps her pull off the sympathetic but still pretty criminal character. Despite the fact that the audience generally seemed to believe that the real Barbara Graham had committed murder, Hayward succeeded in turning her into a tragic figure.

Susan Hayward's character and performance in I Want To Live! reminds one a bit of Charlize Theron's role as Aileen Wuornos in 2004's film, Monster. Both films used real letters from their subjects as the basis for characterization, as well. While I do believe that Theron's role is more compelling, both actresses pull off a biographical account of prostitutes who have committed murder. And, most importantly, they make these murderous women likeable and sympathetic.

Interestingly enough, Hayward is one of only a few who have won Oscars for portraying real-life killers. The others include Charlize Theron (as mentioned previously), Estelle Parsons for her role as Blanche Barrow in Bonnie & Clyde, Joe Pesci as Tommy Devito in Goodfellas, and Forest Whitaker as Idi Amin in The Last King of Scotland. The relatively famous gas chamber scene was shot on a soundstage,

and it opened up a dialogue about the ethics of capital punishment. Audiences were shocked by how barbaric and mediaeval the process was. Having a beautiful Hollywood star being the one gassed certainly helped play up sympathies, too. And the sequence truly was the most notable part of the film. A whopping two weeks was spent shooting the execution scene, and director Robert Wise was obsessed with getting every grisly detail correct. Even those who criticised the film for the inaccuracies commended how realistic the execution sequence was. Originally, producer Joseph Mankiewicz wanted to add an explicitly anti-capital punishment message to the end of the film. However, Wise felt that Hayward's performance did enough to sway the audience about the moral issues with the death penalty. Truth be told, he was right.

Hayward's performance is more than just a PSA about capital punishment. She genuinely puts her all into the performance and it is a treat to watch. While the story really isn't that compelling—it was likely far more interesting in the 50s when it was still "ripped from the headlines fresh"—Hayward's acting is a real treat to watch. There's something charming about melodramatic movies like these that still give them a rewatchable quality all these years later, even if they don't land in the same way as they did for audiences back then. Hayward's acting style is absolutely fantastic—who else could pull off the tiger growling scene during the interview with the media?

Admittedly, the movie feels a bit ridiculous to watch now. While Hayward definitely gives the role her all, the actual story is just a little too hokey and melodramatic.

Essentially, the film doesn't age well. Still, it is a pretty fascinating flick, if only to learn a little bit more about this sensationalised true story. It's also an interesting look at the politics of the era surrounding capital punishment. And, of course, Susan Hayward is great, so it's worth watching just for her!

After this success, Susan Hayward's filmography narrowed to one film a year and in 1972 she appeared in her final film called The Revengers. Three years later she tragically passed away from brain cancer. Her whole life she competed with other actresses for various roles and awards and the Oscar seemed to be something she desired. Rightfully so. It's as if, when she finally got it, she could relax.

Simone Signoret

When you think of a French woman, you envision this unapologetically unfiltered, cultured and liberated woman. With a cigarette in one hand and a vintage edition of Sartre or De Beauvoir in the other. This was Simone Signoret. She was a wildly fascinating woman. Her life was so colourful with ups and downs as if she was the main character of her own life. We can regard her as a pioneer of female liberation and icon of transatlantic cinema. Not many wanted her to succeed and she proved them wrong.

Growing up in Nazi occupied France during WWII, after fleeing Germany since her father was a Jew, it was far from easy for Simone growing up. She changed her last name from Kaminker which indicated her Jewish heritage to her mother's maiden name Signoret. She would sneak out of the house and visit the Left Bank cafes to mingle with the eclectic crowds of writers, artists, musicians and filmmakers. Nazi's would not go there. Simone in her late teens and early 20s stood out in the crowd already. Her unique hooded blue eyes and her love for film and all things art related made other artists notice her. She would even help hide thousands of French films from Nazi destruction.

Through her connections in the arts world, she started acting in small roles in the early 1940s. She worked illegally without a permit and eventually acted in the films of leading French directors like Bunuel and Clouzot. From the get-go, Simone infused her roles with fierce tenacity. Already provoking the status quo of how limited women's roles were. Simone was quite similar to Anna Magnani in that she was earthy, genuine and intellectual. Her career took off in the 1950s with appearances in La Ronde, Casque D'or, Les Diabolique and The Crucible in theatres.

"I collect all the reviews of the films I turned down. And when they're bad—I have to smile."

1959 was Simone's big break. She was cast in the independent British New Wave film called Room At The Top. This film won her numerous awards, including best actress at Cannes and when the time came for the nominees for Best Actress Oscar to be announced, Simone was included. Hedda Hopper, the most popular right wing celebrity columnist in Hollywood, detested the fact that Simone, a left wing liberal, was advancing into the Hollywood realm, and on top of that was getting considered for an Oscar. Hopper did whatever it took to not get Signoret a moment to shine. But who was Hedda Hopper to come in the way of a well-established European actress from getting an award!

At the 1960 Academy Awards Signoret was up against Audrey Hepburn and Katherine Hepburn. Ultimately Signoret found herself rushing up to the stage to accept her award. She was the second French-born actress, after Claudette Colbert, and the first fully French, non-American actress to win the Best Actress Oscar.

Simone Signoret

The riveting love triangle at the centre of Room at the Top won over both critics and general audiences. The film takes place in England, and stars Laurence Harvey as Joe, a young man who plans to move up the social ladder by marrying the daughter of the rich Brown family. However, Joe quickly ends up falling for Alice Aisgill, an older woman who is in an abusive relationship with her husband. Alice is played by the fantastic Simone Signoret in her Oscar-winning performance.

The film is based on the novel of the same name written by John Braine. Originally, producers John and James Woolf had their eyes on Jean Simmons and Stewart Granger for the lead roles. Vivien Leigh had also been offered the part of Alice. Laurence Harvey was also nominated for Best Actor, but he lost to Charlton Heston's performance in Ben-Hur. Notably, Hermione Baddeley was nominated for Best Supporting Actress for her role as Alice's friend, Elspeth. She is only on-screen for two minutes and nineteen seconds, making her performance the shortest to ever be nominated for an acting Oscar.

Room at the Top's various accolades at the Academy Awards were a bit controversial. For starters, the film belonged to a British subgenre called "kitchen-sink realism". These films often had leftist sympathies and the stylings of the genre were inspired by various socialist painters. Signoret herself was a known leftist, and famous right-wing columnist (and a perpetrator of the Hollywood blacklists against suspected communists) Hedda Hopper was rumoured to have quit her position on the Academy's board over Signoret's win.

The film itself clearly shows the upper-class characters as unlikeable and despicable. Alice's husband, played by Allan Cuthbertson, is always shown with an air of superiority. He mistreats Alice and belittles those he considers beneath him on the social ladder. While Joe initially aspired to be a hot shot upper-middle-class man like him, when he eventually achieves those goals, he is left feeling hollow. It doesn't just criticise the upper class though—it skewers the entire class system by showing that Alice and Joe can never be happy within its confines.

Signoret also had the unique position of being the first actress to win the lead acting Oscar without having done any Hollywood films. She was also one of the few French actresses to ever win an Oscar—another French woman didn't win another acting award until Juliette Binoche's Best Supporting Actress win in 1997. The only other French actress to win an acting Oscar before her was Claudette Colbert in It Happened One Night. Ultimately, Room at the Top (and her Oscar win) cemented her place as an international star.

The film's story itself was a hot topic due to its portrayal of sex, as well. Even in England, where there was no Hays Code prohibiting specific portrayals of sex, Room at the Top ended up getting an X rating. The adultery portrayed in the film was also a hot button topic. Still, that spicy rating and the subsequent controversy around it didn't stop the movie from becoming one of the most popular British films that year.

It's also notable that both of the leads in the film are Jewish. This might not seem too revolutionary to audiences now, but at the time, antisemitism was very prominent in the UK. As such, the film was groundbreaking because it had Signoret and Harvey in the lead roles. Harvey initially was not going to be cast, because producers feared that audiences wouldn't approve of the Jewish casting. They ended up casting him in the end, though, of course, and his being Jewish clearly didn't hurt the film too much.

Signoret ended up being nominated for the Best Actress Golden Globe for Room at the Top that year, as well, though she did not win the Globe. Later in 1966, she would be nominated for Best Actress in a Leading Role once again for Ship of Fools. She would also go on to receive much more acclaim in England, where she won three BAFTA awards and was nominated for three more.

Signoret herself was an interesting woman. She didn't adhere to the normal standards that actresses were supposed to adhere to. She made little to no effort to mask her age or try to glamorise herself as she grew older. In fact, she had once commented, "I got old the way women who aren't actresses grow old." She was a bit of a firecracker, once quipping that she saved reviews of all the films she had turned down.
 "When they're bad," she said, "I have to smile."

The star who now was a household name appeared in a few other Hollywood films, but preferred to work in France. Signoret worked all up until her death in 1985. Although her personal life was tumultuous with themes of adultery from her partner's side, it made her even more admired by audiences. On top of her extensive filmography that consisted of films like Term Of Trail, Ship Of Fools, Madame Rosa and I Sent A Letter To My Loves, Signoret managed to indulge in theatre

productions too, and even wrote memoirs and a novel.
Her no-frills attitude, her advocacy for ageing naturally and gracefully and her human approach to acting is to this day a rare and admirable combination to have in such a widely popular actress. She said, "I got old the way that women who aren't actresses grow old." After spending 4 decades in the business of film, we can safely say that Simone Signoret is a highly identifiable, and one-of-a-kind leading lady.

Simone Signoret

"I've been through it all, baby, I'm mother courage."

Elizabeth Taylor

As we enter the 1960s, we notice lots of changes happening in Hollywood. As I have said before, each decade brings a big wave of change that progresses the entertainment industry as a whole. The biggest being the demise of the Hollywood Star System in the 60s. After decades of abuse, constant exchange, breach of contract and manipulation from the movie studios (like MGM or Paramount to name a few big ones) film stars provoked this system, and it eventually crumbled. Elizabeth Taylor was probably the last to come out of this system and establish herself as a celebrity and a worldwide icon of style and acting. Elizabeth Taylor was born in England and moved to Los Angeles right before the outbreak of WWII. With both her parents' work firmly planted in the arts world, her father an art dealer and her mother a former stage actress, Elizabeth found herself getting introduced to Hollywood execs early on. Elizabeth Taylor became a child actor, like Jodie Foster or Natalie Portman, for example.

At the age of 10 she starred in her film debut in There's One Born Every Minute in 1942, followed by Lassie Come Home in 1943 and National Velvet in 44, her breakout role. She spent her teens honing the craft of acting and setting herself up for a lifetime of success in film acting. By her late teens, she took on more mature roles like in Life With Father, Little Women and Father Of The Bride. She always had a look and aura of maturity about her and that made her transition to more provocative and serious roles effortlessly.

A Place In The Sun in 1951, Ivanhoe in 1952, The Last Time I Saw Paris in 1954, Giant in 1956 and Raintree Country in 1957, for which she was nominated for an Oscar for the first time, were all wildly successful films. These were films that made her a sought-after actress in Hollywood. And she starred in them all by the age of 24.

Taylor was known as a striking beauty, with eyes so blue that they gave off a violet tint. The raven-haired beauty was nominated for the Oscar again in 1959 for her widely known role in Tennessee Williams film rendition of his play called Cat On A Hot Tin Roof. Taylor managed to get nominated her third time in 1959 for her role in Suddenly Last Summer.

It made sense as to who would win the Best Actress Oscar in 1961. After three consecutive nominations the years before. Elizabeth Taylor took home the significant prize for her role in Butterfield 8. The provocative and suggestive content and characters of the film was another reason for the deterioration of the Hollywood Production Code, which was soon to be over. Elizabeth Taylor was known for her risqué´ choice of acting jobs that pushed the boundaries of the female experience and what it was to be a woman. There was more that Taylor could offer than being just a pretty face. In addition to Taylor's big moves in her work, she held people's attention with her celebrity status. Her never-ending list of marriages and divorces kept everyone interested and her love for diamonds and jewels made her a style icon of luxury.

The 1960s were Taylor's golden years. Her fanbase was strong and her power in the media was legendary. Similar to Mary Pickford, a legend of the silent era, Taylor

Elizabeth Taylor

would get swarmed, photographed and escorted by security every time she was in public. This celebrity life is what everybody runs for nowadays, but for Elizabeth it was merely part of her job.

1963 in particular was a prosperous year for Elizabeth Taylor as she was cast as Cleopatra in the movie of the same name. She was the first actress to ever get paid 1 million dollars for acting in a film and on top of that she got 10 percent of the film's gross profit, which added up to 7 million dollars. In today's numbers it would almost be 60 million dollars. Elizabeth once said, "If someone's dumb enough to offer me a million dollars to make a picture, I'm certainly not dumb enough to turn it down."

This confident, almost entitled way of being, got Taylor her second Best Actress Oscar win in 1967 for her role in Who's Afraid of Virginia Woolf. She got paid a million dollars for this job too. Her volatile and bitter performance in the film is lauded as her best ever. She even gained 25 pounds and used makeup to age herself 15 years older than she really was. Taylor was only 34 at that time. At the time, this film was too controversial for its frankness and vulgarity in the seemingly naive and tame American community.

If there is one thing that the Academy Awards are a sucker for, it was seeing a glamorous actress like Elizabeth Taylor get frumped-up to play a nasty middle-aged woman. Taylor truly proved the range of her acting with her performance in the 1966 film adaptation of Who's Afraid of Virginia Woolf? Taylor played Martha, a delusional and vicious middle-aged woman who has plenty of uncomfortable outbursts during a dinner party.

Who's Afraid of Virginia Woolf? is a chamber drama that showcases its actors perfectly. It has only four characters on-screen throughout its running time. Martha and her husband George (Richard Burton) invite Nick (George Segal) and Honey (Sandy Dennis) over for drinks. Of course, this is no fun evening romp. As the gang starts drinking, Martha and George begin to verbally abuse one another. Over time, Nick and Honey wind up going from uncomfortable bystanders to actively participating in the drama.

It's a terse film that shocked conversative movie-goers in 1966. The Production Code censorship was only just beginning to wind down, so audiences weren't quite used to such frank depictions of abuse, alcoholism and unhappy marriages. They certainly weren't prepared for all the swearing in the film, either! The film was actually seized from theatres in Nashville because it was considered to break obscenity laws because of lines like, "monkey nipples" and "hump the hostess". Still, the movie was a financial and critical success, despite the controversy. It's kind of funny to think about the stir the film caused—even though it is still genuinely unsettling to watch today, the language in the film pales in comparison to, say, your average HBO show.

Taylor's performance was quite a shock to audiences, too. She is famously known for her stunning beauty, so when she gained thirty pounds to play the haggy Martha, the world took notice. One tagline for the film even boasted about how much the performance deviated from the norm: "The Violet-Eyed Venus Becomes a Boozing, Tired, Greying "Virago!"

The 34-year-old was playing a character in her 50s, and to the untrained eye, Elizabeth Taylor seems like a miscast. Once the film hit theatres, though, her performance was universally acclaimed. Clearly, she was the best person for the role. Now that the film has cemented itself so deeply into the film canon, it's hard to imagine anyone other than Taylor playing Martha. Yes, Taylor absolutely nailed the performance. It's difficult to play a character as acidic as Martha and keep her from becoming grating, but Taylor manages to strike the perfect balance between caustic and sympathetic. Martha is a deeply layered character—despite her abusive behaviours, she genuinely loves her husband. "I gave everything I had to give," Taylor said of the role. "I think that was my favourite role because I really had to get my finger out and act."

Taylor has said that Martha is her personal favourite performance, and it's easy to see why. She truly does bring her all to play the character. Critics generally agree that this is Taylor at her best, as well. Variety noted in their review that Taylor's "characterization is at once sensual, spiteful, cynical, pitiable, loathsome, lustful and tender." Taylor plays Martha with incredible nuance that makes the movie difficult to forget. Martha is also extremely quotable. Not only is the script writing fantastic, but Taylor's line delivery makes all of Martha's barbs so much more enticing. A few of the best Martha lines are as follows: "You're all flops. I am the Earth Mother, and you are all flops."

"You make me puke!"

"What a dump!" (This particular quote comes from Martha doing an exaggerated re-enactment of Bette Davis's line from 1949's Beyond the Forest. Funnily enough, Davis did not say the line with that mannerism at all, but Taylor's line reading has become much more iconic. Many people tend to believe that that is actually how the line is delivered!)

Elizabeth Taylor isn't the only performance worth praising here. In fact, all four main actors were nominated for an Academy Award in acting. It is one of only two films that have had a cast member represented in each acting category. Burton and Segal did not win in their categories, but Dennis did nab the Best Supporting Actress Oscar.

Elizabeth Taylor

On that note, the film was also nominated for awards in other categories as well, including Best Picture. It was nominated for a total of 13 Academy Awards.

Who's Afraid of Virginia Woolf? is a fantastic film all around, and it really is a testament to the power of acting. The story is, essentially, just four people yelling at each other. That doesn't really work if the cast can't sell it. The fact that the film is so utterly engrossing shows that the performances are top-notch. Martha's character is the glue that holds it all together, and with Taylor at the centre of it all, the film is a whirlwind of emotional triumph.

The following years, Taylor starred in more successful films like Taming Of The Shrew, Boom! and The Only Game In Town to name a few major ones. Taylor still starred in many films all the way into the late 1990s. But her philanthropic work took centre stage in the 1980s when she co-founded the American Foundation of AIDS. This dedicated activism will always be applauded and mentioned.

Elizabeth Taylor was Hollywood Royalty. And rightfully so, because she was the full package. She not only was a fantastic actress, but she starred in many influential films. Her support for the LGBT community will always be valued. She had style, class and charisma on and off screen. And her fearless attitude accompanied by her powerful feminine presence made her stand out. She once said, "I feel very adventurous. There are so many doors to be opened, and I'm not afraid to look behind them."

Sophia Loren

Sophia Loren's bold yet timeless Mediterranean beauty and style is imitated to this day. Sophia Loren introduced a different type of Italian woman in comparison to Anna Magnani; a more glamorous and sensual type of woman who still possesses the earthiness and volatility that Magnani personified. Sophia Loren's beauty exceeds the physical. Her way of living and aura makes her incredibly admired.

Loren's career beginnings started in the early 50s in Italian movies. Carlo Ponti, a film producer who scouted Loren in her late teens, would be her key to success for he helped forge Loren into the superstar we know of today. The two would eventually marry and become a power couple in the film industry. Her English-speaking Hollywood debut was in the movie Boy On A Dolphin in 1957. She was 23 at that time and by this point was a well-known star in Italy due to her extensive list of films.

Loren then made a departure from playing the female sidekick to a male hero and decided to revamp her star image and lead in her most important film yet. We see as we progress through each Oscar winner in this book, that many share a similar career milestone. It is the fact that once they chose a role quite different to what they did before, that is when they get rewarded. This leap of faith into the unknown would be most valuable to them. And eventually would bring them to an Oscar. This was in fact the case for Sophia Loren.

"Everything you see I owe to spaghetti."

Two Women serves as a poignant reminder of the dark times of World War II. Two Women, originally titled La Ciociara, is an ultimate collaboration of influential Italian talent that proves the power of European cinema in Hollywood. The film is a 1960 war drama set in 1944 during the fascist invasion of Italy, which included Moroccan Goumiers who allied with the Germans. The film, adapted from Alberto Moravia's fictional novel of the same name, was directed by none other than Vittorio de Sica and produced by Carlo Ponti. Although the characters were fictional, the events that would unfold were certainly close to the truth.

Sophia Loren, the star of the film, plays a young mother and shop owner in Rome, Cesira. She escapes the bombings of Rome with her 12-year-old daughter, Rosetta to find solace and shelter in her native home nestled in the rural settlements of Ciociaria, a vast mountainous region in central Italy. As the duo makes a run for survival, they experience the threat of Nazi's roaming the hills and pillaging the villages in all of Ciociaria.

The mother daughter duo finally arrive at Cesira's native village where they are welcomed to a simple dinner. There they meet Michele, played by Jean-Paul Belmondo, a deep thinker with an appreciation for communism. With Jean Paul Belmondo serving as a sort of friend slash love interest to Cesira and a father figure to Rosetta, he inspires them to not be afraid of the fascists with his rebellious ideologies.

Sophia Loren

But the cruelty that attaches itself to the power of the fascists and their allies results in the simple folk of Ciociaria falling to their feet. The most shocking scene comes close to the ending of this film, where a rape scene takes place in an abandoned church where Cesira and Rosetta stop by to rest on their way back to Rome. The word for this act is marocchinate: this term refers to the mass rape and killing of innocent Italian women, girls and sometimes boys by Moroccan Goumiers.

Sophia Loren

Two Women is about loss of innocence, trauma and the strength to persevere no matter the hardships in life. Sophia Loren, at only 25 years old, managed to play a mother and a survivor. Her maturity was very convincing along with her acts of despair for survival for her and her daughter. This movie proves that a parent will go to great lengths to protect their child. This Italian movie was also the first to win a major Academy Award for a non-English-language performance at the 1962 Academy Awards. And this award was for Loren. Although she did not attend she was very proud and thrilled.

Sophia Loren

She said, "I decided that I could not bear the ordeal of sitting in plain view of millions of viewers while my fate was being judged. If I lost, I might faint from disappointment. If I won, I would also very likely faint with joy. I decided it would be better to faint at home." Overall Sophia won 22 awards for this role in Two Women. She continued to make major motion pictures in the US and Europe. And won many more awards for films like The Fall of the Roman Empire, Yesterday, Today and Tomorrow and Marriage Italian Style to name a few.

There are many awards and titles to Sophia Loren's name. She continues to work on films to this day. Her zest and fire will never diminish. She says, "There Is a Fountain of Youth: It is your mind, your talents, the creativity you bring to your life and the lives of the people you love. When you learn to tap this source, you will truly have defeated age." To this day Sophia Loren's exotic and ultra-feminine image captivates everyone. A woman of many talents, who can act, dance, sing and speak multiple languages. She remains to be one of the most identifiable and beloved actresses for all generations.

"Girls should go on thinking that there is a world out there and that it is theirs for the taking."

Anne Bancroft

She was one of the most versatile actresses of the 1960s who graced the stage, screen and TV. She was somebody who won many coveted awards and most notably the Best Actress Oscar in 1963. Since the 1950s she had carved a career in acting and worked all the way into the early 2000s. But it was Bancroft's talent in reinvention and an unconventional career track that makes her very interesting to discover more about. She may be known for a role that overshadows most of her other work and we will delve into the details of her life and what makes her so significant.

Anne Bancroft was born Anna Maria Louisa Italiano to Italian immigrants in the Bronx. After finishing high school Anne attended HB Studio, the American Academy of Dramatic Arts, the Actors Studio and the American Film Institute's Directing Workshop for Women at UCLA. This education was invaluable to her as it was her training to enter the entertainment business. By this point, the acting style in the business was different. The star system was crumbling and therefore the acting approach and style was getting taken over by more individualistic and introspective acting styles. Take method actors like James Dean and Marlon Brando for example.

It was the early 1950s and Bancroft was in her early 20s and securing small and insignificant roles on screen. Her debut was in Don't Bother To Knock in 1952. The next five years consisted of minor roles that Bancroft was dissatisfied with. The whole glamorous and sultry role was never for her. She wanted depth, which she could not get in Hollywood. In fact, she decided to exit the film business and work on stage.

She spent another five years from 1957–1962 on Broadway and found her luck there. She got to work with major names in the business-like Arthur Penn, William Gibson and Henry Fonda. The collaborations brought Bancroft two Tony Awards for her roles in Two For The Seesaw in 1958 and The Miracle Worker in 1960.

By the time The Miracle Worker was getting cast for a film version in 1962, it took a lot of convincing film producers to cast Bancroft as the lead of Anne Sullivan. But they wanted bigger names Like Elizabeth Taylor. Eventually the decision was made to cast Bancroft who knew the material and characters inside out because of her experience playing it on stage. Bancroft played Anne Sullivan, a blind instructor to Helen Keller played by Patty Duke. This physically demanding and intense role was prepared extensively by Bancroft. Method acting was her approach. To this day, this film is highly rated and admired. And for this dedicated and emotional performance Bancroft won the Best Actress Award in 1963.

Anne Bancroft and Patty Duke both give whirlwind performances in the 1962 adaptation of The Miracle Worker. Both actors had previously played the roles on Broadway—in fact, Bancroft won the Tony Award for Best Performance by a Leading Actress prior to the film version. At the Academy Awards that year, both Bancroft and Duke walked away with Academy Awards: Best Actress for Bancroft and Best Supporting Actress for Duke. Interestingly enough, both Bancroft and Duke almost didn't get the part in the movie. Despite Bancroft's award-winning stage performance, United Artists studio wanted a bigger name for the film. The execs told director Arthur Penn that he could get a $5 million budget if he agreed to cast Elizabeth Taylor (another Academy Award winning actress!) as Anne instead. Penn refused, and as a result, only received a $500,000 budget.

Meanwhile, Duke was considered too old for the role by that point. By the time filming started, Duke was already fifteen years old, which was a bit too old to be playing a seven-year-old version of Helen Keller. However, once Bancroft was in, it seemed natural to have Duke reprise her role as well. Interestingly enough, Patty Duke would later actually go on to play Annie Sullivan in the television adaptation of The Miracle Worker. Truly, both of them turned out incredible performances. As a young

Anne Bancroft

girl, Helen Keller was prone to violent outburst due to the frustration she has about being unable to communicate. In the film, Bancroft and Duke really do engage in physical altercations with one another, to the point where they both would wear heavy padding under their costumes in order to prevent any injuries or bruising. The chemistry and trust between the two actresses was undeniable.

The basis of The Miracle Worker is, of course, the unbelievable story of how Annie Sullivan was able to get through to Helen Keller despite her deafness and blindness. Bancroft had the difficult task of not only being beaten by Duke (as Keller), but she had to really make the audiences believe that she was capable of performing a "miracle". It truly is amazing how well the two actresses are able to work with one another and really make that connection feel real.

The role of Annie also really shows how versatile Anne Bancroft is as an actress. The role that she is perhaps the most well-known for is that of Mrs. Robinson in The Graduate. In that film, she is a seductress—very much the opposite of Annie Sullivan. Annie also wears sunglasses for the majority of the film, too, which makes it all the more impressive that Bancroft is able to show Annie's emotions so clearly. Much of the time, she isn't actually speaking to Helen, which means she must get her emotions and frustrations out primarily through her body language.

The movie is one of the few films to have a perfect 100% score on Rotten Tomatoes. It really is a stunning, intimate film, and of course, it only works because of its two stars' incredibly bold and vulnerable performances. By definition, a biopic like this needs a strong set of actresses. Patty Duke herself commented that she did not win the Oscar, "the part won the Oscar". Both stars would go on to pick up awards at various other ceremonies as well. Bancroft won Best Foreign Actress at the British Academy Film Awards, and Patty Duke earned Most Promising Newcomer at the Golden Globes. Bancroft also won Best Actress at San Sebastián International Film Festival and the National Board of Review Awards.

Anne Bancroft

There was a bit of drama around Bancroft's win at the Academy Award that year, though it didn't necessarily involve Bancroft herself. Since she was busy doing a play during the ceremony, Joan Crawford stepped up to accept the award instead. Crawford had starred in What Ever Happened to Baby Jane? that year, and while she was not nominated, her co-star Bette Davis was. Davis lost to Bancroft, and to rub it in, Crawford accepted the award. Davis and Crawford famously did not get along too well.

This Academy Award was the only one that Bancroft actually won. That being said, she earned herself quite a few more nominations for Best Actress over the years, including, of course, The Graduate. Her roles in 1965's The Pumpkin Eater, 1978's The Turning Point and 1985's Agnes of God also earned her Oscar nods. On the other hand, this was Patty Duke's only Academy Award nomination—though she still starred in iconic roles in films like Valley of the Dolls and of course helmed The Patty Duke Show.

It was a very interesting career trajectory for sure, because Bancroft was already sprinkling her name in film since the early 1950s, as I mentioned before, but was never under the spotlight until this moment. This was the perfect moment for her to re-enter the film business and get the roles she always wanted. After this Oscar win, Bancroft combined stage and film acting in her repertoire. Her appearances in The Devil And The Little Foxes were successful plays and her roles in movies like The Pumpkin Eater, The Graduate, The Turning Point and Agnes Of God all nominated her for the Oscar.

The Graduate, opposite Dustin Hoffman, which came out in 1967, is Bancroft's most memorable role. She believed it often overshadowed her other work. Bancroft plays a much older woman who seduces Hoffman's character, but she was actually only 6 years older than Hoffman.

Eventually Bancroft became one of the few people to win Emmys, Tony's and an Oscar. This is known as the Triple Crown of Acting. Bancroft's list of projects seems to be never-ending. This woman clearly loved to act on stage, film and TV. It just proves how talented and chameleon-like she was. She even wrote and directed a comedy drama called Fatso in 1980.

It is clear that Anne Bancroft was not in it for the fame, the glamour and publicity. She said, "Film critics said I gave a voice to the fear we all have: that we'll reach a point in our lives, look around and realise that all the things we said we'd do and become will never come to be—and that we're ordinary."

She was a very content and happy person, much of this came from her doing work that she loved, her down to earth personality and her beloved husband Mel Brooks, a famous director and actor, a big name in 70s cinema, whom she met in 1961. She said, "When he comes home at night and I hear his key in the lock, I say to myself, 'Oh good! The party's about to begin.'" Their relationship was a very big aspect of their lives and they stayed together until Mel passed away. Anne Bancroft to this day remains a big name in cinema and somebody who can be admired for just being themselves.

"I may be a dumb blonde, but I'm not that blonde."

Patricia Neal

Many Hollywood stars go through tumultuous times in their personal lives. It was tricky for a star to keep private about their hardships. Patricia Neal was hit by a string of tragedies in her life. On the flip side this woman achieved many awards because of her variety of acting jobs in film and stage. Patricia's story is certainly a bittersweet one, but it's worth mentioning what made her leave a long-lasting stamp on film history.

Growing up in Knoxville, Tennessee, Neal knew she was destined for a bigger and brighter future. And she knew she would be an actress since her childhood. After graduating as a theatre major from Northwestern University, just like Jennifer Jones, who I've covered before, Neal relocated to New York City and worked as an understudy on Broadway. Patricia found her footing quickly and secured a role on Broadway in the play called Another Part Of The Forest in 1946. She was only 20. This extraordinary performance led to an extraordinary achievement for Neal. She won a Tony Award for Best Featured Actress in a Play. Neal, now an overnight success story, joined the Actors Studio in NYC that churned out big names like Anne Bancroft, Jane Fonda and Sissy Spacek, who all won Best Actress Oscars in their careers.

The young Neal was instantly approached by Hollywood execs like David O. Selznick, who famously fashioned Jennifer Jones' career. And he later married her. He convinced Neal that he will secure her an Oscar, while trying to get her into bed: the former obviously would come true, but the latter ··· hmmm not so much! But it was Neal's earnest and sombre acting, clearly influenced by a more naturalistic acting style, that secured her roles instantly in films like John Loves Mary, The Day The Earth Stood Still, The Fountain Head and Bright Leaf, both opposite Gary Cooper,

But it was not long until the bad side of Hollywood really started creeping in. Gary Cooper was one of many already married womanisers in Hollywood. And when Patricia Neal fell pregnant by Cooper, it meant that she had to abort, illegally and secretly. It's not surprising that many Hollywood actresses went through this, as if it were a rite of passage. This moment led the bitter and broken Neal to depart Hollywood and back to New York City. But this moment, although very traumatic, was a blessing in disguise.

Neal plunged into darker roles on Broadway. With connections from her time on Broadway and Actors Studio she went on to act in The Children's Hour, Cat On A Hot Tin Roof, Suddenly Last Summer, A Face In The Crowd and Miracle Worker. All of the stage productions were eventually adapted to film by the way. In 1953 Neal met Roald Dahl and they got married and started a family. Those were the 50s for Neal.

The early 60s saw the revival of Neal's film career. She starred opposite Audrey Hepburn in Breakfast at Tiffany's in 1961. And in 1963 she starred in Hud opposite Paul Newman. The most memorable and celebrated role of Neal because this film earned her many awards. Although considered to be a minor role for her appearance only being 25 minutes, Neal still won a BAFTA, Laurel, National Board Of Review, New York Film Critics Circle and Academy Award in the year 1964.

Hud focuses on the Texas ranch life of Hud Bannon played by Paul Newman, his nephew and older father the ranch owner. Patricia Neal plays Alma Brown, the housekeeper, who resists the rugged and dangerous charm of Hud even though they flirt constantly. Alma is someone who clearly has lived a little; she is not afraid of speaking up, she is a mature woman who knows how to cook and how to deal with rugged Texan men. Hud, a big drinker who enjoys fighting, teaches his nephew life lessons and makes him his protege. Women in the small town almost

throw themselves at Hud, he is known as womaniser in the area and unapologetically carries this title with pride. The only person who he fails to seduce is Alma. After a boozy night at the bar, Hud breaks into Alma's room and tries to rape her. He forces himself onto her and overpowers her. Unable to protect herself, she grows weak under his body. At the last moment, Hud's nephew breaks in and rips his off Alma and saves her. The following day she packs her bags and leaves for good from the town. Hud hungover, but more sane, apologises to Alma as she boards the bus. She accepts his apology and as a final goodbye Hud tells her that she may the "one that got away".

Patricia Neal

In 1968, Neal was nominated again for an Oscar for her role in The Subject Of Roses. Although the 1960's were revolutionary for Neal. Those years were infused with disaster. Neal and Dahl's 7-month-old son was hit by a car and got brain damage from which he was rehabilitating for two years. This was in 1960 and in 1962, their 7-year-old daughter passed away from measles. Moreover Neal suffered three burst cerebral aneurysms while pregnant in 1965 and was in a coma for three weeks. She had to rehabilitate and luckily gave birth to a healthy daughter. Neal's work was spread thinly since the 70s and her final film appearance was in 2009 in Flying By.

Her drive and talent pulled in projects that made her one of the most successful actresses on stage and film in the 1950s and 1960s. The best actress Oscar was the cherry on the cake to prove that it was not that she needed Hollywood but Hollywood needed her. But none of the dramatic films or plays she was in, stand anywhere near the heart wrenching story of her life. Only somebody strong and relentless would live a life Patricia Neal had lived.

Julie Andrews

Julie Andrews' most successful films are to this day watched and loved by children and adults. The actress who personified an airy, wholesome and squeaky-clean image found it difficult to step out of this mould. But that did not stop her from starring in various types of films. Dame Julie Andrews also serves as a great example of a musical hero.

Growing up with a pianist mother and singer stepfather, Julie was musical since early childhood. She was a natural. But her childhood was very poor. The family kept relocating to different decrepit areas around London and Surrey to survive. Although her stepfather was a raging alcoholic, his connections in the arts world got the young Julie singing lessons. Julie and her parents toured Britain together, singing to World War II troops. She was around ten years old.

By her teens, she was singing in London shows, at events and on the radio . And by her late teens she was performing on the West End in shows like Aladdin, Humpty Dumpty, Jack And The Beanstalk and Cinderella. Thanks to her parents in pushing her to early stage success and her undeniable talent, she eventually got an opportunity to appear on Broadway the day before her 19th birthday in 1954.

The Boyfriend was her debut. And soon after Andrews got the part of Eliza Doolittle in the Broadway production of My Fair Lady. In 1957 Andrews was nominated for an Emmy for her performance for a live TV version of Cinderella. This culminated in Andrews appearing on TV regularly. In 1960 Julie, now 25, appeared in the period musical called Camelot. When the film version of My Fair Lady was in the casting process Julie was overlooked as an option to reprise the famous character but now on screen. Julie was only known in the theatre world and was unknown in Hollywood. So Audrey Hepburn was cast.

"Sometimes I'm so sweet even I can't stand it."

But this quickly changed when Walt Disney approached Andrews to star in Mary Poppins. Julie was hesitant to take on this job because she was due to give birth and still had her hopes up for the film role of Eliza Doolittle. Disney reassured her that "we will wait for you". Clearly, he really wanted Julie to be the star. Andrews eventually took on the debut role of Mary Poppins in 1964. This film obviously became a major hit. The 1960s brought back the trend of musicals and Andrews was the trailblazer of this resurgence of film musicals. The financial and audience success of this film got Andrews many awards: a Golden Globe, A Grammy, A BAFTA, A Laurel and of course the Best Actress Oscar.

Julie Andrews

Julie Andrews won the Best Actress Academy Award in 1965 for Mary Poppins, and for good reason—Mary Poppins has become a pop culture icon and one of the most recognizable characters of all time. It's difficult to put into words just how utterly iconic Andrews' performance really is. Realistically, it doesn't need to be put into words. Unless you were living under a rock for the past sixty years, you know all about Mary Poppins and the joys that Andrew brought to the role.

Disney's Mary Poppins tells the story of a magical nanny who takes two children on a fantastical journey. The cockney chimney sweeper, Bert (Dick Van Dyke), joins them along for the ride. From there, it's a musical journey filled with magical purses, flying via umbrella, dancing penguins, and supercalifragilisticexpialidocious. The various songs throughout the film are classics, including "Spoonful of Sugar," "Jolly Holiday," and "Let's Go Fly A Kite." The film's legacy has persisted all these decades later, and it even had a sequel in 2018. Prior to choosing Julie Andrews, Disney had considered actresses Angela Lansbury and Bette Davis for the role. At the time, they were basing the character solely off of the original book series' characterization of Mary Poppins, which was colder and more rigid. Once the studio had decided to soften the character up and make her warmer, though, they knew they wanted Andrews. She was three months pregnant at the time, so she was initially hesitant to take the role. It's hard to imagine what Mary Poppins would have been without Andrews, and clearly Disney understood how essential she was to the film. They told her that they would wait until after she gave birth in order to ensure she could play the part.

Julie Andrews took her role as Mary Poppins very seriously and was incredibly dedicated. In order to perfect the lullaby "Stay Awake," she took almost fifty takes in the Disney recording studio before she mastered the soft, whispery quality of the song. All her work paid off, of course, as her role was critically acclaimed and the author of the Mary Poppins books herself (P.L. Travers) approved of her casting. Andrews contributed more to the film than being the lead role, too. She was also the robin who provided the birdsong harmony for "A Spoonful of Sugar" and voiced one of the Pearly singers in "Supercalifragilisticexpialidocious".

Though P.L. Travers approved of the casting of Andrews, she actually ended up absolutely hating the Disney film. In fact, she reportedly left the premiere in tears. She did not like the character changes and wholly disapproved of the film's ending. Later on, in a 1977 interview, Travers admitted that she did think the film was well made. However, she felt that it had changed her original property so much that it no longer felt like her story. She held ill will towards Disney for a long time, though apparently never had any issues with Julie Andrews herself.

Julie Andrews wasn't the only person getting props at the Academy Awards for the film. The film won the awards for Best Original Score for its fantastic and memorable soundtrack, as well as winning Best Visual Effects and Best Film Editing for the way it blends animation with live-action. In addition to those wins, Mary Poppins was also nominated for Best Picture, Best Costume Design, Best Director, Best Adapted Screenplay, Best Cinematography, Best Production Design, AND Best Sound Mixing. Seriously, the wonder of this film is so incredible that nearly every aspect of the movie is worthy of recognition.

Julie Andrews would go on to be nominated for Best Actress twice more. In 1966, she was nominated for The Sound of Music and in 1983 for Victor/Victoria. Andrews' career flourished after this and she starred in more major movie successes like The Americanization Of Emily, The Sound Of Music, Torn Curtain and Thoroughly Modern

Millie. But by the end of the 1960s her reputation as a film actress went downhill after appearing in two flops: Star! and Darling Lili.

Julie focused more on TV shows and variety shows that featured her as a host during the 70s. Only appearing in two other films The Tamarind Seed and 10. These roles were Andrews; indication that she wanted to play more provocative roles than her previous goody two shoes ones. And with the help of her second husband Blake Edwards, they shot films together all the time and framed Andrews as a more sophisticated and darker type of character on screen.

Julie Andrews

In 1982, she starred in Victor/Victoria and then latter appeared in That's life! and Duet for One, both in 1986. All films were successful. The 1990s once again mainly consisted of TV appearances. And in the early 2000s Andrews revived her film career in light-hearted children and teen films like The Princess Diaries, Shrek and Despicable Me to name a few. It seems that Julie Andrews was born to play in light-hearted things aimed at young people.

Julie Andrews presence on screen is one of class, purity and simplicity. Her crystal-clear voice and bright character always brings luminosity in all of her films. With a career in show business spanning since her childhood, Julie is a veteran on film, stage and TV. Someone who preferred to sing songs that were bright and sunny, I think these two words describe her perfectly.

"Men don't want any responsibility, and neither do I."

Julie Christie

In the year 1966, another British actress won the best actress Oscar. The unfussy yet cool Julie Christie stood out in a crowd of glamour. A rule-breaker by nature, she did not expect to win but found herself on stage accepting the golden statuette in a matching golden gown. It was the first time the Oscars were televised in colour, the perfect way to present the vibrancy of the 1960s and Julie Christie's charm. With an amazing filmography and wonderful style, she will go down in history as an icon, especially of the 1960s era.

Born to upper middle class English parents in India, where they owned a tea plantation, Julie moved to England to go to school. Showing her free-spirited side at an early age, she would skip school and meet random people on the street. She met an actor and decided to become one herself. She was enamoured by the bohemian lifestyle and eventually went on to study at the Central School of Speech and Drama in London.

Soon after, at the age of 21, Julie appeared in her first film, A For Andromeda. Then she appeared in a couple comedies. She was even getting considered to play Bond girl Honey Rider in Dr No, the very first bond film. But her breakout role was in the film Billy Liar in 1963. The director, John Schlesinger, became sort of her mentor. Julie's role in this film made her popular in Britain as an icon of the swinging sixties. It was a time where the Beatles, Twiggy, Michael Cain, Marianne Faithful, The Twist dance and psychedelic prints were in full swing. London was changing: the fashion, music, art, film and way of life became more bohemian. It was a cultural reset.

Christie then starred in Young Cassidy in 1965. And after this her career took a major step up. Schlesinger got together again with Christie to bring the movie Darling to the screens in 1965 too. She starred opposite Lawrence Harvey and Dirk Bogarde, two of the most prominent British actors of the 60s era. This film catapulted Christie into international fame.

Darling follows the story of free spirited, immoral London model Diana Scott, played by Christie. She entangles romantically with three men throughout the story that help her become relevant in the public and successful in her own right. But they are never good enough for her; she desires freedom and fun. Diana is always pulled back to the London lifestyle even when she is shooting adverts in sunny Italy or going on a weekend party trip to Paris. She is an "it girl" whose rise to fame is helped by the three men she meets. She begins romances with all three men, but her desire for freedom and to not be shackled by the confines of domestic life makes her break up with all of them. Ultimately she marries an Italian prince who she meets at a shoot. She reluctantly returns to their estate after fleeing. But her responsibilities as a princess now overpower her own opinion. She has no choice but to adapt to her new life.

Julie Christie

This film, a true swinging 1960s film for its cinematography, promotion of the bohemian lifestyle and the inclusion of 60s icons, won many awards and earned Julie many too. The most prominent being the Best Actress Oscar at the 1966 Academy Awards. Julie resisted coming to the ceremony because she did not want to be in the hustle and bustle of Hollywood, which she clearly was not a fan of. But nonetheless, upon the uttering of her name as the winner, she was thrilled. After the ceremony she got her well-deserved holiday in palm springs. She later said this about Hollywood:

"I could never really see the point of being high-profile when I loathed it so much. Every now and then, you can go to something like an Oscars ceremony, but nobody is holding a gun to your head. The rules were the same 40 years ago as they are now. You can either choose your spotlight—or you can stay at home."

That same year Christie starred in Doctor Zhivago which was a major success too. She went on to star in a list of more incredible films like Fahrenheit 451, Far from the Madding Crowd, McCabe & Mrs. Miller, Don't Look Now and Shampoo.

This is the appeal of Julie Christie: from the very start of her acting career, she had her eye on only film roles and film roles that were interesting, alluring and memorable. This taste in film combined with her refrain from the Hollywood scene makes her very charming. Her compelling performances that varied from one film to another, proved her talent. That is why she still acts to this day. She starred in contemporary films like Troy, Harry Potter and the Prisoner of Azkaban, Finding Neverland, Away from Her and New York I Love You.

One of the few actresses who do not sugar-coat their life and achievements. Somebody who lives a life for herself and does what she enjoys. Julie Christie has made a name for herself as a beautiful and memorable actress in cinema. She said, "I've never been terribly ambitious. Of course that's easy to say when you've achieved other people's wildest ambitions. But I've never really been a driven, dedicated actress. I prefer an easier life." This brutally honest yet nonconformist way of being is what makes Julie Christie so iconic.

Julie Christie

Barbra Streisand

Barbra Streisand's career has been a fruitful one, for which she has received lots of honours. She's the true definition of a star. A natural born leader who did things her way from the very start, Barbra Streisand to this day has that je ne sais quoi that commands people's attention always on her.

Born and bred in Brooklyn, New York and raised in a very Jewish household, Barbra knew that her future would be in show business early on. She went to theatre school and eventually started singing in local Manhattan nightclubs and cabarets after graduation. She started paving her way in the New York theatre crowd and eventually stole the show in her Broadway debut playing a small comedic role in I Can Get It for You Wholesale in 1962, at the age of 20. She appeared on TV shows simultaneously. This was her ticket to instant stardom, as it was followed immediately with a record deal to produce music albums. The Barbra Streisand Album was her first in 1963 which won Grammy for best album of the year, best female vocal performance and best album cover. That same year she released her Second Barbra Streisand Album.

Barbra, now the best female singer and most exciting newcomer to show business, took it upon herself to star on Broadway. In 1964 she starred as Fanny Brice in Funny Girl. This show cemented Streisand as a force to be reckoned with not only in the studio but also on the stage. She spent the following years touring the musical and headlining her own solo television shows like My Name is Barbra and Color Me Barbra.

Refusing to fix her nose, name and Brooklyn accent, Barbra stood out like a sore thumb. But in the best possible way because she was aware of her unconventional image. But after finally getting cast as the lead in the film version of Funny Girl, Streisand took this opportunity to show everyone that she was a leader and not just a performer. People she worked with on the set of Funny Girl said that she was difficult, outspoken and rude. It's hard to believe these claims because she was merely setting boundaries, pushing for creative control and demanding respect.

"When I sing, people shut up."

Barbra Streisand

The Jewish Streisand playing an obviously Jewish character is also incredibly important. Streisand helped destroy stereotypes surrounding Jewish women with her performance. By playing Fanny with such bravura and nuance, it helped eliminate stereotypes that Jewish women were simply dependent on men. Joyce Antler writes about Streisand's performances in her book Talking Back: Images of Jewish Women in American Popular Culture, and notes that Streisand "takes the battle between the sexes, the double standard, and sexuality in a funny and shrewd way by stretching the boundaries beyond respectability and behaving in unladylike ways."

That isn't to say that Streisand's role in Funny Girl is only important to the Jewish community. Her performance is ultra-memorable in every way, so naturally audiences of every kind latched onto the fantastic character that is Fanny Brice. Notably, the film was selected by the Library of Congress to be preserved because it is "culturally, historically, or aesthetically significant".

It's an incredibly important film that has made a lasting impact on pop culture far and wide. Have you ever seen a film where a character sensually utters the line, "Hello, gorgeous"? That actually comes from Funny Girl! Those are the first lines uttered by Streisand in the film, and right from the opening she managed to enter herself into the pop culture lexicon. Fans of Glee might also recall that Lea Michele's character, Rachel Berry, frequently references Funny Girl and notes Barbra Streisand as an inspiration. Streisand's role as Fanny Brice is enduring, and she truly deserved every single award that came her way for it.
The combination of Omar Sharif, an Egyptian, and Streisand, a Jew, made headlines. And the sheer quality of the film made it the second highest grossing film of the year, following Kubrick's 2001- Space Odyssey. When the 1969 Oscars came around, Barbra won the Best Actress Oscar for Funny Girl. This win was a tie—the only in Oscar history—between Barbra and Katherine Hepburn for The Lion In Winter. Katherine, in her typical fashion, did not attend, but Barbra stumbled up the stage in a semi see-through pant suit. Fun fact, she had to choose between two Oscar outfits, the one she wore, and another, more demure one. She chose the scandalous one and decided to save the demure one for the next time she won an Oscar. Her predictions were right, because she did win a second Oscar, but not for Best Actress and rather Best Original Song for the song called "Evergreen" from the soundtrack of A Star Is Born.

Funny Girl was an instant media sensation once it was released in 1968. Even folks who aren't super into musicals are familiar with the Streisand classics from this film— "Don't Rain on My Parade" is the standout. Streisand won the Academy Award for her knock-out performance, though notably she actually tied with Katherine Hepburn that year. Personally, I think they both deserved the award equally, and the tie in no way cheapens either of the women's accomplishments.

Funny Girl tells one of the greatest love stories ever told. The film opens with Fanny Brice waiting for her husband Nicky to get out of prison. Most of the story is told via extended flashbacks, not unlike how 1945's Mildred Pierce is told. It details Fanny's rise to fame and her eventual marriage to Nicky. The story is very loosely based on the real-life actress and comedian Fanny Brice, but notably the story takes quite a few storytelling liberties.

Streisand's acting in the film truly is outstanding. Funny Girl director William Wyler said, "I wouldn't have done the picture without her." As the film's title suggested, the role of Fanny requires a great deal of comedic timing, and Streisand completely nailed it. Her delivery of jokes is impeccable.

Of course, Streisand wows with her singing voice as well! She sings with such passion, and every stanza is dripping with charm. It's darn near impossible not to smile the whole time she belts out "Don't Rain On My Parade!" Her talent is truly unmistakable here. It's worth noting that the soundtrack for the film is featured on Billboard's Greatest Albums of All Time list, and NPR's "The Greatest Albums Made By Women" list.

It's also interesting to remember that Streisand was once thought to be "too ugly" to become a star. Biographer Neal Gabler noted that much of Hollywood considered Streisand to be "too ethnic, too Jewish" and notes that the odds were very much against her. Imagine the talent we would have missed out on if the hateful bigots won here. The fact that she had been expected to fail by many makes her

Barbra Streisand

Academy Award win all the more impressive and incredible.

Omar Sharif was similarly considered a "risky" casting choice. The Egyptian actor plays opposite Streisand as Nicky Arnstein. Hollywood execs tried to pressure Wyler to replace Sharif after the Six-Day War between Israel and Egypt broke out, but Wyler refused. On top of that, Streisand had threatened to quit if Sharif was replaced. This adds an interesting political element to the film's casting choices—though originally not intentional, pairing a Jewish actress and Egyptian actor together like that was a pretty big deal.

Entering the 1970s, Barbra became a superstar and a spokesperson of Women's Rights and Civil Rights. She starred in movies like Hello Dolly!, On a Clear Day You Can See Forever, Up The Sandbox, The Way We Were and A Star Is Born throughout the decade. She was the voice of the generation and gladly took on the role of singer, songwriter, actor, producer and director. She conquered the world of entertainment and launched the production company called First Artists alongside Paul Neman and Sidney Poitier. Much like Mary Pickford who launched

Barbra Streisand

United Artists.
In 1983, Streisand directed, produced, co-wrote and starred in the romantic musical drama titled Yentl. This movie won many awards including an Oscar for Best Adaptation Score. On top of that Barbra became the first woman to receive a Golden Globe for Best Director for a film.

Barbra persisted in leading more productions like The Price Of Tides and The Mirror Has Two Faces. She continued releasing albums and starring in movies. To this day, she works on great projects. There was nothing that Barbra could not do, but that doesn't mean that there were no vultures out there trying to take her down.

Basically, men in the industry who saw her as a threat did not like that she was succeeding in the male dominated realm. She said, "A man is commanding—a woman is demanding. A man is forceful——a woman is pushy. A man is uncompromising—a woman is a ballbreaker. A man is a perfectionist—a woman's a pain in the ass. He's assertive—she's aggressive. He strategizes—she manipulates. He shows leadership—she's controlling. He's committed—she's obsessed. He's persevering—she's relentless. He sticks to his guns—she's stubborn. If a man wants to get it right, he's looked up to and respected. If a woman wants to get it right, it's difficult and impossible."

Barbra Streisand to this day remains a superstar loved by many. Her multi-talent, relentless attitude mixed with a warm inviting personality attracts everybody. She proves that women can be anything and everything all at once. There can only be one Barbra Streisand.

Maggie Smith

Everybody knows Dame Maggie Smith as the actress that played Professor McGonagall in the Harry Potter franchise, but there is a long journey of film and theatre achievements made by Smith that are often overlooked by her more contemporary work. It was her confidence and professionalism that set her apart from others and a special type of acting that keeps her in the spotlight to this day.

Maggie Smith was born to a Scottish mother and English father. Having grown up with the idea of not being pretty enough to be an actress by her mother and grandmother, Maggie's childhood dream of being an actress would come to fruition in her late teens, much to the dismay of her family. The strict and uptight upbringing gave Maggie a stern and relentless drive to achieve all of her dreams and prove people wrong. She entered the Oxford Playhouse to play stage roles in classics like Twelfth Night and Cinderella at the age of 17. A few years later she started appearing in TV and film roles, but minor ones. Her first role was in Child In The House in 1956. That same year she had her Broadway debut. In fact, in 1959, she received the first of her 18 BAFTA nominations for her role in the film Nowhere to Go.

The 1960s were Maggie's years of carving out a reputation as a diverse talent for film, tv and stage. Her appearances opposite previous best actress Oscar winners seemed to have foreshadowed her own future, in films like The VIP's, The Pumpkin Eater, Young Cassidy and The Honeypot.

"When you get into the granny era, you're lucky to get anything."

It was Smith's performance in Othello, the film version opposite Lawrence Olivier that earned her the first of her Oscar nominations in 1966. Having finally mustered up this reputation of a predominantly supporting actress on screen, which we can notice that this is her favourite type of role in film to this day, rather a headlining role, Maggie was ready to take on a major role in 1969. She was known as a highly professional actress who would dig into her scripts during filming breaks rather than mingle and give actors notes if she did not like their acting. Maggie's moment of international fame came when she was cast as the idealistic, free spirited Miss Jean Brodie in the film version of The Prime Of Miss Jean Brodie.

The exit from the 1960s and the entrance of the 1970s brought a new wave of female driven scripts. New lessons about the female experience, the liberation and equality for women were themes that were ever present in this film. And for this memorable performance, Maggie secured the best actress Oscar in 1970.

The character of Jean Brodie is rather fascinating. The film takes place in 1930s Scotland at the Marcia Blaine School for Girls, where Brodie is a teacher. Brodie is an ⋯ unconventional teacher, to put it mildly, rarely following the school's actual curriculum and routinely speaking highly of fascist leaders like Francisco Franco. She also plays favourites, to the point where the four girls she spends the most time with are called "the Brodie Set". Brodie prides herself on her ability to shape young girls, saying, "Give me a girl at an impressionable age, and she is mine for life." She's a warped character that warns viewers of the conceited and self-absorbed adults who can manipulate children on a whim.

Maggie Smith

While some of her students are enamoured with her, the staff of Marcia Blaine School for Girls are much less impressed. Much of the movie is about the tension between Brodie and Miss Mackay, played by Celia Johnson. Miss Mackay resents Brodie for, well, a variety of reasons—she's a bad teacher, for one, and often humiliates her students whom she does not respect—but cannot get her fired due to Brodie's tenure. There's a compelling bit of school politics that underlines the movie, and much of it serves as a microcosm for global politics.

Smith brings a certain charisma to the character and makes Brodie's influence over her students very believable. Though the things she says are often obviously off-kilter to adult viewers, her charm and self-assurance makes it easy for the girls to fight for her approval. Brodie herself is a symbolism for fascism and the ways it can worm its way into the minds of the innocent or impressionable.

Smith has the magnetism of a cult leader in this movie, and in a sense, Brodie sort of is similar to a cult leader. She's full of herself and intent on moulding her followers (in this case, her selected students). The British drama is well-written, too, and it's the perfect script to really let Smith's acting prowess shine. You can see Smith carefully timing her performance and letting that sinister calculation flash in Brodie's eyes to really sell the character. It's a fantastically well-done performance that, as Dave Kehr puts it, "The British are so damn good at."

The Prime of Miss Jean Brodie was a novel first that was adapted into a play. Originally, the stage version was offered to Maggie Smith, though she had to decline the part due to other film commitments. Vanessa Redgrave played Jean Brodie on the stage instead. Then, when the movie adaptation was being developed, Redgrave was unable to accept the offer. Director Ronald Neame was reportedly happy she declined, because he wanted Smith instead. Prior to Smith signing on to the film, the role was also offered to Julie Andrews.

Maggie Smith herself was unable to attend the Academy Awards that year, and so actress Alice Ghostley accepted on her behalf. In addition to the Best Actress win, the film was also nominated for Best Original Song, though it lost to Butch Cassidy and the Sundance Kid's "Raindrops Keep Fallin' On My Head". Though it didn't get the Oscar, "Jean" did end up nabbing the Best Original Song award at the Golden Globes that year instead.

Smith also earned a few other wins and nominations for her performance. She won Best Actress at the 23rd British Academy Film Awards, and her co-star Celia Johnson won Best Supporting Actress at the Awards, as well. Pamela Franklin also earned a nomination, and won Best Supporting Actress at the National Board of Review Awards. Finally, Maggie Smith was runner-up for Best Actress at both the New York Film Critics Circle Awards and

As a final fun fact about the film, Maggie Smith and Robert Stephens, who plays Miss Brodie's ex-lover, were actually married at the time of filming. Funnily enough, the actors who played Gordon and Miss Lockhart, Gordon Jackson and Rona Anderson, were also married at the time.

After this win, Smith proceeded in her usual fashion of acting simultaneously on film, tv and stage. In 1978, she won the Best Supporting Actress Oscar for her role in California Suite. But it is Maggie's decision to not be flashy and living in Hollywood but rather remain on her home turf of England with her family that makes her very admired. It proves that you don't have to be in the Hollywood buzz giving interviews and photoshoots left right and centre in order to be on everyone's radar. She once said, "It's true I don't tolerate fools but then they don't tolerate me, so I am spiky. Maybe that's why I'm quite good at playing spiky elderly ladies."

Maggie Smith delivered even more great and award-winning performances in films, TV series and plays such as Room With A View, Three Tall Women, Sister Act, Gosford Park, Downton Abbey, Harry Potter, The Best Exotic Marigold Hotel and Lady In The Van to name only a few.

Maggie Smith's exceptional work in all acting mediums, deserves a standing ovation. Her long standing career proves her timeless presence on screen that can adapt to any genre, cast and story. That is what makes Maggie Smith so unique, her versatility and smart taste in projects. Her image makes her very memorable and respected, especially to film and theatre lovers.

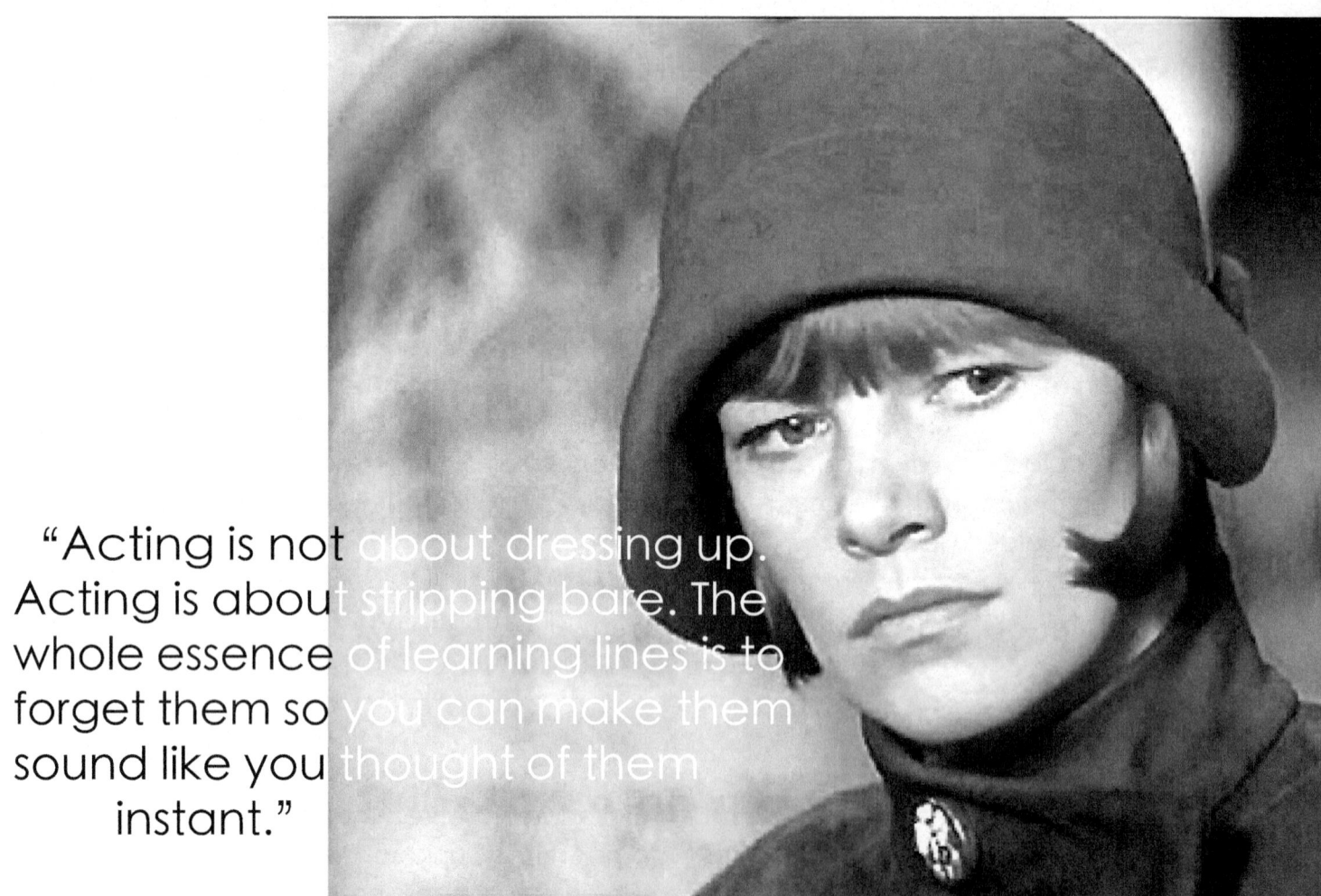

"Acting is not about dressing up. Acting is about stripping bare. The whole essence of learning lines is to forget them so you can make them sound like you thought of them instant."

Glenda Jackson

Glenda Jackson's mission, much like Anne Bancroft's and Maggie Smith's, who I have covered previously, was not to become rich and famous, but to really hone the craft of acting and become a master of it. We can safely say that Glenda Jackson's mission was successful. She was yet another English actress who made a significant mark on 70s cinema with her emancipated female characters who held their own in a male ruled world. In addition, her participation in politics makes her a very powerful boss woman.

But before this happened, Glenda worked hard to even get any acting roles in her early 20s. She joined London's Royal Academy of Dramatic Art as a theatre student and persevered until securing legitimate acting gigs on stage and film. Her first stage role was in Separate Tables in 1957 and first film role in This Sporting Life in 1963. She then worked on the stage production of Marat/Sade in 1964 on the West End and eventually made her Broadway debut when touring this play. Soon after she was cast in the film adaptation of it in 1967. This work, also paired with Jackson's work in Hamlet on stage, put her on the map as a highly skilled and memorable actress in the British entertainment sphere.

In 1968, she stole the show in the film called Negatives. It was the following year that really gave Glenda Jackson a moment to shine. D.H. Lawrence's classic novel Women in Love was adapted into a film in 1969. The movie was nominated for four Academy Awards, and star Glenda Jackson walked away from the 43rd Academy Awards with the statuette for Best Lead Actress. The film overall was a major success and paired with a fantastic cast made it a classic in British cinema.

Women in Love focuses on two sisters, Ursula and Gudrun Brangwen, as they navigate the world of romance and commitment in post-World War I England. Eventually, they meet two men, Rupert and Gerald, and each begin to pursue relationships with them. Glenda Jackson plays Gudrun, who is romantically linked with Gerald, played by Oliver Reed. Jackson's character, Gudrun, is the more prominent of the two sisters, and for this reason, other big shot actresses turned down the role of Ursula. Faye Dunaway and Vanessa Redgrave both turned the role down because they didn't want to be overshadowed by Jackson.

Oliver Reed and Glenda Jackson actually didn't get along on set at first. Their personalities clashed: Jackson's Shakespearian theatre sensibilities didn't jell well with Reed. Despite their initial awkwardness, Reed would later write that he greatly

admired Jackson: "Once there's a spark there's always a fire, depending on where the wind blows and how much water you put on it. With good movement of air there is always combustion, and Glenda will always be Glenda."

Director Ken Russell had commented that the casting for this film was "difficult" because he wasn't used to working with professional actors. His main body of work up until that point was television, where he primarily worked with amateur actors. Producer Larry Kramer was set on getting Glenda Jackson because of her well-established reputation amongst stage actors. Apparently, United Artists studio originally rejected the casting, saying that she wasn't attractive enough to play the character. Russell himself wasn't sold on her either—that is, until he saw her performance in Peter Weiss's play, Marat/Sade. This would be the first of six films that Jackson would work on with Russell.

At the time, Jackson didn't have much film experience. This

would be her first lead role in a movie, making it all the more impressive that she was able to win an Oscar for it. Women in Love would serve to kickstart the film careers of both Jackson and Russell. Women in Love was also notable for being a very sexy film, with plenty of nude scenes. Glenda Jackson was actually pregnant at the time of filming, and joked that this made her look better naked. She reportedly said she had never seen herself with such a "wonderful bosom" before. Jackson would become the first actress to win an Academy Award for a role that included a nude scene.

Glenda Jackson would later star in Ken Russell's 1971 film The Music Lovers. Funnily enough, there's a line in Women in Love between Gudrun and the character Loerke (Vladek Sheybal) where she jokingly proclaims to be a nymphomaniac married to the Russian composer, Pyotr Ilyich Tchaikovsky. Loerke joked back that Tchaikovsky was gay. In a fun turn of events, Jackson would end up playing a nympho married to a homosexual in The Music Lovers!

Jackson's views on acting and the Oscar itself were a bit cynical. She commented that she had "no real ambition about acting" but that she knew "there had to be something better than the bloody chemist's shop". Despite what she said, though, she remains active today, with two upcoming films in production at the time of writing. She noted that "the more you realise how painfully easy it is to be lousy and how very difficult to be good." Still, she was judgemental of the star system of Hollywood. She herself stated that she was never a part of the "glitzy, glamory, show-bizzy part of the entertainment world.

  While she appreciated her Academy Award accolades, she felt that the Academy was not all it was cracked up to be. "My mother polishes them to within an inch of their lives until the metal shows," Jackson said of her Oscar. "That sums up the Academy Awards—all glitter on the outside and base metal coming through. Nice presents for the day. But they don't make you any better."

Jackson would actually win a second Academy Award after Women in Love for 1973's A Touch of Class. She did not expect to win a second time. She wasn't even at that ceremony, as she was working on another project at the time. She was going to turn the television off and felt that the ceremony wasn't really worth it. "No one should have a chance to see so much desire, so much need for a prize, and so much pain when it was not given." She said, "I was quite happy when I got the second Oscar. Now my mum has a proper set of bookends." It was a romantic comedy, in which Jackson could still play her signature role of a free-spirited woman but with a light-hearted touch. In fact this film stood out for its feminist undertones.

Throughout the 1970s Jackson worked on major projects that brought her many awards. She eventually achieved the Triple Crown Of Acting which consists of the academy, Emmy and tony award. Some of her successes were in her portrayal of Queen Elizabeth the first in a BBC series called Elizabeth R and in the film Mary, Queen Of Scots, her role in the film Sunday, Bloody Sunday, Hedda, House Calls and Hopscotch. All of these projects proved Jackson's versatility and ability to maintain her status of playing complex characters in thought provoking stories.

She continued working throughout the 1980s and by the 1990s she departed acting altogether. She made a big move to politics and stood for election to the House of Commons in the 1992 general election, subsequently becoming the Labour MP for Hampstead and Highgate. This became Jackson's full time undertaking. She mentioned once, "One of the most depressing remarks that was made when I first came to the House of Commons was made by an MP who said, "What d'you want to come here for? You're famous already." Being outspoken about current affairs and problems in the world makes Jackson a valuable individual in the leftist community. After taking a 23-year hiatus, Jackson returned to the stage at the age of 80 to play in King Lear. She said before, "An actor can do Hamlet right through to Lear, men of every age and every step of spiritual development. Where's the equivalent for women? I don't fancy hanging around to play Nurse in Romeo and Juliet. Life's too short."

But she proved even herself wrong when she returned to acting and resurrected her star status without having to take on that nurse role. She still has the drive to keep acting to this day. Glenda Jackson's energy and optimism is very inspiring and the variety of highly admired work she has done makes her very special.

"It's never too late – never late to start over, never late to be happy."

Jane Fonda

One of the longest standing members of the entertainment industry as well as one of the most prominent human rights activists to this day, Jane Fonda certainly has lots of stories to tell. Coming from an already famous family, Jane realised her passion in acting since her teens. With her father Henry Fonda, an already established actor in Hollywood, it did not take long for Jane to get her foot in the door.

Raised by her father after her mother committed suicide when Jane was only 12, Henry became Jane's biggest support and mentor. After dropping out of college, modelling here and there and studying art in Paris for 6 months and then returning to the US, Jane met Lee Strasberg of The Actors Studio and decided to pursue acting full time. She said,

"I went to the Actors Studio and Lee Strasberg told me I had talent. Real talent. It was the first time that anyone, except my father —who had to say so—told me I was good. At anything. It was a turning point in my life. I went to bed thinking about acting. I woke up thinking about acting. It was like the roof had come off my life!"

In 1960, at the age of 22, Jane made her film debut in Tall Story, opposite Anthony Perkins. Joshua Logan, the director, was close friends with Henry Fonda and was excited to debut Jane as a newcomer to Hollywood. The film may have demonstrated the potential of young Jane, but she recalled sleepless nights, bulimia and tension during filming on top of her fears of feeling unworthy and plain. In addition, she and Logan were in love with Perkins which caused even more tension on set. However, soon enough, Jane featured opposite big names in films like Walk On The Wild Side and Period Off Adjustment for which she won a Golden Globe for most promising newcomer.

It took a few hits and misses in terms of film successes for Jane to finally establish herself as a major name in film. Especially with the tag of being the daughter of one of the most famous actors ever, she had a lot of proving to do. The same was said for her younger brother Peter Fonda, who was simultaneously carving out his own name in Hollywood as a more outwardly nonconformist and anti-establishment figure. It was only at the end of the 1960s when the brother sister duo became key figures of such counter culture movements, which we will get back to soon.

But in 1965, Jane starred in her most prominent film yet: Cat Ballou. It was one of the top grossing films that year which was nominated for multiple Oscars and won a Best Actor Oscar. Finally Jane became a bankable star. More successes followed. The 1960s showed Fonda's acting range like in The Chase, Any Wednesday, Barefoot In The Park, Barbarella and They Shoot Horses, Don't They?

Fonda was highly praised for her role in They Shoot Horses, Don't They? which came out in 1969 and she even won the New York Film Critics Circle Award for Best Actress and was nominated for Best Actress Oscar in 1970. 1969 also saw the release of Easy Rider which starred Henry Fonda. The success of Easy Rider helped spark the New Hollywood era of filmmaking during the early 1970s. It was a message to the counterculture of America. Jane would assume her position in this movement a couple years later.

It was in 1971 that Jane starred in her most provocative role yet: in the movie Klute directed by Alan J. Pakula. Klute was the first of what was known as the "paranoia trilogy". The other two films are The Parallax View (1974) and All the President's Men (1976). Jane played the titular role of a call girl opposite Donald Sutherland in this classic crime film. Jane hesitated to take on this role, because she felt that she was not qualified to play a prostitute due to her feminist views. Jane was just getting into the feminist movement and regarded the role

as too out of her depth. But with Pakula's insistence, friends advice and her own extensive research she eventually mesmerised everybody after starring in this film.

Thus was the beginning of Jane's prominence in social justice. Possibly Jane's outward political actions during most of the 1970s went hand in hand with her film success slowly dwindling after the success of Klute. But nonetheless, Jane was still in the spotlight; her name was now bigger than ever due to her anti-Vietnam war protests, feminist rallies and public arrests. She was ahead of her time with her outspokenness and being someone who not only stood in solidarity but actually went out to help anti-establishment and anti-war causes.

The films she starred in during the 70s were perhaps her most acclaimed: despite controversy around her political views and an eventual blacklisting by Hollywood following the "Hanoi Jane" mishap, she still managed to cement herself as an actress of high calibre. And it was for her performance in 1971's Klute that she won her first Academy Award for Best Actress.

Jane Fonda

The film follows Bree Daniels, a call girl and aspiring actress, as she begins to face harassment from a stalker. Detective John Klute (Donald Sutherland) steps in to investigate the blackmail alongside a missing persons case. As the film goes on, a tentative romance between Klute and Bree begins to unfold. Famous film critic Roger Ebert gave the film 3.5 out of 4 stars and noted that the film should have been called Bree instead of Klute. And, really, he's right. The movie should be called Bree. It's not that Donald Sutherland doesn't do a great job as John Klute—he is clearly very in tune with the character and his performance—but Fonda and her character have a certain magnetism. At the end of the day, Bree is the linchpin of the film.

Fonda plays the role of Bree with stunning depth. By taking great care to avoid the stereotypical "damsel in distress" or "hooker with a heart of gold" tropes, Fonda really makes Bree her own. The scenes that really flesh out Bree's psyche and her insecurities are the scenes that take place in the psychiatrist's office. These portions were actually almost entirely improvised. This means Fonda herself was truly the one who added that complexity to Bree. The fact that she was able to rattle off these unscripted lines, seemingly effortlessly, is a testament to just how talented of an actress she is and to just how in tune with the character of Bree Daniels she really was.

Let's be real, the majority of the films about sex work out there are generally very un-feminist. They tend to reduce characters working in sex work (male or female, really) to little more than an object. With Fonda's performance, however, the film is able to transcend stereotypes or misogynistic hurdles. In fact, most of the feminist undertones explored in the film were largely Fonda's idea. It's in the psychiatrist office scenes where Bree is able to explore her conflicted thoughts about her desires to be a sexual force and the hatred she feels for a patriarchal society that exploits her. These scenes help keep Klute relevant and wholly watchable to this day. Now, that isn't to say that Andy and Dave Lewis aren't responsible for some of Bree's brilliance, but Fonda took serious consideration for the subject matter in a way two male writers likely couldn't. In fact, Fonda recounted to Criterion in an interview that she actually reached out to her feminist friends in order to make sure she could tastefully handle the subject matter.

Fonda even consulted with various call girls and madams before taking on the role. Funnily enough, she was initially worried that she wouldn't be able to play Bree convincingly and tried to convince Pakula to hire Faye Dunaway. He refused, which led her to investigate her role more thoroughly by spending a week observing high class call girls in New York City. Clearly, the research paid off, as Fonda nails the character with grace. The performance reveals a certain smartness and emotional intelligence within Fonda. To this day, it's hard to find other performances that manage to shape a character so well. The view of sex work presented by Klute was truly ahead of its time. The performances from both Fonda and Sutherland and their subtle yet wholly believable chemistry really elevates the film into a must-watch.

Overall, her performance is difficult to take your eyes off of. Fonda plays Bree with incredible range, going from confident seductress to neurotic and terrified. Of course, Jane Fonda's acting chops were no secret at this point. She certainly brought her A-game to that film as the cynical and desperate character, but Klute gave her the chance to show off even more of her range. Thus, she won her first Academy Award for Klute and later she won Best Actress again, in 1978 for Coming Home. This film was a major success for its performances that were set in a very appropriate premise surrounding the Vietnam War.

More successful films gave Fonda a revived film career. She starred in The China Syndrome, another major success. And that was followed by California Suite, On Golden Pond and Agnes Of God, which all actually co-starred previous Best Actress Oscar Winners.

In the early 1980s Fonda released her famously successful workout video series: Jane Fonda's Workout. VHS/VCR was a cutting-edge system in the early 80s and Fonda's release of her aerobic video workouts lent to the explosion of VCR. She would subsequently release 23 workout videos with the series selling a total of 17 million copies combined, more than any other exercise series.

To this day Jane Fonda stars in movies, does exercise videos and participates in philanthropy and political activism. There is nothing that this woman cannot do. Her most memorable contemporary role is from 2005's Monster-In-Law.

It must take a lot of drive and passion for someone to even attempt all of the achievements that Jane Fonda has done. Someone who experienced health problems and loss makes Jane Fonda an even more impregnable individual. Jane Fonda is celebrated to this day, and rightfully so, as a true leading lady.

Liza Minnelli

Liza Minnelli followed in her mother's footsteps to become a world renown singer and actress. Judy Garland, with her husband Vincente Minnelli, paved the way for their daughter to become a star herself. Liza, since childhood, would perform with her mother on stage and in small roles in Hollywood films. Born into the Hollywood world, Liza's career seemed to be arranged already, but she won over audiences on her own terms, and set herself apart from other entertainers including her mother. She even won a Best Actress Oscar, something her mother only dreamed of winning.

Liza's first film appearance was at the age of 3 with her mother in the musical film called In The Good Old Summertime in 1949. She basically grew up on the sets of MGM, seeing all of the major stars of the 1950s and 1960s rehearsing, getting styled and shooting major motion pictures. She later said:
  "My family's been in show business since the 1700s. I traced them. I'm bred to this. Like a racehorse. A thoroughbred. Look at my parents, my God. But it was my curiosity that made me do this. Because you could also say,
  'Look at Frank Sinatra Jr.' It's not like a natural thing that happens. You gotta work."

At the age of 15, Liza dropped out of high school and moved to New York City to study acting. Soon after she won a supporting role in the Off-Broadway revival of the 1941 musical called Best Foot Forward in 1963. She would then join her mother performing at the London Palladium, The Ed Sullivan Show, Judy Garland Show and The Tonight Show. Everybody watched Liza grow up from a child to a young woman.

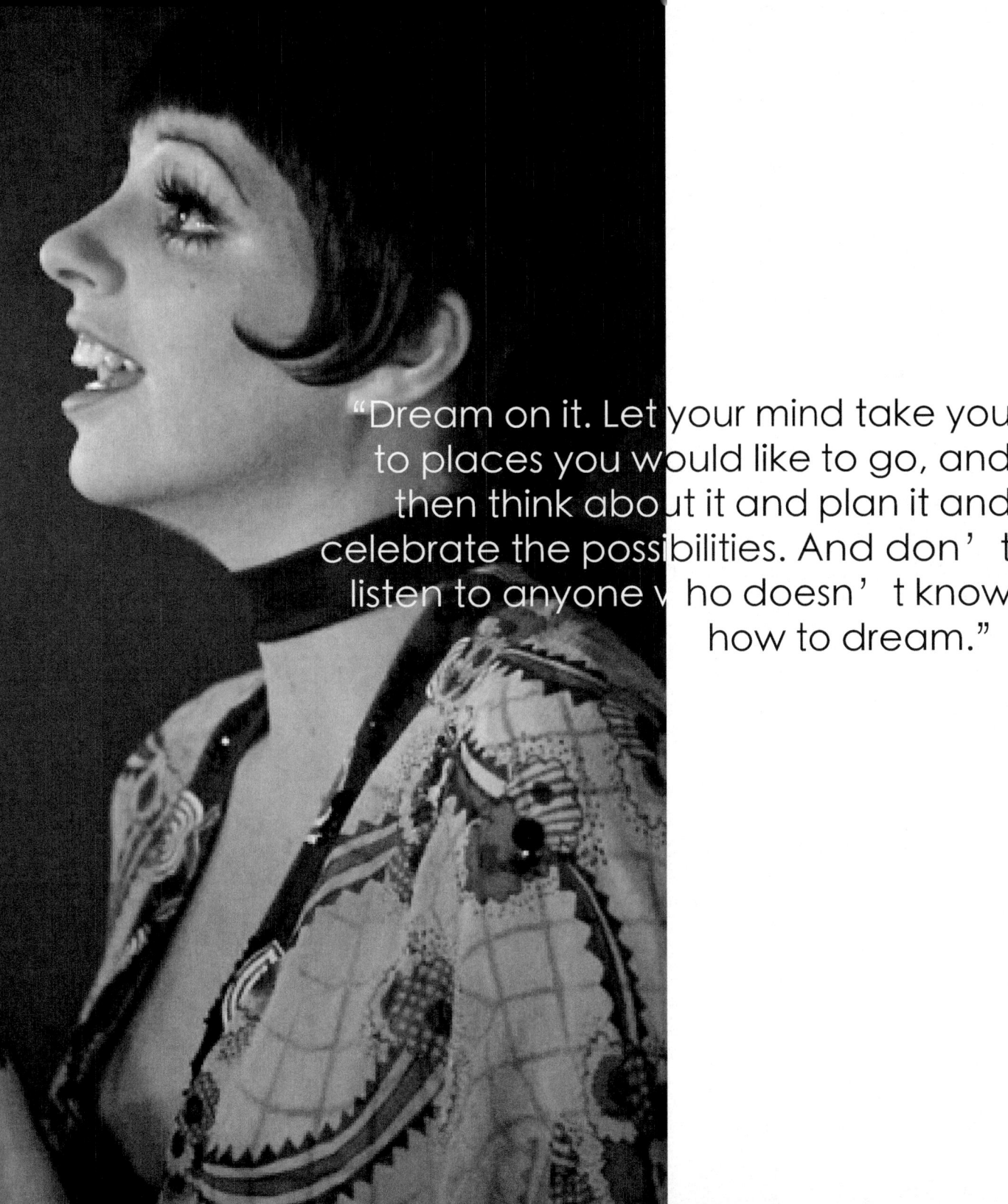

"Dream on it. Let your mind take you to places you would like to go, and then think about it and plan it and celebrate the possibilities. And don't listen to anyone who doesn't know how to dream."

By the age of 19, Liza was singing in various nightclubs all over the US and even won a Tony Award for Leading Actress for the 1965 musical Flora the Red Menace. This succession of achievements led to Liza starting her recording artist career and recorded her first albums through Capitol records starting in 1964.

With small film roles here and there and varied TV appearances, Liza's film career took a serious turn in 1969 when she appeared in The Sterile Cuckoo, directed by Alan J. Pakula. It was his first feature film, and it got Liza nominated for Best Actress Oscar in 1970. Minnelli was only 23 years old. In fact Pakula's later film Klute, earned Jane Fonda her first Oscar win in 1972. Liza continued her journey of playing eccentric characters like in Tell Me That You Love Me and Junie Moon. But in

Liza Minnelli

1972, she appeared in her most successful role to this day playing a vampy 1930s performer Sally Bowles in the musical film directed by Bob Fosse called Cabaret. This film earned Minnelli countless awards, the most important being the Best Actress Oscar in 1973.

The city is Berlin. The year, 1931. In the Kit Kat Klub, immersed in darkness and smoke, Sally Bowles opens the curtains and makes her way to a chair in the centre of the stage. She wears black: from the elegant vest to the fierce boots to the tiny derby hat. Every musical note is reflected in a minimal yet sharp movement, detached and restrained. Sally Bowles and the Kit Kat dancers perform the cynical song of love Mein Herr. And it becomes canonical: for Liza Minnelli, for Bob Fosse, for the 1970s and onwards. Cabaret, along with its crazy creators, is now placed within the great history of cinema.

In this now-legendary musical film set in 1930s Germany, when the Nazis are on the rise to power, Sally Bowles is an aspiring actress who longs to live for the moment and desires to look, feel and be special. Liza Minnelli creates a character who is at the same time strong, confident and vulnerable, sensitive. Sally is tragic, androgynous, funny, limited and free—all within one character. Sally Bowles, through Liza Minnelli, will live forever. And Liza's Oscar for the role is one of many recognitions of this wonderful accomplishment.

It must be acknowledged that at the 1973 Oscars, Minnelli had substantial competition in the Best Actress in a leading role category with impressive performances by Cicely Tyson, Diana Ross, Liv Ullmann and Maggie Smith. So, what made the young star stand out? Cabaret itself was an unusual musical for the time. It was much darker than the traditional films in the genre and tackled complex socio-political topics while at the same time realising Bob Fosse's unconventional vision and choreography. Minnelli as Sally Bowles managed to capture a woman of many nuances living in a complicated time, struggling between her cravings for success, sexual and romantic experiences, love, rejection and confusion. She's forced to be someone on stage by the fascinated gazing audience, but at the same time she's free to express herself through her artistry. Sally has a number of personas: from the seductress in the club to the young woman outside of it with innocent dreams and somewhat illusory perceptions. The character was multi-layered and executed by the winning actress with brilliant skills: melodic voice, sensual moves, quirky presence, charisma and nerve, and last but not least, memorable hair and make-up choices. This symbiosis turned out enough to earn Liza the Academy Award and, even more importantly, a special legacy in the world of cinema. Sally Bowles has been copied, imitated, impersonated and honoured numerous times in art and culture. This might be Liza Minnelli's biggest achievement in Cabaret: giving eternal life to an unforgettable fictional lady.

We could count the 1973 Oscars as the most memorable and mentioned ceremony to this day—if we put aside the 2017 ceremony of the Moonlight vs La La Land mix-up, which we will eventually come to when we get to Emma Stone's Oscar win. But this 1973 ceremony was major: it was the year The Godfather was nominated, among other major films. Liza Minnelli's Oscar was somewhat upstaged when Marlon Brando won the Best Actor Oscar for The Godfather. He had a Native American Activist Sacheen Littlefeather go up to respectfully decline the award on his behalf and to speak about the treatment of Native Americans in the entertainment industry, only to be booed off the stage.

The night concluded with The Godfather winning best picture and Cabaret winning 8 Oscars. To this day, Cabaret holds the record of the most Oscars won without winning Best Picture. After this major year in cinema history, Liza's career began to dwindle; she starred in more flops than successes, but nonetheless very memorable roles in films like Lucky Lady, A Matter Of Time and New York, New York. However, Arthur in 1981 was a major hit. It even won two Oscars.

Liza Minnelli's career has spanned for many decades and she returned to Broadway, recording albums and appearing in TV shows. She pushed through personal hardships with substance abuse that also ended her mother's life prematurely. Liza made it known how much her parents meant to her and honours them to this day as her biggest support and inspiration. She said: "My mother gave me my drive but my father gave me my dreams." Liza was born to perform, and Cabaret, made Liza Minnelli's image iconic and frozen in time. She still has that dazzling and contrasted look about her to this day.

Ellen Burstyn

Ellen Burstyn's filmography comprises serious roles that show the complexities of being a woman. Her mature and complex performances make her a very remarkable and timeless actress. Some of her films to this day are classics that everybody must see. Burstyn's versatile yet human portrayals on screen truly resonated with women in the early 70s due to the feminist messages that helped push the feminist movement. And to this day Ellen is a very respected and quite underestimated actress.

Raised in Detroit in a very abusive family, Ellen, then Edna Rae Gillooly, left home at the age of 18 without finishing high school. She made ends meet by working as a dancer and model in Dallas and Montreal. Her dream since childhood was to be an actress, and by the age of 22, she relocated to New York City and secured small TV roles. Wanting to act since childhood and dreaming of winning an Oscar one day, Ellen started working her way up on Broadway and studied at the Actors Studio.

Ellen spent the 1960s working tirelessly on various TV shows. She still appears in many TV shows to this day. Film roles were done sparingly for Ellen. It was only in the 1970s when she really had a chance to bloom into a well-known actress.

At the same time, Ellen's personal life was not perfect either; her marriages would always fail, and she even ended up with abusive and stalker husbands. Since childhood, she suffered from many forms of suffering and abuse, and took it all the way into her adult life. Later in life she said, "You will thank your mother and father or whoever it was that brought you up for your difficult childhood. Because it all becomes fodder for your creative experience and expression."

"It's been awhile. My Oscar is getting kind of tarnished. I looked at it a couple of years ago and thought I really needed a new one."

By early 1970s, now on the cusp of turning 40, Ellen welcomed a flow of film roles like in Tropic Cancer, The Last Picture Show and The King Of Marvin Gardens. These films launched Burstyn's film career. Ellen was a real woman, not the glamorised, perfectly manicured girl with the perfect life, that doesn't exist; she was somebody who was 3 times divorced and a single mother. The film community liked this aspect of Ellen because she was at the right place at the right time. The hippie movement as well as the female liberation movement was in full force by the early 1970's and Ellen's honest and flawed image was very fitting.

In 1973, Ellen appeared in one of her most famous roles in the movie The Exorcist. This film's significance on popular culture was tremendous, as it became the biggest horror movie since Psycho. It won two Oscars and was the highest grossing R-rated horror film until IT in 2017. The little-known Burstyn, who was now all over the world on the big screen, was soon given another huge opportunity.

Ellen put on her producer's hat when looking to collaborate

with talented artists to get the film Alice Doesn't Live Here Anymore on the screen. She said, "It was early in the women's movement, and we were all just waking up and having a look at the pattern of our lives and wanting it to be different ... I wanted to make a different kind of film. A film from a woman's point of view, but a woman that I recognised, that I knew. And not just myself, but my friends, what we were all going through at the time. So my agent found Alice Doesn't Live Here Anymore ... When I read it I liked it a lot. I sent it to Warner Brothers and they agreed to do it. Then they asked who I wanted to direct it. I said that I didn't know, but I wanted somebody new and young and exciting."

And that led to Ellen choosing Martin Scorsese to direct the film. This production was the catapult that launched Scorsese into the commercial realm of cinema, for he was so new to the industry. He was unknown at that time after directing Mean Streets and upon Francis Ford Coppola's recommendation, Ellen and Martin started their collaboration, which was Martin's first Hollywood studio production. Ellen stated that this production was the best experience she ever had. The two agreed that this story was about "emotions and feelings and relationships and people in chaos".

Ellen Burstyn

And they succeeded in portraying that with Burstyn as the lead. For her portrayal of a single, jobless, widowed mother of a little boy, who is on the road to find a better life, she won the Best Actress Oscar in 1975. Ellen's childhood dream came true when she heard her name uttered on TV, but unable to attend, she celebrated on her own. This film was special to Ellen as it very much resembled her own life.

Alice Doesn't Live Here Anymore, is as raw, gritty and emotional as can be. Burstyn's character Alice flees her home with her son to start a new life after her husband is killed in a car crash. The widowed

Alice is on a mission to provide for herself and her son but also to pursue her childhood dream of being a singer. Upon arriving in Tucson, Arizona as a temporary spot on the way to her childhood home of Monterey, California, Alice settles down and begins working as a singer in a seedy local bar and as a waitress at a diner. Along the way she meets a variety of love interests, who she shows her vulnerability and intimacy, only for this to result in arguments and hostile conflicts with the likes of younger Ben, played by Harvey Keitel and David, a ranch owner played by Kris Kristofferson. Her weakness is men, for she finds solace in the company and affection of a man. But the lack of compatibility with these men is overshadowed by their simple desire for closeness and intimacy.

Alice's rocky relationship with David comes to a head when he storms into the diner to profess his love for her. He tells her that he will do anything for her and that he will follow her to Monterey to pursue her dreams. They reconcile after breaking up over their goals and desires. Ultimately, we as an audience hope for a fresh, new and exciting start for Alice and her son, yet we are left with a bittersweet ending. It's really more bitter than sweet, as we watch Alice walk down the busting street of Tucson with her son, indicating that they are staying in Tucson to live with David.

Alice is an interesting character, for she is strong and weak at the same time. Her girlish naivety and desire for freedom combined with her motherly instinct and longing for a serious relationship makes her a complex character. We often think of her as such a fool for her choices in men and her unrealistic expectations of her singing career. Yet we hope she finally finds peace and true love after all the trauma she faced.

Ellen Burstyn was bound to win the Best Actress Oscar for this film. The character of her on-screen son was also performed on a masterful level. This mastery of acting would continue to be seen in further work. Ellen went on to appear in more movies as the decades went on as well as TV. But it was not until the year 2000 that really challenged Burstyn.

Darren Aranofsky's arguably most intense film, Requiem For A Dream, starred Jared Leto, Jennifer Connelly and of course Ellen Burstyn. The whole cast went through gruelling physical changes and preparation for their roles and Ellen even stated, "I don't think I've ever been this challenged in a role—it was harder than The Exorcist." The complete chaos, disturbing imagery and storyline of this film with Burstyn's performance that many still cannot get out of their heads, saw Burstyn nominated for Best Actress in 2001, but she lost to Julia Roberts in Erin Brockovich. To many film fans, this award felt like a steal from Burstyn, who might have deserved the win more.

Ellen Burstyn still appears on TV and film to this day, like in Pieces of a Woman. She is known as somebody who plays physically and emotionally demanding roles that show her range of acting talent. Her ability to show the vulnerable and fragile aspect of being a woman is something not many actresses can do. She holds a lot of power on and off the screen which makes her very respected.

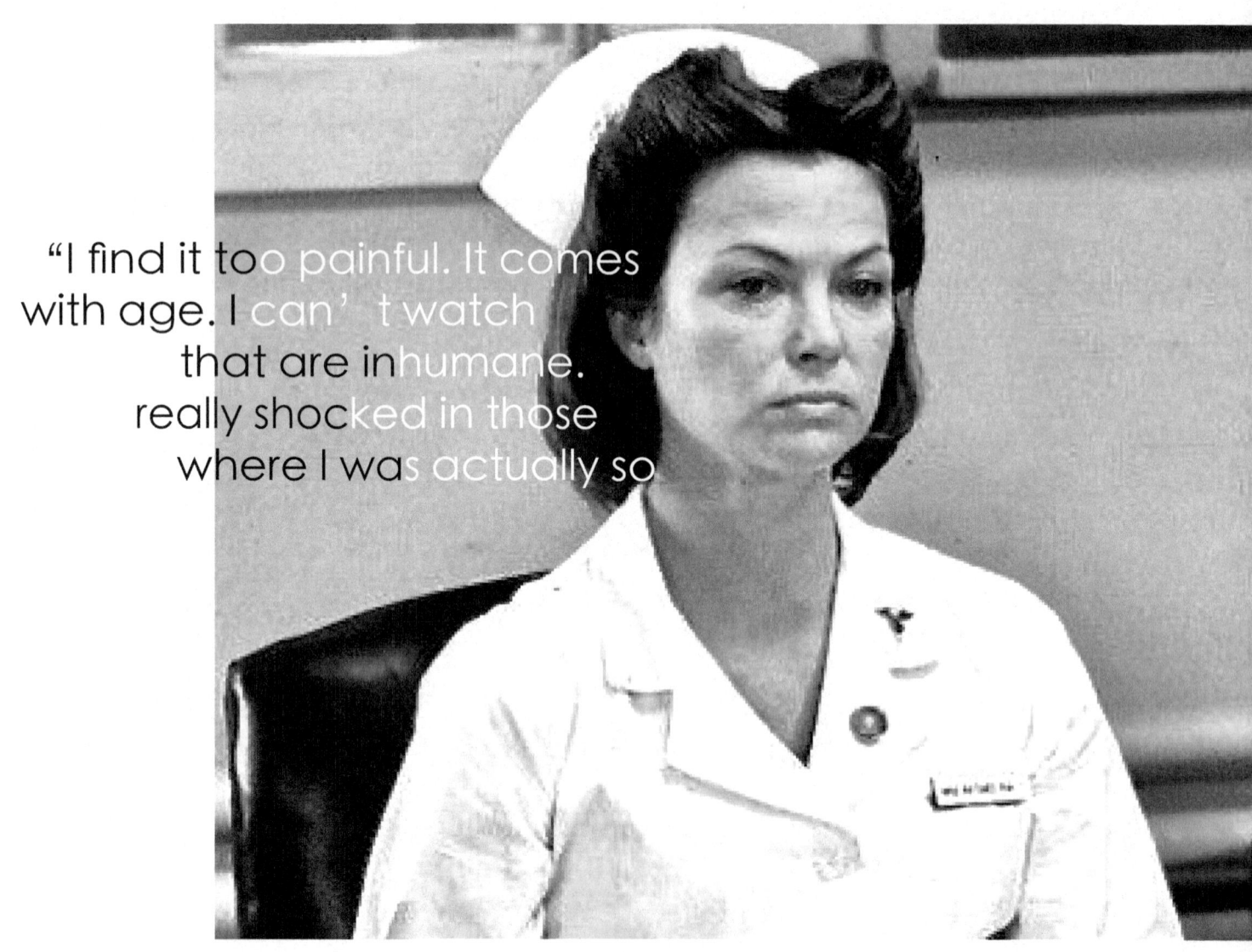

"I find it too painful. It comes with age. I can't watch that are inhumane. really shocked in those where I was actually so

Louise Fletcher

Louise Fletcher's rise to become a Best Actress winner was unconventional. It was only after her second legitimate film role that she won the Best Actress Oscar. She played a villain who was so iconic that after this role, there was no other role that could top that. Louise Fletcher came from a modest life to playing a role many people still cannot forget.

Louise Fletcher grew up in Alabama to deaf or hard-of-hearing parents with three other siblings. They were taught to speak English by their aunt. Louise was influenced by this aunt to pursue acting. And consequently, upon finishing high school, Louise studied acting at the University of North Carolina. She then moved to Los Angeles and just like other Oscar-winning actresses who were starting off in Hollywood, Fletcher would work as a waitress to make ends meet. Fletcher, being 5'10 in stature, towered over most actors and found it difficult to find any roles other than in Westerns, since the male actors were taller than her.

It was the end of the 50s and Fletcher found success in TV shows like Lawman, Untouchables, Maverick and Perry Mason. She only appeared in one film as an uncredited role in the 1963 film called A Gathering Of Eagles. Louise Fletcher then decided to step away from acting altogether to focus on family. She got married and had two children with Jerry Bick, a film producer.

But after an 11-year hiatus from show business, Fletcher came back stronger than ever and found herself starring in 1974's Thieves Like Us, co-produced by her husband and Robert Altman, who also directed the film. Fletcher had no intention of returning to the screen but upon her husband's insistence that she be in his movie--a dare more likely—she made the best decision ever to return. She was afraid that other actors would scorn her for getting an upper hand due to her being the wife of the producer. This crime film co-starred Shelley Duvall and Fletcher who both actually starred alongside Jack Nicholson in their most prominent film roles: The Shining and One Flew Over The Cuckoo's Nest respectively.

Which leads me to Fletcher getting cast as the female lead of Nurse Ratched opposite Nicholson in the 1975 movie adaptation of One Flew Over The Cuckoo's Nest. This was Fletcher's next serious film role following Thieves Like Us. After Michael Douglas, one of the producers, acquired rights to the book to be adapted, Milos Forman, the director, decided to pursue Louise Fletcher to star in the film after seeing her in Thieves Like Us. Many other major actresses like Anne Bancroft passed on this role due to their belief that this part was anti-feminist. Let's be honest, nobody could play the role of Mildred Ratched like Fletcher could. The antipathy, acid and sadism Fletcher brought to the screen was undeniably anger-inducing to the audience. She's one of the most

memorable and potent villains on screen there ever was. At the time, seeing a female villain was a rarity.

Her performance also demonstrated the ways in which a female villain is different from a male one. The film showed that women can be far more cruel and twisted than most could expect. And this role, paired with Nicholson's portrayal of McMurphy, a foil to Ratched, made this film an instant hit. The rebelliousness of McMurphy could be compared to the 1970's counterculture which clashed with the power of the puritanical conservative America which Ratched symbolised.

Fletcher said this about her character: "Life had stopped for her a long time ago. She was so out of touch with her feelings that she had no joy in her life and no concept of the fact that she could be wrong. She delivered her care

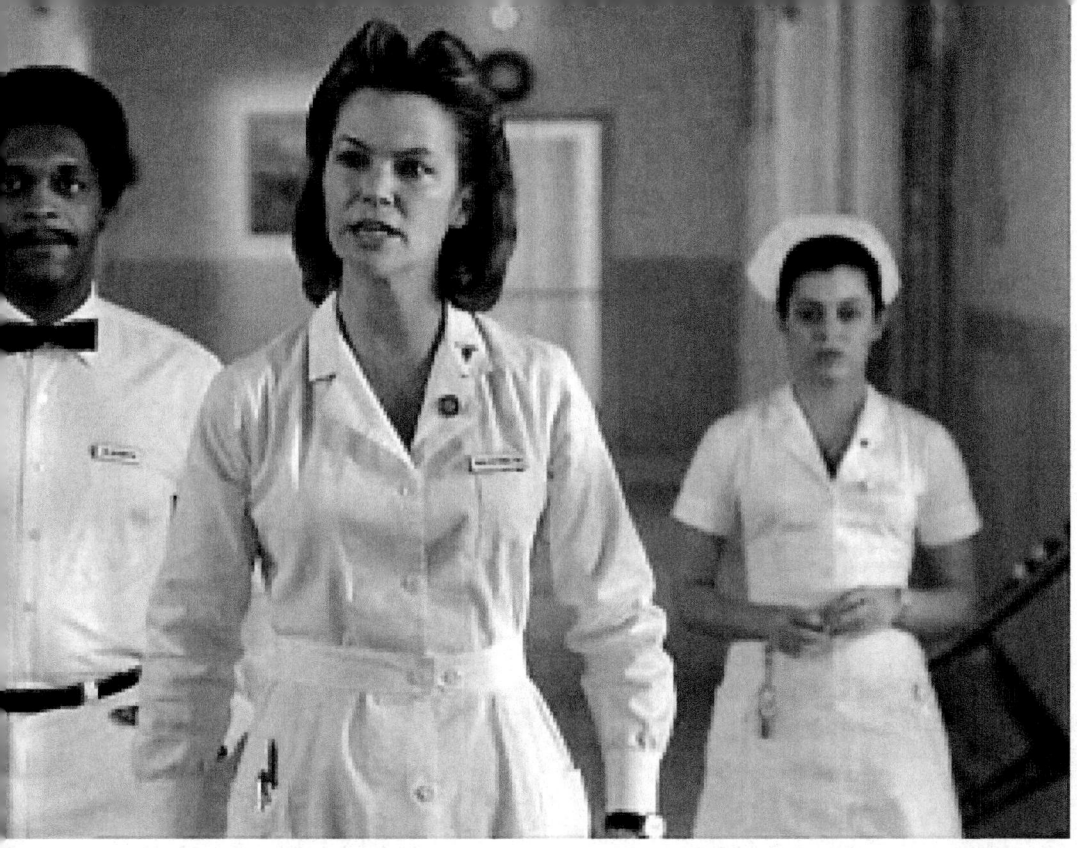

Louise Fletcher

Nurse Ratched has become a go-to reference and symbol of the evils that lurk in hospital bureaucracies. Along with Kathy Bates' performance as Annie in Misery, Nurse Ratched is the iconic evil nurse.

One Flew Over the Cuckoo's Nest tells the story of Jack Nicholson's Randle Patrick McMurphy, who has been transferred into a mental institution after assaulting a teenage girl. He and the other patients are frequently challenged by head nurse Mildred Ratched. She abuses her authority by doing things like sending those who challenge her to shock therapy. McMurphy refuses to accept her dominating personality, and frequently challenges her. Jack Nicholson plays off of Fletcher's performance excellently.

Amazingly, before playing Nurse Ratched, Louise Fletcher had only appeared in a few television shows and two other films—and in one of those films, her performance was uncredited. Fletcher's performance here is so commanding and magnetic, one would think she had already been a long-time veteran of the screen. Fletcher had been cast after other heavy-hitters like Anne Bancroft, Ellen Burstyn and Angela Lansbury turned down the role.

Fletcher had auditioned for the role repeatedly for over six months before finally landing it. Director Milos Forman had continuously told

Louise Fletcher

her that she wasn't approaching the character in quite the right way, but he kept on calling her back. He believed that she was the right pick but needed just a little more of a push—and what do you know, she was in fact the perfect person for the role.

In order to prepare for their roles, Nicholson and Fletcher both witnessed electro-shock therapy being performed on mental hospital patients. Fletcher recalled that this was "heavy" and difficult to watch in an interview with the Guardian. They and the rest of the cast also witnessed patients in the mental hospital they were shooting in as they went about their day-to-day routine.

Fletcher went to great pains to make Nurse Ratched feel like a "real" human being as opposed to a monster. "Making Ratched a human being was no small feat," she said. "I wanted to make her believable as a real person in those circumstances. "Fletcher has stated that she believed Nurse Ratched really did care about her patients, but was too drunk on her own power to actually care for them properly. She has also noted that she drew inspiration from the recent Nixon resignation, and used that as a basis for showing how power can be misused by people who genuinely believe they're doing "the right thing".

Despite the humanization of Nurse Ratched, she is still a wholly unsympathetic character. The fact that Fletcher made her both real and human while still making her this loathsome character is truly incredible. The complexities of Nurse Ratched are certainly not easy to pull off, and Fletcher fully deserves an Academy Award for her fantastic and complicated portrayal. Truly, Nurse Ratched is a sickening character, and Fletcher herself said that she was so disturbed by her own performance that she refused to watch the film herself for years.

Funnily enough, Fletcher had actually created Nurse Ratched's first name herself—she never had the first name Mildred in the original Ken Kasey novel. Nicholson had asked Fletcher what her character's first name was, and then later Nicholson ad-libbed the "Hello, Mildred" line. Fletcher's flustered reaction in that scene is genuinely her being surprised that he referenced her made-up name.

Fletcher's performance was met with universal acclaim, and it was a clear breakthrough for her career. In addition to winning the Academy

Award, she also earned a BAFTA and Golden Globe for her role. Notably, One Flew Over the Cuckoo's Nest won awards in all five major Academy Awards: Best Picture, Best Actor in Lead Role, Best Actress in Lead Role, Best Director, and Best Screenplay. This was only the second film to accomplish this feat, the first being 1934's It Happened One Night. The film is widely considered to be one of the greatest films ever made and by 1993, it was deemed "culturally, historically, or aesthetically significant" and selected to be preserved in the National Film Registry. At the Oscar ceremony, Louise Fletcher billowed up the stage to accept the best actress Oscar and concluded it with a sign language "thank you" to her parents. At this moment Fletcher felt what fame really was. It's especially poignant when you remember that before her stardom she was rejected by 15 talent agencies and only now were the offers were rolling in.

After this legendary role, Fletcher continued acting on film but no role ever came close

in terms of success to the monster she played in One Flew Over The Cuckoo's Nest. She said this looking back on her win: "Just enjoy it: it'll make you wonderfully happy for a night. But don't expect that it'll do anything for your career ... Sure, it changes your life enormously in personal ways, but it was not a guarantee of anything. I'm realistic. I have to be." Her career is rather interesting, as she's starred in huge commercial and critical successes ... but she's also been in a whole lot of flops like Exorcist II: The Heretic and Mama Dracula. Still, her performances are consistently on point, and she did go on to be nominated for various Saturn Awards for her roles in films such as 1987's Flowers in the Attic and the 1997 television movie Breast Men. She also snagged a few Emmy nominations for her guest appearances in Joan of Arcadia and Picket Fences.

Although she worked steadily after her Oscar win, Fletcher's stardom was fleeting. And she accepted this reality. She said, "Frankly, how many parts are out there for people like me? I'm not going to be a person who complains about roles for women; there's a long line of people doing that. I'm working. Even if I don't think something is so great, I still do it. I'm one of those actresses who have to work for a living. I don't have huge savings." Louise Fletcher's arresting performance in one of the most powerful films will forever be valued. Talk about a performance of a lifetime.

Faye Dunaway

Faye Dunaway is to this day considered one of the most beautiful and talented actresses in Hollywood. She defined the New Hollywood era of cinema or the Second Golden Age as some may say. She's a woman who garnered lots of attention and praise for her varied roles because they proved that a woman's life goes further, much further, than housewife, mistress or maid. She is known to be a widely talked about actress due to her reputation of being hot and cold by industry professionals, but with a strong identity on and off screen, Faye Dunaway is one of a kind.

Dunaway decided to transfer from a teaching major from University of Florida to an acting major at Boston University. Showing her acting talents early on, Dunaway had to choose a scholarship to LAMDA or take on Broadway. She chose the latter and appeared in plays like A Man for All Seasons and After the Fall in the early 60s. These stage successes brought Dunaway film roles. Her screen debut was in The Happening in 1967 and that same year she appeared opposite Jane Fonda, in Hurry Sundown.

Merely a few months after the release of these two films, the 26-year-old Dunaway, headlined in her most famous film to this day: Bonnie and Clyde, opposite Warren Beatty. This film activated a new era of filmmaking: the new Hollywood era. More gritty, visually violent and exposed type of films followed suit after Bonnie and Clyde.

The feeling of irresolution, the loose ends never ending getting tied up at the end of these films, was what made audiences come back to the cinema. It was not the producers or studio heads who made all of the decisions but the actors, writer and directors now. Keep in mind the counterculture of the late 1960s coming into the 1970s which affected all of media and art in American society. Think about The Graduate, Klute and McCabe & Mrs Miller to name a few films that starred other Best Actress Oscar winners.

"You can't be ashamed of the work you've done. You make a decision, and then you have to live with the consequences."

Faye became an instant star after this film. Everybody felt her commitment to acting and she got nominated for Best Actress Oscar in 1968. But she did not win, Katharine Hepburn did. In such a short amount of time, Dunaway was at the forefront of new talent. And she continued acting in movies like The Thomas Crown Affair, A Place For Lovers and The Arrangement to name a few. In 1974 she appeared in two box office hits: Chinatown and The Towering Inferno. Faye Dunaway's reputation as a leading lady persisted, there was no holding her back. She appeared in Three Days Of The Condor the following year.

1976's satirical film Network, written by the legendary Paddy Chayefsky and directed by Sidney Lumet, has been widely regarded as one of the best American films. Its performances were especially acclaimed, and the film ended up nabbing three Academy Awards for its actors: Peter Finch (Best Lead Actor), Beatrice Straight (Best Supporting Actress), and Faye Dunaway (Best Actress).

Network tells the story of desperate executives who crave a ratings boost so badly, they exploit one of their mentally unstable anchors for profit. Howard Beale, said deranged anchor, announces that he will kill himself on live TV in order to boost the ratings. At first, the network fires him, but decides to give him one final go on air so that he can have a nice, dignified send-off. Beale uses his time on-air to give a giant rant about how life is bullshit ... and the ratings spike. In steps Diana Christensen, who uses this opportunity to do things like work with terrorists to make docudramas and give Howard his own show as "the mad prophet of the airwaves".

While all the actors knock it out of the park, Faye Dunaway is the focus of this article. Dunaway had been nominated for an Academy Award back in 1967 for playing Bonnie Parker in Bonnie and Clyde. She had also been nominated for Best Actress for her role in 1975's Chinatown, but Network was her first win. In Network, she plays Diana Christensen, the head of the titular network's programming department. William Holden's character Max Schumacher describes Diana the best with this line from the film: "You're television incarnate, Diana—indifferent to suffering, insensitive to joy."

Dunaway had not been the first choice to play Diana. The studio had wanted Jane Fonda, and Chayefsky had wanted the likes of Candice Bergen or Natalie Wood. On the other hand, Lumet had wanted Vanessa Redgrave, but Chayefsky rejected that casting outright based on political differences. Finally, Dunaway was cast in September of 1975, and Lumet told her she was not allowed to make her character feel vulnerable or sympathetic: "I know the first thing you're going to ask me—where's her vulnerability? Don't ask it. She has none. If you try to sneak it in, I'll get rid of it in the editing room, so it'll be a wasted effort."

Faye Dunaway

Dunaway researched cutthroat executives to prepare for her role, and she specifically wanted to study a female exec. Of course, in the 70s, women in such positions were still a rarity. Dunaway ended up modelling her character on NBC's daytime programming Vice President Lin Bolen. Dunaway actually ended up adopting a few of Bolen's mannerisms in her performance—something that Lin Bolen was understandably not happy about. After all, Diana Christensen truly is a completely unlikeable character.

Now, one might think that a character like Diana Christensen would be easy to play because she lacks complexity or sensitivity. On the contrary, making a main character like this be loathsome yet fun to follow is a real challenge. Dunaway has an incredible magnetism to her, and it's delightful to watch her be, well, completely awful! Most of all, her particular brand of sensationalising, exploitative evil is wholly believable. This is really, truly how we perceive network executives, so it works.

Dunaway mentioned that she didn't need to make any adlibs or make any changes to her dialogue in the film because Chyafesky had written it so well. According to her, it was "the only film I ever did that you didn't touch the script because it was almost as if it were written in verse." Truly, it is an incredibly well-written film, to the point where many people who have watched it decades later did not recognize that it was satire at all. Not only is the script spot-on in its criticisms of television, but Lumet's naturalistic lighting makes it feel almost like a documentary.

There is a very famous picture of Faye Dunaway with her Oscar that was taken after her win. She had called over her then-fiancé Terry O'Neill to do a photoshoot. She hadn't slept since accepting the Oscar, so the resulting pictures of her staring off by a hotel pool with her award sitting on a beach table made her look almost bored. It's an incredible set of pictures—the famous one of her slouched in the beach chair has been dubbed "The Morning After".

A final fun fact about the film's Oscar winnings: to this day, Beatrice Straight has the shortest performance to ever win an Oscar. She is only on-screen for five minutes and two seconds. Ned Beatty was nominated for Best Supporting Actor, and similarly, he was only on screen for five minutes and fifty-three seconds. Neither of these are the shortest performances ever nominated, though—that title belongs to Hermione Baddely, who was nominated for her performance in Room at the Top. She was onscreen for a little over two minutes.

Dunaway said this about her win:

"I will never forget the moment, and the feeling, when I heard my name. It was, without question, one of the most wonderful nights of my life. The Oscar represented the epitome of what I had struggled for and dreamt about since I was a child. The emotional rush of getting this accolade, the highest one this industry can award you, just hit me like a bomb. It was the symbol of everything I ever thought I wanted as an actress."

It wasn't until 1981 that Dunaway reminded the public that she was still a force to be reckoned with on screen. She portrayed the iconic Joan Crawford in the film called Mommie Dearest, which highlighted the life of the controversial old Hollywood actress. Faye Dunaway has acted simultaneously on TV and stage since the 1960s, too. But her film career is the most extensive and prominent. She clearly is very proud of her career. Her commitment made her a perfectionist and that may have made some people she worked with tense around her due to their idea that she was capricious. On the contrary, most admired her curiosity and devotion to the art of acting. Dunaway said, "I want to get it right. The fact is a man can be difficult and people applaud him for trying to do a superior job. People say, 'Well gosh, he's got a lot of guts. He's a real man.' And a woman can try to get it right and she's 'a pain' It's my nature to do really good jobs, and I would never have been successful if I hadn't."

Faye Dunaway's films have stood the test of time because they were unique and innovative at the time they were released. They therefore influenced other films. Her collaboration opposite alpha male actors like McQueen, Redford, Newman, Nicholson and Beatty to name a few, solidified her as an alpha female who held her own among these major stars.

Diane Keaton

If there is any Oscar Winning Actress whom you can call eccentric, the frontrunner for that title would have to be Diane Keaton. Much like Katharine Hepburn's masculine personal style, Keaton has become a fashion icon for this look too. Often her personal life and fashion choices overpower her acting career, but nonetheless it all comes together to prove that those who live life to the beat of their own drum usually become icons.

Diane Keaton, originally Diane Hall, studied acting in Santa Ana College in California and at the Neighborhood Playhouse in NYC. She started working in summer stock, which was basically theatre during the summer months when theatre was off season. She understudied on Broadway and eventually got a role in the musical called Hair on Broadway in 1968, but she refused to appear nude in the musical. That same year she was cast in Woody Allen's Broadway play called Play It Again Sam. They started their romance then, too. She was around 23. She later reprised this role on film in 1972.

Keaton made her film debut in 1970 in the film Lovers And Other Strangers. And two years later she starred in her breakout role in 1972's The Godfather, directed by Francis Ford Coppola. She played Kay Adams, Michael Corleone's wife. The film was an obvious success and Keaton continued her character's journey in further The Godfather films. By this point Keaton and Woody Allen had broken up but their professional relationship continued. They collaborated on more movies like Sleeper and Love And Death, in 1973 and 1975 respectively.

But it was 1977 that saw Diane earning a taste of what fame really was like. She and Woody Allen collaborated on yet another film, Annie Hall, and it made Keaton an icon, especially of fashion.

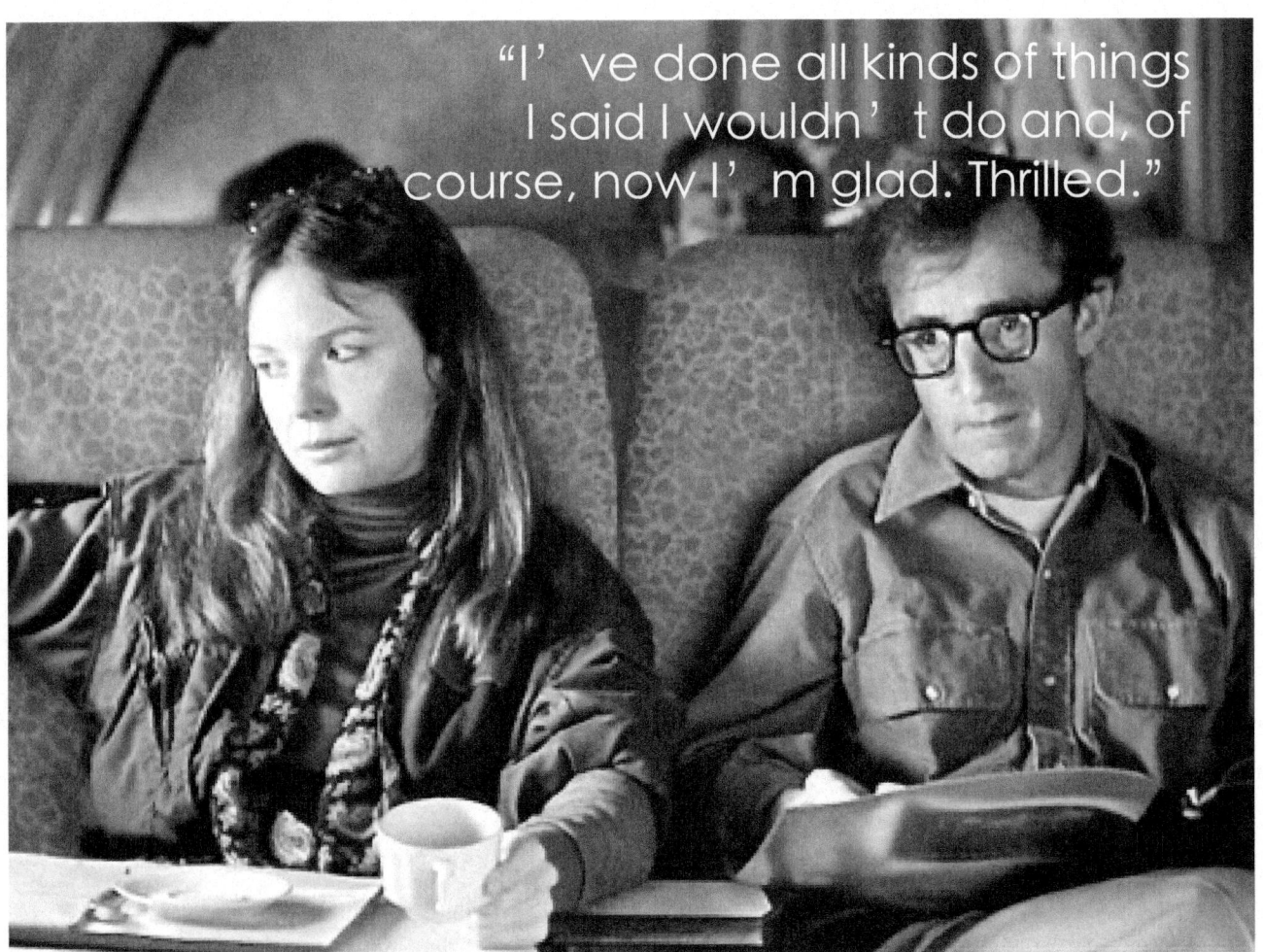

"I've done all kinds of things I said I wouldn't do and, of course, now I'm glad. Thrilled."

Diane Keaton

We may be used to seeing Woody Allen films, they're classics now, but at that time, in the 1970s, his storytelling and dialogue was original and innovative. It took the audience's attention away from the grim post-Vietnam war films and into stories urban life, relationships and self-growth. Audiences were hooked and came back to the cinema over and over again to watch Annie Hall.

Annie Hall is a romantic comedy, an experiment with the cinematic medium and with humour; a thoughtful reflection of philosophical concepts, the female protagonist. Annie is the soul of the New York plot. She makes statements with her speech and vocabulary, repeating words in confused yet important sentences, as well as with her unique 1970s fashion choices. Annie Hall is feminine, masculine, curious, quirky and original. She is what interests and excites us in the film. And just like we do, Woody Allen's Alvy Singer falls in love, fascinated by her personality.

For Diane Keaton, Annie Hall is one of her favourite film parts and this shows when we experience it. She fills her performance with affection and joy, and becomes the perfect partner of a neurotic Alvy (Allen), always wondering about the world, about sexuality and modernism and death. In fact, Allen wrote the part specifically for Keaton and the character (and film, too) is even named after Diane. At times, as a child and young woman, she was called Annie by others and Hall is her middle name. For her portrayal, she won the Academy Award for Best Actress in 1978. And quite certainly, with this role, Keaton and Allen left behind a substantial cinematic and cultural legacy that we now clearly see even after nearly five decades.

Diane Keaton creates the peculiar and charming Annie Hall—a woman with human needs and relatable insecurities, doubts that we feel as we watch. At the same time, she is somewhat resilient—open-minded to the world, others and Alvy and yet defending her own points of view and opinions. One of the best qualities Diane Keaton incorporates in Annie Hall is her desire and capability to love. To love passionately and quietly, to know the longing to start a relationship and the sadness when its end is near.

The emotionally charged universe that Annie Hall exists in can affect the viewer on many levels: from the warm humanity to the oddly attractive behaviour and clothes; from her crazy driving to the welcoming smile that shines from this film adventure's protagonist.

Diane Keaton has shared that because of her collaborative work with Woody Allen, she has learnt how to not take her acting incredibly seriously and how to be able to relax and perform with enjoyment in front of the camera. Together, these two artists enriched their creative projects and Annie Hall is exemplary in this regard. An intimate New York tale of love and the fading of love. Genuine and heartfelt. As is Annie Hall herself. "La-di-da!" exclaims Diane's character—and we accept it, repeat it, sing it and imagine sweet intellectual encounters with a man with glasses or a woman with a tie in 1970's New York.

More collaborations between Allen and Keaton followed: Interiors, Manhattan, Radio Days and Manhattan Murder Mystery. To this day Keaton and Allen are dear friends who stand by each other even during controversial times, like Allen's abuse allegations.

Keaton worked throughout the 1980s and 1990s in films like Reds, The Little Drummer Girl, Baby Boom and Father Of The Bride to name a few. The 2000s followed with more rom-coms like Something's Gotta Give, And So It Goes and Book Club to name a few. That really is her favourite genre to be in: romantic, light-hearted comedies revolving around family, relationships and personal growth.

Diane Keaton

Diane Keaton maintained her ability to transform the fashion landscape with her oversized mens suits and unisex clothes. Although she tried to pull away from romantic comedy type roles later in her career, her image of an endearing and quirky woman is her niche. She said, "I've always loved independent women, outspoken women, eccentric women, funny women, flawed women. When someone says about a woman, 'I'm sorry, that's just wrong,' I tend to think she must be doing something right."

On top of Keaton's extensive career in film, which to this day is thriving, she is known for her personal choices of remaining unmarried and adopting two children in her 50s. What we notice based on her previous quotes is that she truly enjoys getting older and that with age comes wisdom, freedom and beauty in a woman. My favourite quote by Keaton, which I think applies to all aspects of life is: "Here is my biggest takeaway after 60 years on the planet: There is great value in being fearless. For too much of my life, I

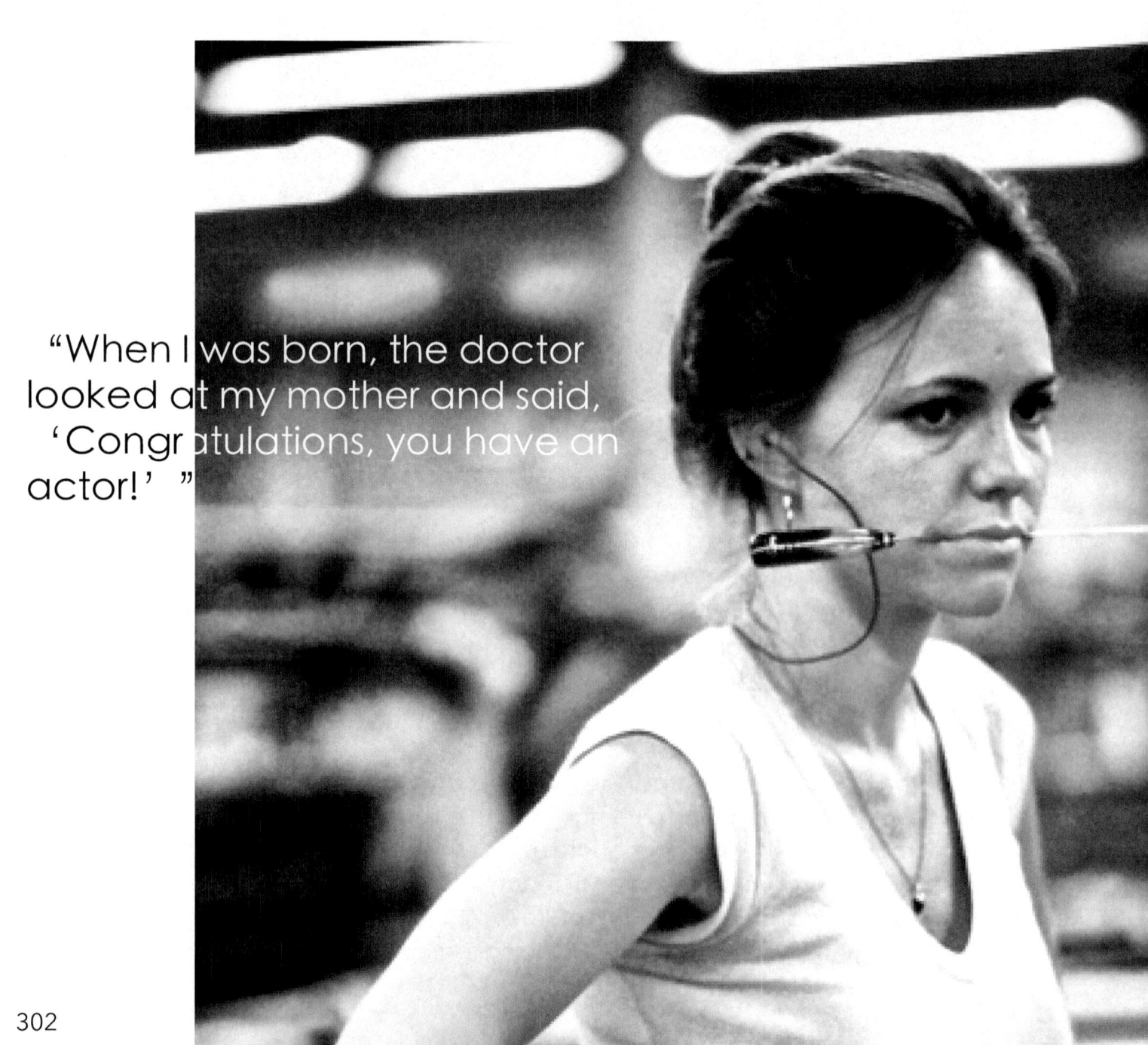

"When I was born, the doctor looked at my mother and said, 'Congratulations, you have an actor!'"

Sally Field

As one of the most decorated stars of film and TV, Sally Field has always been a widely loved actress. Her variety of leading and supporting roles in iconic films will forever be remembered. But just like many other Oscars Leading Ladies, Sally Field had to start from scratch and begin her rise to worldwide fame and critical acclaim.

Growing up in California, mainly Pasadena and Van Nuys, Field was exposed to LA life early on, especially with a mother who was an actress herself and a stepfather who was a stuntman. Much later in life, Sally wrote a memoir called In Pieces which came out in 2018 that exposed secrets from her early life, including her tumultuous relationships with her late mother and sexually abusive stepfather.

Field's outlet to let out her emotions was through acting; this was her calling in her late teens and she pursued acting to run away from family problems. In her memoir she said, "I was able to feel something I didn't feel before. I heard my voice. And I wondered what would have happened if I hadn't. How long would it have taken me to feel that I had a right to be outraged?"

After drama classes at school and attending an actors workshop at Columbia Studios, Field won the starring role in the series called Gidget in 1965. Field was only 18 when the series debuted. It was mega popular, although it was cancelled after one season. Sally then appeared in the series called Flying Nun. This series was written especially for Field to lead in. And it lasted for 3 seasons from 1967 to 1970. Sally Field basically grew up on screen, going from a teen star to a young lady. While filming Flying Nun, Field married her high school sweetheart and eventually, by the age of 23, was hiding her baby bump on set.

Field starred in more TV shows and TV movies going into the 1970s. But none made her stand out as much as her inaugurated roles. Her film debut was in the Way West in 1967. After noticing that she was getting typecast as the girl next door, California girl, Field took on acting lessons at the Actors Studio under Lee Strasberg's mentorship around 1974.

1976 was a breakthrough year for Field as she returned to film and TV with more serious roles. She starred in Sybil, a series opposite Joanne Woodward, a previous Best Actress Oscar winner. Field played a woman suffering from multiple personality disorder. In fact Woodward won her

Sally Field

own Oscar for a role much similar to Field's in Sybil. For this role in Sybil, Field won an Emmy in 1977. In addition Field starred in the movie Stay Hungry. From this year onward, Sally's film work would spread far and wide, making her a big name in show business.

She starred in major films opposite her then boyfriend, Burt Reynolds, like Smokey And The Bandit, The End and Hooper in 1977 and 1978. She also appeared in Heroes in 1977. 1979 was a serious step for Fields' career as she starred in her most critically acclaimed role in a drama film, Norma Rae. The film was based on the true story of Crystal Lee Sutton, which was told in the 1975 book Crystal Lee, A Woman of Inheritance by reporter Henry P. Leifermann of The New York Times.

Norma Rae is a story about never giving up, standing up for your rights and needs and coming together as a community to make change for the better. Set in 1970s Alabama, cotton mill worker Norma Rae is a single mother of two. She is young, lively and opinionated. The harsh and long working conditions that she and her mother work at the mill are the only way for them to put food on the table. Norma is often courted by men in the small Christian town, due to her history of going out and dating different men. Yet her reputation only signs good and she marries once again to a fellow mill worker.

Then a new individual comes to the close-knit town: Reuben Warshowsky, played by Ron Leibman. He is a union organiser from New York City and is on a mission to get all labourers to join the union movement. Norma Rae eventually teams up with Ruben and the two embark on a promotion of the union effort, much to the dismay of grumpy factory bosses and too-scared-to- speak-up workers.

The duo rally people and advise them on the benefits and outcomes of starting the union. The more Norma involves herself in the movement, the more distant she becomes from her family and she starts to neglects her motherly and wife duties. When her father, a factory worker, dies suddenly from a heart attack due to the long and gruelling work hours, Norma is even more determined to promote the union.

Eventually, Norma rebels at the factory and holds up a piece of paper that she writes on and it says "UNION". She holds it up high while standing up on a table in the factory for all to see. This scene is particularly iconic and it's very powerful. One by one, starting from her mother, the workers shut down their cotton machines and drop all of their work as a sign of rebelliousness and refuse to work until they are given the right treatment. Feisty and unstoppable, Norma is manhandled by the police and taken away. Ultimately an election is held to unionise the factory. This becomes a televised and deported event. As the ballots come in, workers crowd together, hoping for the best. With only 100 votes difference, the votes in favour to unionise win and the workers rejoice, including Norma and Reuben. The two, who have now become friends, part ways.

This successful film brought a lot of attention to Sally's artistry, and she consequently won a multitude of Best Actress awards, most notably the Best Actress Oscar in 1980. She marched up the stage jubilantly to accept her award. The following years were loaded with more film roles like in Back Roads, Absence Of Malice and Kiss Me Goodbye in 1981 and 1982.

But Sally Field was not done yet with the Oscars spotlight. She returned to that stage to accept her second Best Actress win in 1985 for her role in Places In The Heart. This was a role reminiscent of her first Oscar winning one, as it conveyed a woman taking charge of her family and life to better it. Set in Texas during the Great Depression, Edna Spalding played by Field takes charge of her family and farm when her husband dies. This time she was confident in her power as an actress.

Sally Field continued with more various film roles. Her most iconic roles are in Steel Magnolias, Mrs Doubtfire and Forrest Gump. In 2013 she was nominated for the Best Supporting Actress Oscar for her role in Lincoln.

I think it's Sally Fields' authenticity on and off screen that captures audiences. The vulnerability that she portrays in her characters is not so easy to emulate. And with a memoir that details her hardships growing up, it adds another layer of sincerity and humanity to her reputable career.

"Fame sweeps you away. I had to go home every six months to remember who I am."

Sissy Spacek

Born in Texas as Mary Elizabeth Spacek, Mary was given the nickname "Sissy' by her brothers. Sissy Spacek initially aspired to be a singer and so she moved to New York City, but after taking acting lessons, modelling and starring as an extra in films, Sissy swiftly switched her career to acting. This was the beginning of her journey to become a widely praised and striking actress.

With the help of her actor cousin, Rip Torn, Sissy got her foot in the door by taking acting lessons at the Actors Studio. She consequently had her film debut in Prime Cut in 1972. Various TV roles followed. But it was her film career that truly took off. Only a year later in 1973, the 23-year-old Spacek landed her breakthrough role in a Terrence Malick film called Badlands, opposite Martin Sheen. There she met her soon to be husband Zack Fisk, a production designer. They would work together on more movies.

A few years later she appeared in her most famous role, and to this day we associate her with this film: Carrie. It was the first film adaptation of the Steven King book of the same name. Sissy Spacek did whatever it took to secure this role. She was actually 26 when the film came out, a whole 10 years older than the character she played, but she played the younger role very convincingly. Brian de Palma, the director, had no choice but to cast Spacek because of her dedication to the character. This film is a cult classic worth watching. Spacek is unforgettable in it. And because of this, she was nominated for the Best Actress Oscar in 1977.

The following years consisted of establishing Spacek as a high value star. She appeared in Welcome to LA, 3 Women and Heart Beat. Spacek had a chance to showcase her versatility in Coal Miner's Daughter in 1980. It was a biopic about the life of country singer Loretta Lynn. Loretta Lynn picked Spacek out of a stack of other actresses to play her on screen. This film was universally successful and Spacek was the centre of attention.

Coal Miner's Daughter chronicles the life of Loretta Lynn as she goes from living in a poor family to becoming one of the most successful country music stars of all time. The film is based on George Vecsey's biography of Lynn. In 2019, the National Film Registry selected it to be preserved after the U.S. Library of Congress deemed it to be "culturally, historically, or aesthetically" significant.

Spacek truly gave her all in this performance—she actually sings all of the Lynn hits on the soundtrack. In order to keep everything authentic, director Michael Apted actually had Spacek and her co-star Beverly D'Angelo perform their songs live. Spacek doing

her own singing here was almost definitely a huge part of why she won the Oscar–after all, that amount of dedication and talent is simply too impressive to go unawarded.

Not only was the film's soundtrack certified gold by the RIAA, it also ended up being nominated for a Grammy Award for Best Female Country Vocal Performance. As if all that wasn't enough of an achievement, the soundtrack won the Country Music Association's Award for Album of the Year—the only other soundtrack that nabbed that award was the 2001 soundtrack for O Brother, Where Art Thou?

Loretta Lynn herself was quite impressed with Spacek's performance. Although she had picked Spacek for the role, she chose her solely based on a photograph and she was unfamiliar with Spacek's other film roles. The original director who was set to helm the film, Joseph Sargent, did not approve of the casting because he felt the two didn't look enough alike. The production studio, Universal Pictures, on the other hand, loved the casting and got so fed up with Sargent's refusal that they bought out his contract and replaced him with director Michael Apted. Later, Meryl Streep wound up auditioning for the role of Loretta Lynn, and it was one of the few times the star was ever turned down for a role. The studio really had their eyes set on Sissy Spacek.

Despite all the push for Spacek, though, she actually initially turned the film down. She wasn't particularly a fan of country music, so she felt that the role wasn't right for her—that is, until she met with Lynn. Spacek was so charmed by Lynn's personality that she changed her mind. Lynn and Spacek spent plenty of time together leading up to the film's shoot, and Spacek even followed Lynn on tour in order to get a feeling for her various mannerisms. On top of that, Spacek also spent time with the legendary music producer Owen Bradley, who had produced many of Lynn's records. Bradley actually gave final approval on the soundtrack, and the fact that Lynn's own producer approved of Spacek's singing says a lot about how well she nailed the performance.

In Spacek's memoir, My Extraordinary Ordinary Life, she says that she would tape-record Lynn so that she could study her speech patterns. Reportedly, she never broke character while on-set and would constantly speak in Lynn's accent. It got to the point where crew members and visitors actually believed that was her natural way of speaking!

Conversely, Lynn's husband Dolittle wanted little to do with Tommy Lee Jones, who was portraying him in the film. Dolittle distanced himself from Jones until he heard that the actor had gotten arrested for drunk driving and speeding in a Jeep. Dolittle decided that he liked him after that, and warmed up to Jones right as shooting began. In fact, Doolittle wound up taking Jones out in his Jeep later on and showed him how to speed more efficiently!

Coal Miner's Daughter truly does a fantastic job of bringing Loretta Lynn's life to the screen. In addition to Spacek's fantastic job portraying her, Apted took great care to emulate the setting of Lynn's childhood. He clearly researched further than just the "hillbilly" stereotypes, and Spacek herself commended Apted for taking great care to present the poverty of Kentucky in a way that felt realistic. Critics also commended the set design and costuming and praised the fact that they didn't opt to show Lynn's

Sissy Spacek

childhood home as some overdramatic, desolate home of squalor.

That year's Academy Awards was graced with the presence of Loretta Lynn herself. She was out in the audience while Spacek accepted her award. Having the real-life subject of a biopic in the audience of an awards ceremony is pretty rare, and amazingly, Lynn wasn't the only subject in the audience that night. Robert De Niro won Best Actor that year for his portrayal of boxer Jake LaMotta in Raging Bull, and LaMotta was also in the audience!

Spacek's ability to sing the songs herself, rather than lip sync, emulate Lynn's specific accent and transform from a teenager to a middle-aged woman in the span of the film's runtime was most advantageous to her success. She proved that playing a real-life person never comes easy, but if done right, it certainly will bring lots of attention and rewards.

There is just something about actresses like Sissy Spacek, Shelly Duvall, Audrey Hepburn and even Mia Farrow that is intrinsic to their personas, and therefore their characters in film. It's this ambivalence of whether they are a woman or child. They possess a youthful, gamine energy that

Sissy Spacek

makes them one of a kind regardless of how old they are. They can play teenagers when they're in their mid-30s and old women when they're in their 20s. That's something really rare.
Sissy, now in her early 30s, starred in more highly successful films in the 1980s like in Missing, The River, Night Mother (opposite Anne Bancroft) and Crimes Of The Heart (opposite Diane Keaton and Jessica Lange.) She took a few years off from acting to spend time with family and returned to the big screen in 1990 in the movie The Long Walk Home opposite Whoopi Goldberg. Since then, Spacek's filmography has been ever-growing. It is filled with successes like JFK, Affliction, The Straight Story and In The Bedroom. Her more fairly recent highlights were in Deadfall, The Old Man and The Gun, so far her most recent film and The Help. Also an adaptation worth watching. And since the early 1970s, Spacek has had an ongoing TV career. Although this has consisted of more TV films and a few series roles, it is clear just how prominent her film career has been.
Spacek is multi-talented and her ability to transform proves her versatility. Her ability to mix the dark and light of a character is very appealing. That is why she has won three Golden Globes, an Oscar and has even been got nominated five more times on top of that for the Best Actress Oscar. She's someone who stays out of the spotlight, lives on a farm in Virginia with her two daughters and husband. There is a lot about Sissy Spacek that is very endearing and level-headed.

"All that attention to the perfect lighting, the perfect this, the perfect that, I find terribly annoying."

Meryl Streep

Meryl Streep is probably one of the most famous and decorated actresses of all time. She has accumulated 21 Oscar nominations and of those 21, she has won 3: one Supporting Actress and two Best Actress. She is Hollywood royalty and she is highly respected and in demand. But this respect was not so evident in her early career when producers would claim her as unattractive. But with her obvious passion for performance and inner determination, Meryl Streep became a cinematic icon.

We can spend hours talking about all of her achievements and films but the mission of this book is to highlight each actress's life journey, their most prominent career moves and what makes them so special.

Not quite invested in performing arts in school, Meryl Streep realised her potential in college. Her extensive work on stage during her college years made her proficient in memorising lines, doing various accents and singing. Streep made her Broadway debut in 1975, at the age of 26, in Trelawny of the "Wells".

Two years later she made her film debut opposite Jane Fonda, who I've covered before, in Julia. But it was the gritty Michael Cimino directorial called Deer Hunter where Meryl showed her ability to play emotional and deep roles. Although the role was minor, Meryl illuminated the male dominated cast which included Robert De Niro, Christopher Walken and her then real-life boyfriend John Cazale, who was already terminally ill with cancer. She actually decided to take on this role to be close to Cazale. This was in 1978.

Streep built her reputation as a worthy actress in the late 1970s and early 1980s, as she starred in Woody Allen's Manhattan, The Seduction Of Joe Tynan and of course Kramer Vs Kramer. Kramer vs Kramer obviously brought a lot of attention to Streep. The film's themes were focused on topics of gender roles, divorce, conflicting parents and relationships. It was the highest grossing film of 1979. And in 1980, the film won many major Oscars which included Meryl winning her one and only Best Supporting Actress Oscar. Three years later she won the Best Actress Oscar for her role in Sophie's Choice, probably her most celebrated role to this day. The heart wrenching story was Meryl Streep's triumph.

Streep built her reputation as a worthy actress in the late 1970s and early 1980s, as she starred in Woody Allen's Manhattan, The Seduction Of Joe Tynan and of course Kramer Vs Kramer. Kramer vs Kramer obviously brought a lot of attention to Streep. The film's themes were focused on topics of gender roles, divorce, conflicting parents and relationships. It was the highest grossing film of 1979. And in 1980, the film won many major Oscars which included Meryl winning her one and only Best Supporting Actress Oscar. Three years later she won the Best Actress Oscar for her role in Sophie's Choice, probably her most celebrated role to this day. The heart wrenching story was Meryl

Streep's triumph.

Sophie's Choice is a film concerned with the slow but enchanting reveal of its main characters' heart. Its artistic strength is in how carefully this voyage is crafted, giving us a sense of discovering something concealed while always keeping the viewer at arm's length, reassessing what they think they know. It's often heavy, plodding, and dry in its delivery, but the haunting emotional shock of what is discovered resonates vividly in the hours and days after viewing the film. What unfolds between our two main characters, Nathan (Kevin Kline) and Sophie (Meryl Streep), isn't particularly "story" focused. A synopsis of the film itself would be unremarkable and simple, but the dynamics of their relationship, both with each other and their pasts, is where the journey takes place. We show up after the story has already happened. And so, each new revelation of the characters leads us backward to reconsider what we've already seen, until the devastating final sequence.

Our narrator and unofficial tour guide into the troubled lives of the couple is Stingo, an aspiring writer played by Peter MacNicol. The actor carries off the role of subdued and introspective southern scribe without a hitch, but there's an added element of strangeness for viewers more familiar with his comedic work (which is what he has primarily done in the nearly four decades since Sophie's Choice.) His character of the timid, somewhat ineffectual tenant to the dysfunctional couple isn't a radical departure from the types of characters he usually plays, he just exists in a different world.

Stingo comes looking to rent a room, but ends up becoming close friends with the constantly warring couple. Sophie is a playful and somewhat whimsical personality who is gracious and charming but carries a heavy sadness with her that we get scattered glimpses of. Her live-in boyfriend Nathan, on the other hand, exudes strength, seriousness, and a flare for the dramatic. He seems to compliment Sophie's nature, and like her, has a sense of turmoil beneath the surface. His has a more dangerous feeling to it, however. Though his passionate speech and lust for knowledge is exhilarating to Stingo, there is a flip side to this nature that is jealous, vicious, and a little unpredictable.

The sheer power and command that Meryl Streep seizes from her first appearance make it apparent that this entire narrative is going to ride on the shoulders of her acting talents. The film is set in 1947, and much of the production has the muted, sedated feel that many films focused on this era have. This comes across in the elements of the set design, wardrobe, and performance style alike. Everything has a very stagey, almost overly proper tone, as if the film doesn't want to be much more than a vehicle for its words and poetic perspective. Whether intentional or not, something about its style captures the simplicity of television and film of the time. It is also very literary and loaded with dialog almost relentlessly. When characters are not conversing, Stingo is giving us voiceover narration, but everything is done in a manner reminiscent of a play. The only time this buttoned-down feel is disrupted is when we get brief glances of the photos that Nazi-obsessed Nathan has around the home. Horrific images from the death camp stir the calm on the film's surface.

The most dramatic break in style comes late in the third act, when there is a sharp turn away from the mood of 1950s melodrama to something more akin to an Ingmar Berman movie. When Nathan becomes increasingly absorbed in what is believed to be important scientific work, Sophie seeks companionship in Stingo. The relationship is non-sexual, though there is a strong sense of feelings being restrained and sought-after intimacy being indulged through

Meryl Streep

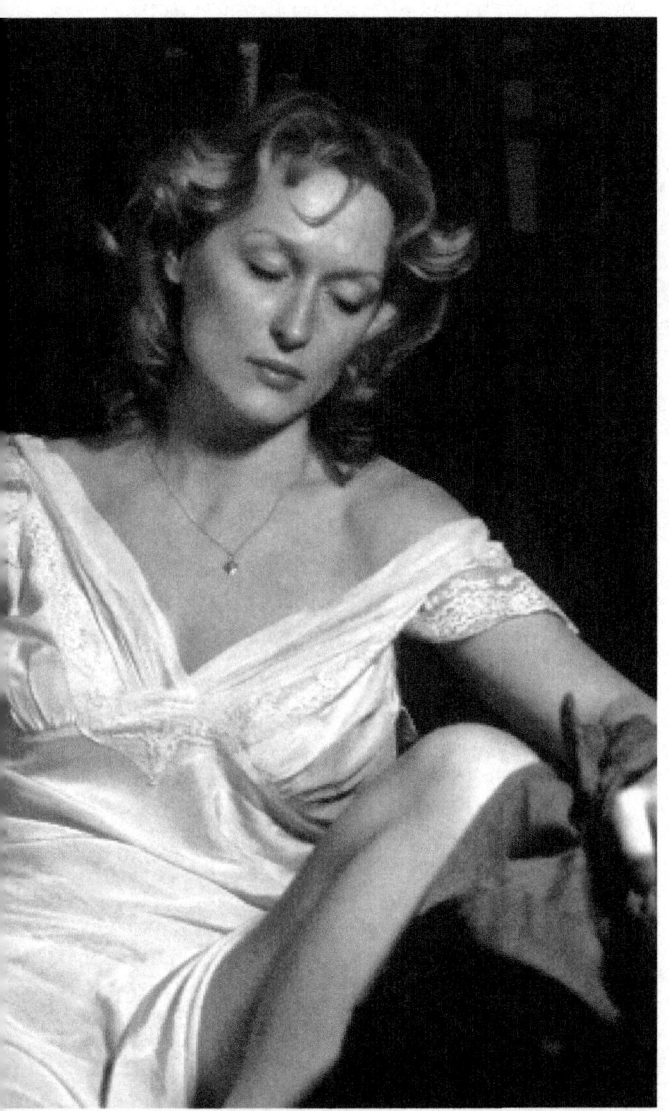

conversation. Sophie reveals her troubled past as a Polish interpreter during Nazi occupation, and the horrors that she witnessed as she was shuffled around the upper crust of SS households after being taken prisoner. The camera holds on her face in an invasive and sometimes uncomfortable way as she brings us into her pain. It's impossible to imagine the film working without an actress of Streep's calibre, and the final sequence rests entirely on her authenticity as we see the moment of her spiritual death. The final, horrific story which she reveals exposes an unbearable weight and trauma from which she will never be free. Though the film itself can be extremely dull and a bit of a challenge to push through, Streep fills the characters' words with a heart-breaking potency that elevates it to a memorable and moving work.

Meryl Streep

As the years went by Meryl managed to get married and have children on top of her ever-growing list of fantastically memorable and diverse roles. Her no-frills attitude towards conveying the emotional range of a character while transforming on screen was her signature. If you wanted your film to be a hit, then you would hire Meryl Streep. Films like Silkwood, Falling in Love and Out Of Africa showed her amazing range.

But by the early 1990's Streep wanted to convey that her range could be extended to more comedic and absurd roles like those in She Devil, Death Becomes Her and Postcards From The Edge. More movies followed in the mid 1990s to early 2000s like The Bridges of Madison Country, Music Of The Heart and The Hours. But it was in 2006 that Streep renewed her image of a strong female character to attract modern, more younger audiences who were not too familiar with her older work. Devil Wears Prada. Her character is unforgettable, in your face type of boss woman.

Streep's succession of diverse film roles proved her versatility regardless of her age, like those in Mamma Mia!, Doubt and Julie And Julia, which proved that she will never be pigeonholed. In 2012, Streep won her second Best Actress Oscar for her uncanny rendering of Margaret

Thatcher in Iron Lady. Then more film roles followed: Its Complicated, The Post, August: Osage County, Into The Woods and Suffragette. Her more recent works are in The Laundromat and Little Women.

Meryl Streep has done TV sporadically and her most recent TV role was in Big Little Lies. The same goes for theatre: the mid- to late-1970s is when she really embraced the stage before taking on film.

Some claim Meryl Streep is a living legend, some may argue that she is overrated. But what is undeniable is her choice of performances. I don't think there is anyone else that can match her extensive list of successful films as well as versatile roles. Her ability to create remarkable women on screen is most admirable, especially when at times strong female roles were scarce. Meryl has the magic power to project a strong female character in all her roles.

Shirley MacLaine

Shirley MacLaine's curiosity and free spirit pushed her to become a well-known and respected actress in her early 20s. She has been in the entertainment industry for a very long time and her career has stood the test of time. Why? Because she was transforming with the industry. A performer by nature, Shirley MacLaine brought humour, softness, vulnerability and zest to her roles that gave her an opportunity to utilise her singing, dancing and off course acting skills.

Shirley MacLaine started her collaborations with big names early on in her working career. With an extensive background in dance, mainly ballet, Shirley who towered over most male dancers at 5 '7 and possessed unconventional looks struggled to find luck in professional dance. But her relentless attitude and enthusiasm to learn new skills got her to pursue acting instead. Broadway was the move. Her younger brother Warren Beatty was also starting his journey as an actor.

Barely out of high school, Shirley made her debut in the chorus line in the musical Oklahoma. She then took part in the dancing ensemble of Me and Juliet on Broadway. Before you know it Shirley MacLaine stole the spotlight in The Pyjama Party. She was the understudy but replaced the actress who got injured. Shirley was instantly approached by film producer Hal B. Wallis to sign her to Paramount in 1954. She was only 20 years old at the time.

Shirley represented a different type of female: a more mischievous, pixie-like character rather than the glamorous and seductive one that was promoted in Hollywood in the 1950s. Shirley made her film debut under Alfred Hitchcock's direction in The Trouble With Harry in 1955. At the time, she was a novelty in Hollywood. She even won a Golden Globe Award for New Star of the Year for her debut performance.

A string of successful films in the 50s, which showed off Shirley's talents, followed like Artists and Models, Around The World In 80 Days, The Matchmaker, Some Came Running and Hot Spell. MacLaine had already garnered her first Oscar nomination for Some Came Running in 1958.

"The person who knows how to laugh at himself will never cease to be amused."

Shirley was learning quickly in the fast-paced environment. The variety of roles and movie genres she was in proved how versatile she was. Her collaborations and ultimately friendships with already big names like Frank Sinatra, Dean Martin and Vicente Minnelli also gave her an opportunity to get insight into the life of actors. These men became almost like mentors to her.

The 1960s brought even more significant roles like those in Oceans 11, Can Can and The Apartment. The Apartment, in particular, was a major success. It was nominated for 10 Oscars and won 5 of those. This 1960 film solidified MacLaine as a serious actress even though she did not win the Oscar for this film. It was only her second nomination.

Shirley worked on more major films in the following years like in The Children's Hour (opposite Audrey Hepburn), Irma La Douce (for which she was nominated for the Oscar her third time), Two For The Seesaw, What A Way To Go! (in which she replaced Marylin Monroe as the lead) and Gambit (where she plays a Eurasian woman). All of these films are now considered cult classics. 1966's Gambit was the third movie in which Shirley played an Asian character: Around The World In 80 Days in 1956 and My Geisha in 1962 were the other two.

In 1969, Shirley brought in her choreographer friend, Bob Fosse to direct his first feature film, Sweet Charity, a musical in which Shirley headlined in. Shirley had the ability to entertain yet bring emotion to her characters, whether they were happy or sad. She said, "If you really play the character truthfully. Everything is the truth. Then the comedy will be funnier and the drama will be sadder."

The 1970s came rolling in and Shirley's work ethic did not decline. As she matured, so did her roles. She was nominated her fourth time for the Oscar in 1977 in the film called The Turning Point (opposite Anne Bancroft). The 1980s then came flooding in and still no Oscar win. After almost three decades working tirelessly and successfully in the film industry, it did not make sense as to why, at this point, the iconic Shirley MacLaine had not won!

But a win was just around the corner. In the year 1984 Shirley got to claim her Best Actress Oscar. She has spoken of her discipline (which she inherited through her training as a dancer) and I think it is exactly this discipline mixed with her endless curiosity which has kept her relevant for so many years. MacLaine appeared in her Oscar winning film called Terms Of Endearment in 1983. To this day MacLaine claims the character she played in this family comedy drama, Aurora Greenway, as her favourite.

At the 56th Academy Awards, James L. Brooks' Terms of Endearment made quite the splash. It boasted a star-studded cast: not only is there the fantastic Shirley MacLaine, but the film also includes Jack Nicholson, Danny DeVito, Debra Winger, Jeff Daniels, and John Lithgow. The film ended up becoming the second highest grossing film of that year, and was of course a huge critical success. In addition to MacLaine's Academy win, the film was nominated for eleven awards overall and won Best Adapted Screenplay, Best Supporting Actor (for Nicholson), Best Picture, and Best Director. Terms Of Endearment was also the second highest grossing film of 83 following Return of the Jedi.

Shirley MacLaine

The film primarily deals with the relationship between Aurora Greenway (MacLaine) and her daughter, Emma (Debra Winger). Emma tries to get away from her controlling mother and winds up marrying a college professor in order to escape her. Still, despite their issues, they share a close, if not somewhat strained, relationship. The movie also follows the relationship between Emma and her husband (Jeff Daniels), as well as Aurora's romance with Garrett (Jack Nicholson).

Originally, actual mother-daughter duo Janet Leigh and Jamie Lee Curtis were considered for the roles of Aurora and Emma. Sissy Spacek had also been in the running to play Emma, but other commitments kept her from taking on the role. According to Brooks, the reason he ultimately cast MacLaine was because she was the only actress who approached the film "like a comedy". MacLaine actually turned down a role in the cult film Poltergeist to play Aurora.

Infamously, MacLaine and Winger's relationship on set was taut. Winger was battling with a severe cocaine addiction, which caused her to be quite confrontational. The two actually got into a shoving match on set. On top of that, MacLaine chronicled in her autobiography that Winger literally lifted up her skirt and farted in her face at one point.

In a later interview, MacLaine called the set "chaotic" and claimed that director James L. Brooks thrived on that tense energy. MacLaine also claimed that Brooks liked to play "mind games" with the cast and that it got so frustrating for her (and everyone else in production, for that matter), she left set one day with the intention of driving to the airport and quitting.

Despite Winger and MacLaine's strained relationship on set, the two shared a pretty cute moment at the Academy Awards. Winger had actually also been nominated for Best Actress, but of course, MacLaine won. When MacLaine's name was called, she reportedly turned to Winger and whispered, "Half of this belongs to you." Winger responded, "I'll take half."

The actresses' bizarre relationship with one another likely helped to bring out their performances, however. Brooks encouraged everyone to play practical jokes on one another in order to keep their performances spontaneous and genuine. There are a few parallels with the pair's real-life relationship and the characters' as well—strained yet uniquely close.

On the other hand, MacLaine seemed to have a better relationship with Jack Nicholson. According to an interview she did with Fox, she believes Nicholson's spontaneity and tendency to improvise helped build her own performance. The two would get up to goofy antics on set together, like showing up nearly naked. The majority of their scenes

together were improvised. For example, when Garrett puts his hands down Aurora's dress on the beach, that was all Nicholson's idea. Their chemistry is great and they clearly work well together, and both MacLaine and Nicholson are very much deserving of their Academy Awards.

MacLaine not only delivers a powerfully emotional performance, but she nails the comedic timing of each scene as well. As bittersweet as the relationship at the centre of the film is, it still very much has comedic moments that lighten up the movie. Leonard Maltin called the movie "unpredictable" with a "wonderful mix of humour and heartbreak".

A later film, Steel Magnolias in 1989, was another worldwide success for MacLaine. She starred opposite major actresses like Sally Field (who won the Oscar too), Dolly Parton, Daryl Hannah, Olympia Dukakis and Julia Roberts (who was just starting out in the film industry). This union of leading ladies on screen was just as strong off screen as it was on

screen. MacLaine recalls a universal camaraderie between these actresses, saying that working on Steel Magnolias was free of any cattiness or competition.

In 1990 MacLaine starred in Postcards From The Edge opposite Meryl Streep. In 1996 a sequel to Terms Of Endearment was released called The Evening Star. Most people forget this film even happened, and for good reason: it was a critical and commercial failure, despite MacLaine and Nicholson reprising their roles. The characters' developments were contrived and felt unrealistic, but MacLaine's performance is still top-notch. Unfortunately, the writing is so clunky that her and Nicholson's performances are dulled because of it.

Shirley continued working on films opposite other Oscar-winning actresses like in These Old Broads, which happened to be Elizabeth Taylor's final film appearance. She starred in Bewitched opposite Nicole Kidman and Wild Oats with Jessica Lange. She has also appeared in a sprinkling of TV shows, like Downton Abbey, opposite Maggie Smith.

Geraldine Page

It was a long and winding road to Oscar success for Geraldine Page. Much like Marie Dressler and Shirley Booth, who won Oscars late in their acting career, Geraldine Page won hers at the age of 61. She suddenly passed away a year after her win, but she left a legacy of Oscar worthy performances that made her an underrated actress. Today, not many may know of Geraldine Page so let's delve into the story of her life and career.

After years of extensive studying of drama at various universities and institutes in the midwest, Geraldine relocated to the hub of theatre, New York City. She simultaneously studied under Uta Hagen's direction and then Lee Strasberg's method acting. To support her aspirations, she worked various jobs like a coat check girl, theatre usher and lingerie model. At the time, Page was in her early 20s and had nothing to lose.

Her stage debut was in 1945 in Seven Mirrors. More productions followed that established her theatre career like Yerma in 1952 but most notably, the Tennessee William's production of Summer & Smoke. Geraldine became a relevant name in the off-Broadway movement.

Film and TV gigs followed in the early 50s. Hondo, opposite John Wayne in 1953, was Geraldine's official film debut. And she'd already ticked off her first Best Supporting Actress Oscar nomination for her role in the film. But her hopes to become a film legend were suddenly halted when she was blacklisted for eight years from Hollywood due to her association with Uta Hagen, from whom she studied acting. The Hollywood Blacklist was at its height and Uta Hagen was one of many on the Red Channels list: a list of anyone associated with alleged communism supporters or sympathisers, who were then barred from working and contributing to the entertainment industry.

"I have played old ladies since I was 17 years old, and very convincingly. I've always looked funny and was too tall to play the leads and so had to play the grandmothers."

Therefore, Geraldine Page turned her attention to theatre and TV for the remainder of the 1950s. She worked on major Broadway plays like The Rainmaker, The Immoralist, Separate Tables and Sweet Birds of Youth opposite major actors like James Dean and Paul Newman. Her TV performances were did not go unnoticed either, like that in the series Playhouse 90, for which she got nominated for an Emmy in 1959.

Geraldine entered the 1960s with a succession of film adaptations from previous plays she had worked on in the 1950s. She rekindled her film career with movies like Summer & Smoke, Sweet Bird Of Youth and The Three Sisters. She also appeared in widely memorable films like Toys In The Attic, Dear Heart and You're A Big Boy Now.
Geraldine Page was truly unstoppable. She was loved by audiences and film critics. She

was considered "one of the finest actors of her generation". The 1960s transitioned to the 1970s and the 1970s transitioned into the 1980s. And Geraldine was giving more and more phenomenal performances on film, stage and TV. It was her deep dive into the universe of her characters that made her performances detailed and intrinsic.

She once said, "The main thing is the ability to control your instrument, which, in the actor, is yourself. Look the way you want the character to look. Sound the way you want the character to sound. Once you've trained the instrument to do what you want, you're in control, and you're free."

It did not make sense as to why Geraldine, one of the greatest most seasoned actresses of her time, had not won an Oscar. But Geraldine was always a stage actress first and foremost, Broadway being her place of power. She once remarked, "I didn't want to be a Hollywood actress who every often does a Broadway play. I wanted to be a Broadway actress who every so often does a movie." So it's possible that she was indifferent to an Oscar win, but after seven overall Best Actress and Best Supporting nominations, she struck gold in 1986. The Trip To Bountiful became Page's penultimate production and her most rewarding one. All the stars aligned to make Geraldine the Best Actress Oscar winner in 1986, one year before her sudden death in 1987. This win was certainly anticipated, for Page had a string of Best Leading and Best Supporting Oscar nominations under her wing since the 1950s.

The Trip To Bountiful is a slow burn, a quiet film focused on one woman and her story only. It is really a character study that lets us glimpse into the world of an elderly woman coming to terms with her past, her present and her future during life post World War II. It is a beautiful film, directed by Peter Masterson and adapted from Horton Foote's stage play of the same name.

We follow the bus trip journey of Mrs Carrie Watts, a soft spoken yet steadfast old woman, who will stop at nothing to give a final visit to her childhood home: a small cottage house nestled in a long-forgotten settlement named Bountiful. Mrs. Watts sneaks out of her simpleton son's and his snarky wife's house, where she lives with in Houston, and sets off on her final adventure to Bountiful and also gives her old friend Callie Davis a visit.

Mrs. Watts befriends a young woman named Thelma on the night ride to Bountiful and they share their life stories which lead to Mrs. Watts breaking down in tears about her past mistakes and losses. When her son and daughter in law set out to find her, Mrs. Watts tries to get to Bountiful before they find her and take her back to Houston. It's a cat-and-mouse chase, and this time Mrs Watts succeeds at running free from her son and daughter-in-law who have been holding her in a tight grasp so she can't run away.

Despite having heart problems that lead to her having multiple episodes of fainting, Mrs. Watts is determined to visit Bountiful only to arrive at an overgrown place with vast greenery and her childhood home decrepit, as well as finding out that Callie Davis had passed away a couple days before.

The film is about the experience of ageing, revisiting the past and coming to terms with the ups and downs with life. After all, A Trip To Bountiful is an ode to seeing beauty in the simple, human things in life and realising how important it is to live your truth and experience life to the fullest, even if it means taking risks. Page's performance is nuanced, not a loud-mouthed granny who struts with a sense of entitlement, but rather a soft girly voiced of a retired southern belle who is lonely but still has the fire in herself to pursue her goal. She finds blessing in nothing more than humming a song from church, or a warm-hearted conversation with a stranger about birds. Page truly brings humanity and colour to the film.
It was her performance in the film A Trip To Bountiful in 1985 that captured Geraldine in the most vulnerable and gritty state on screen. In fact, the sound of Geraldine

Page's name being called as the recipient of the Best Actress Oscar resulted in a standing ovation. Three more films followed suit, Riders To The Sea being her final one. A year after her long-awaited Oscar win, Page suffered a fatal heart attack. Geraldine Page was certainly a legendary woman who touched many people with her deeply moving performances.

Her only daughter from her marriage to Rip Torn, the actor, Angelica Page, also an actress, and she wrote and performed a monologue play about her late mother. She said this that I think proves just how fantastic Page was: "I grew up in the centre of her sparkling career. As her only daughter I feel compelled to share her lessons and gifts with others who did and did not have the opportunity to know her magic intimately. She was a true rebel and trail blazer. A masterful woman who was ahead of her time and should not be forgotten anytime soon."

Marlee Matlin

Not only is Marlee Matlin, to this day, the youngest ever winner of the Best Actress Oscar, which she won at the age of 21, but she was also the first woman with a disability to win. In the already major category of Best Actress, Marlee, a newcomer, was up against Hollywood heavyweights like Jane Fonda, Sissy Spacek, Kathleen Turner and Sigourney Weaver at the 1987 ceremony. Marlee Matlin made sure that nothing would stand in her way from reaching her dreams. Her pursuit of being a deaf actress is off course what is intrinsic to her life but also her characters on screen but that does not stop from giving an amazing performance and being a role model to anyone with any sort of disability from going after their dreams.

Marlee Matlin lost most of her hearing as a baby and was the only one in her family that was deaf. She was introduced to acting on stage as early as seven years old in children's theatre in Chicago, even winning an award for her acting as a teen. But she went on to study criminal justice after graduation. But she soon realised that a career in this sphere was not for her and resumed her acting ambitions after graduation from Harper College in Illinois.

After performing at the International Center on Deafness and the Arts in 1985 in the production of Children Of A Lesser God, she was scouted by Henry Winkler, who gave her a nudge to pursue film acting. Consequently, Matlin won the main role in the movie version of Children Of A Lesser God. And it became her film debut. The film was directed by Randa Haines and co-starred William Hurt.

Set in wet, cold and windy New England, James Leeds, played by William Hurt, a hearing man with a dry sense of humour and outgoing personality, gets hired as a teacher at a school for deaf youth. His unorthodox yet effective ways of teaching helps hard-of-hearing teenagers build confidence. There he meets the enigmatic Sarah Norman, played by Matlin, who is a deaf and mute janitor at the school. She is young, rebellious and independent.

"The handicap of deafness is not in the ear; it is in the mind."

The plot of Children Of A Lesser God revolves around the heated and ultimately rocky romantic relationship between James and Sarah. James, clearly struck by Sarah's beauty and fiery personality, makes it a mission of his to help her use her voice to speak out loud, something she has not done for a very long time.

The relationship dynamic is problematic from the get-go due to James' manipulative behaviour to get Sarah to do what he wants. The manipulations begin with him seeing her swimming naked at the school swimming pool after hours and jumping in to have sex with her. Then he makes her quit her job to live with him, knowing how much she likes her job, and finally blaming her for his not being able to enjoy listening to classical music anymore because he is sad that she cannot hear music with him.

James believes that his purpose is to help Sarah and somewhat own her in order to mould her into the woman of his dreams. As Sarah opens up about her past trauma with boys, sex and childhood, we notice that she shows vulnerability to James, yet we do not see this same vulnerability coming from him, regardless of the fact that he professes his love for her, takes care of her and takes her on dates. He always tries to change her to be the woman he wants her to be.

The relationship comes to a head when Sarah and James argue due to his determination to hear her speak. She realises his coercions will not work on her; she is far too strong to do something she doesn't want to do. She leaves him and returns to her estranged mothers home to start a new life away from James and the school. James keeps trying to get hold of Sarah and she dodges his advances. Yet, at a school dance, the two meet up and decide to reconcile, realising that they love each other and will work not their relationship.

Marlee Matlin

Marlee Matlin

The film came out in 1986, when Matlin was only 21. She and Hurt started dating during the filming of this movie and their union was toxic. Matlin was introduced to drugs and alcohol through Hurt, and they eventually split and Matlin went to rehab, but only after her career defining moment. One of the most unexpected wins in Oscar history was Marlee Matlin's. At the 1987 Oscars, when Matlin won the Best Actress Oscar for her role in Children Of A Lesser God, Hurt actually presented the award.

Matlin added various film and TV roles to her resume that showed off her dramatic and comedic talent. She proved that being a person with a disability does not have to be the defining quality of her characters; that such a person is beyond their restrictions and just happens to have a disability rather than being governed by it. The idea that being a victim of one's differences was and is something that Matlin refuses to promote.

Matlin's TV career is actually far more extensive than her film career. She appeared in major shows like Seinfeld, Picket Fences, Reasonable Doubts, Law And Order, Desperate Housewives and My Name Is Earl to name a few.

There are other respectable distinctions in Matlin's career. Like in 2009, Matlin released an autobiography called I'll Scream. She described her substance abuse, her abusive relationship with Hurt and the sexual abuse she suffered from her babysitter when she was a child. Furthermore she has and continues to take part in charitable organisations and foundations, for AIDS, Jewish communities and deaf communities to name a few.
Marlee Matlin is still relevant today, and she speaks up on humanitarian causes especially the rights of deaf people. Her dedication to make the world a better and more inclusive place is an aspect that makes her stand out. Marlee Matlin is certainly a ray of light in and out of the entertainment industry.

"Women are the real architects of society."

Cher

There is a lot to unpack about Cher and her life. Her career has been a fruitful one since the 1960s. And since then it has been full steam ahead. Originally born Cherilyn Sarkisian, Cher was a leading lady since childhood. And everyone around her knew that she was going to be a star.

"The Goddess Of Pop" was a natural born performer and leader. She did not go to college, nor did she have any training or connections. She dropped out of high school at the age of 16, moved to LA and made ends meet by working random jobs. Cher was smart and fearless; she was not hesitant to approach those who would help start her entertainment career. Two years later after her big move, in 1962, Cher met Sonny Bono, a performer. They started recording music together and eventually became a couple. By 1965, the couple promoted themselves as the iconic "Sonny & Cher" singing duo. This was their breakthrough which led to the Sonny & Cher Comedy Hour on CBS in 71. The larger-than-life costumes, set design and sketch comedy proved that Cher was a talented actress, on top being a unique singer.

The destruction of Cher's personal life at the beginning of the 1970s came hand in hand with her career. Her eventual divorce from Sonny in 1975 made the public lose interest in her and when the two paired up amicably once again in 1976 for the Sonny and Cher Show, it was clear that the novelty of them as a spectacular power couple was no more. Plus, the trend of musical variety shows was not in fashion anymore. This signalled Cher to focus on her career and hers only. Music wasn't doing it for Cher: her music career was on a decline and it was time to reinvent.

The 1980s were revolutionary for Cher. She was in her 30s and disappointed with how Hollywood was unimpressed with her couple of early unsuccessful films from the 1960s. She credits Robert Altman for launching her acting career—a serious acting career. He cast her in the Broadway production of Come Back to the Five and Dime, Jimmy Dean, Jimmy Dean in 1982. She said, "Without Bob [Robert Altman] I would have never had a film career. Everyone told him not to cast me ... I am convinced that Bob was the only one who was brave enough to do it."

Cher consequently appeared in the film version of the play in 1982. She then appeared opposite Meryl Streep, who to this day is a good friend of hers, in Silkwood in 1983. She recalls that people laughed when her name showed up on the screen credits at one of the film's previews. Regardless of what some thought of her she won a Golden Globe for her performance in Silkwood. She said, "I've always taken risks, and never worried what the world might really think of me."

More successes followed like in Mask, Suspect and The Witches of Eastwick. Although getting lots of praise and recognition for her work on Mask in 1985, she was not nominated for Best Actress the following year at the Oscars. To show her disapproval at the Academy and their choice to omit her from even getting a nomination she rocked up in pure Cher fabulousness to present one of the awards that night. She showed up in this. A showstopper to say the least.

In 1987 Cher appeared in Moonstruck, a role she was hesitant to take on but eventually one that led her to become an Oscar winner. Cher brought magic to the screen opposite Nicholas Cage and Best Supporting Actress Winner that year too, Olympia Dukakis. Once again Cher appeared in a more controlled outfit than that of a few years back, but nonetheless nothing short of exquisite at the 1988 awards to accept her statuette.

Moonstruck is about Loretta Castorini, played by Cher, who is newly engaged to an older man, Johnny. While away on a trip to his homeland, Sicily, to say his goodbye to his mother on his deathbed, Loretta is given the responsibility of reaching out to his estranged younger brother, Ronny (Nicholas Cage) to invite him to their fast-approaching wedding.

This being Loretta's second marriage, she is hellbent on making this marriage work. The Italian community in New York City is very tight-knit so when Loretta connects with her fiancé's rugged and outspoken brother, they start a secret romance, only to be caught by her own father when attending an opera on a date together. And so, Loretta is torn between going through with this marriage with the older man, which is a safe bet for her future, or following her lust for Ronny.

When Nicholas Cage is cast in any film, he adds an element of unserious ridiculousness. His image and acting style is not the best quality and I believe the casting choice of Cher with Cage does not work very effectively. Despite being styled to look more homely and "regular" Cher still is a striking woman. You can put a potato sack on her and she still would love breath-taking. And with Cage's rugged yet dopey image, Cher overpowers him and therefore makes their on-screen relationship not believable. For this disbalance I question the final outcome of the film: Loretta deciding to marry Ronnie when Johnny changes his mind to marry her.

Nonetheless, this film proved Cher's natural talent for dramatic acting, she totally shined on screen.

Cher's film career tapered as the years went by but nonetheless she still appeared in memorable films like Mermaids, Tea With Mussolini and Burlesque. To this day, Cher simultaneously juggles acting and music and impresses us with her fervour and fashion, proving that age is just a number. Cher is an icon and a beautiful woman. She famously said, "Until you're ready to look foolish, you'll never have the possibility of being great."

Cher's trademark is her extravagant style, her outspoken feminist attitude and relentless nature. It is hard to ignore her achievements. Her adventurous and quite controversial antics make her a remarkable and real person. She has had a larger-than-life presence since the 60s which proves her ability to transform and be a trendsetter simultaneously.

"I have, in some ways, saved characters that have been marginalised by society by playing them – and having them still have dignity and still survive, still get through it."

Jodie Foster

Jodie Foster did not have a typical childhood. The child prodigy who spoke French fluently since childhood learned to read at age three and appeared in her first jobs at age 3, which is far from normal. Her single mother pushed Foster to keep booking jobs early on and helped carve the girl into a child actor. But with a good head on her shoulders and safety all around growing up on set, Foster always aimed higher than just acting; she went to Yale University to study literature while taking a break from acting. Jodie Foster's story is a very interesting one full of ups and downs.

Jodie along with her older siblings were constantly appearing in advertisements and TV shows since childhood. Eventually she and her older brother became primary breadwinners in the family by the age of 12. Foster appeared in a string of TV shows throughout the 60s and 70s. Her first being Mayberry RFD in 1968 followed by over 50 more shows in total.

Foster simultaneously began appearing in films in the 70s: her film debut was in Napoleon and Samantha in 1972 at the age of 10. A few more films followed but her appearance in Martin Scorsese's film Alice Doesn't Live Here Anymore opposite Ellen Burstyn, an Oscar winner, was Foster's real taste of true filmmaking and serious roles.

Two years later Scorsese cast Foster in the classic Taxi Driver opposite Robert De Niro. Foster, who was 12 upon casting, was assessed psychologically to see whether she could handle being on set of this film due to its violent content. Foster's maturity and potential to play serious roles proved that her future was bright. De Niro noticed this and rehearsed extensively with Foster during the filming of Taxi Driver. Foster later said, "The idea that everybody thinks if a kid's going to be an actress it means that she has to play Shirley Temple or someone's little sister." It was on set of this film that Foster realised that filmmaking and acting was a craft that one must chisel at in order to do a good job. It's not just fun and games. Foster was nominated for best supporting actress Oscar for her role in this film.

Foster furthered her film career in Echoes Of The Summer, Bugsy Malone, The Little Girl Who Lives Down the Lane and Freaky Friday. And she showcased her acting skills in European films like Moi, fleur bleue and Casotto as well as Candleshoe, Foxes and Carny.

Foster was swiftly taking on more adult roles. Her mother was adamant that she start promoting herself as a fully grown adult, even going as far as arranging a partially-nude photoshoot when Foster turned 16. Foster's mother and the wife of the photographer were present on set.

But Foster had a plan of her own, a more sensible one. After finishing high school she took a break from acting and focused on her studies at Yale University. Taking the moment to live a more normal life as a student and discover oneself was exciting for the young Jodie. Nonetheless she worked on films during the summer holidays.

Foster's dream of living a quieter, publicity-free life was already crushed during freshman year of college. Her risqué role in Taxi Driver seemed to make quite an impression on fully grown creepy men, most notably John W. Hinckley, Jr. who had been obsessed with Foster all these years. He started stalking Foster on campus, sending her letters and calling her. The unhinged Hinkley decided then to recreate his own Taxi Driver movie. He decided to get Foster's attention by attempting to assassinate newly elected President Ronald Reagan in 1981.

Hinckley's notes to Foster went as follows: "Over the past seven months I've left you dozens of poems, letters and love messages in the faint hope that you could develop an interest in me. Although we talked on the phone a couple of times I never had the nerve to simply approach you and introduce myself ... The reason I'm going ahead with this attempt now is because I cannot wait any longer to impress you." After the assassination attempt that left Reagan wounded, Hinckley was sent to jail and then to psychiatric care.

Foster tried to retract from media attention regarding this incident and finally graduated Yale in 1985. Although she appeared in a handful of mediocre films during college, it was difficult for Foster to re-establish the level of success she had before college.

But it was in 1988 that things took a positive turn. Foster, now 26, appeared in the gritty and visually disturbing film, The Accused. The film ended up being groundbreaking for that time because of its intense subject matter. It brought to light the subject of rape culture. The film was a huge success and Foster was the highlight of this film.

The Accused's subject matter is more relevant than ever during the #MeToo Movement. Themes such as non-consensual sex, harassment, sexual abuse and the public vs the victim are huge in this film. Foster plays Sarah Tobias, a young woman who is raped by three men in one night at a seedy public bar, while being harassed by a much bigger group of men who watch on and enjoy the show. After the traumatic experience, Sarah goes on a journey of redemption, but most importantly reclaiming her power as a woman living in a sexist world. The Accused dives into the bureaucracy and corruption of the justice system and its unfair, lack of moral and systematic way of treating its accused and accuser.

The film teaches us that no matter what the victims reputation was, how they were dressed, what they did or said, it is not a reasonable reason for their rape. Sarah recounts her words during the hearing in court. She recounts herself saying "no!" No is a good enough word for the abuser to stop. Yet to this day a woman's words are not enough for her to defend herself.

Jodie Foster

The flashback of the rape scene to this day remains one of the most controversial cinematic scenes due to it viscerally intense visuals. As harrowing as the scene was, it left cast members emotionally troubled and even physically sick after filming it for 5 consecutive days. Although it was intricately rehearsed in order for the exercise to be less intrusive for the actors, it still left Foster with broken blood vessels in her eye and she recounted that she simply blacked out while filming. Complex ranked the rape scene from the film number 16 on its list of "The 53 Most Hard-To-Watch Scenes in Movie History".

Saying that this film revitalised Foster's film career is an understatement. In 1989 Foster won her first Best Actress Academy Award for her performance in The Accused. This was the perfect way to prove to herself and to the world that she is as fact a Hollywood star—not a child actor anymore but a legitimate actor.

Jodie Foster

Four years later Jodie found herself accepting her second Best Actress Oscar for her role in Silence Of The Lambs, a psychological thriller. She plays Clarice Starling, a young and fearless FBI trainee opposite Anthony Hopkins, who plays an imprisoned cannibal killer Dr. Hannibal Lecter, who helps Clarice find another serial killer on the loose. The film was a major box office hit and remains one of the most iconic films.

Jodie acted and directed her first feature film called Little Man Tate in 1991. She appeared in further memorable films like Shadows And Fog, Sommersby, Maverick and Nell in which she acted and produced. She was nominated for the Oscar once more for her role in Nell.

More successes followed like Contact, Panic Room, Flight Plan and The Brave One. Jodie Foster has directed and acted more films such as The Beaver, Money Monster and episodes of Black Mirror and Orange Is The New Black.

Jodie Foster is relevant to this day as a dedicated and seasoned actress, producer and director. She keeps her personal life private. It is exciting to follow the journey of Jodie Foster from her childhood to now. It proves that natural talent never disappears; it always comes to the surface; and one must take advantage of it.

Jessica Tandy

Jessica Tandy was a well-respected actress in her time. With over 60 years of acting experience on stage, on film and TV, she was finally awarded the best actress Oscar at the age of 80, making her the oldest female winner. It was clearly a long time coming for Jessica, who merged her early English acting experience into an American filmography. Her list for stage and film is long, so we will focus on Tandy's biggest accomplishments and what took so long for her to get that Oscar.

Jessica Tandy started acting in London theatre at the age of 18 after studying acting at the Ben Greet Academy. The 1930s were filled with West End productions focused on Shakespeare's work like Hamlet, Macbeth, Henry V, Midsummer Night's Dream, King Lear and The Tempest. Tandy made her film debut in 1930 in The Indiscretions of Eve, a British film. Only in 1938 did Tandy appear on film again in Murder In The Family, another British film. By the late 1930s and early 1940s Tandy's marriage to her first British actor husband, Jack Hawkins, was coming to an end and her remarriage to Hume Cronyn, in 1942, brought a sort of revitalization to her career in film.

Tandy moved to the US to establish a consistent film and theatre career. On the English stage, Tandy had to fight for roles against other established stage actresses. This competition transferred to the states, which meant Tandy was often overlooked as a leading lady and appeared in smaller roles in films. Her Broadway career was by far more exciting. Her first US film was in The Seventh Cross in 1944. She also appeared opposite Oscar Winner Greer Garson in Valley Of Decision in 1945.

"You are richer for doing things."

For Tandy, Broadway brought exciting opportunities: in 1947, she portrayed the title character of Blanche Dubois in the original production of Tennessee Williams's play called Streetcar Named Desire. For the next two years Tandy, along with Marlon Brando and Kim Hunter, played their respective characters 855 times on stage. At that time Tandy (although she was a mature actress) and Brando were essentially unknown at that time. They were fresh faces in the Broadway community. Jessica Tandy was the only lead actor from the original Broadway production who did not appear in the 1951 film adaptation of Streetcar. Vivien Leigh, a far more marketable star, was cast as Blanche. Vivien won her second Oscar for her adaptation of Blanche, rightfully so, but Tandy once again was put on the back burner of getting cast in major roles on film.

Nonetheless, Tandy did win a Tony for Blanche.
In 1950, Jessica appeared in September Affair opposite Oscar winner Joan Fontaine. Jessica later said, "I think things were much more stereotyped then. You either were a sex symbol, or a beautiful woman, which I wasn't, or you got the dregs of the parts, not the interesting ones. I'd been playing large parts in the theatre for a long time, being the whole cheese in a lot of plays, and I wanted to do more in films than I was offered."

Jessica spent the 1950s all the way into the 1980s making big waves in theatre opposite her husband Hume Cronyn. Much like Oscar winner Anne Bancroft and her comedian husband Mel Brooks would work together happily and successfully, so did Tandy and Cronyn. Their professional collaborations made their relationship stronger. Tandy and Cronyn appeared in Broadway successes like The Fourposter, Honeys and A Delicate Balance to name a few.

In 1963, Tandy appeared in a minor yet memorable role in Hitchcock's film called Birds, opposite Tippi Hedren.

Clearly Tandy had a favourite medium to act in and that was on stage. She said, "I'm most comfortable on the stage. Because of the nature of film and television, you'll very often do the climactic scene on the first day and the other parts weeks later. It's hard to remember exactly what state you were in. It's easier when you start at the beginning and go through to the end. Any new project, new play, new film, you're really starting from square one every time. You can't be sure enough of yourself to say, 'Well, this is just a piece of cake.' It's not like that at all—not for me."

As such, Tandy won her second and third Tony awards in 1978 and 1983 for her roles

in The Gin Game and Foxfire respectively. Both were roles she starred in opposite her husband. In 1994, the couple actually won the Tony Lifetime Achievement Awards. Arm in arm the elderly couple went up to accept their award. That same year of 1994, Tandy passed away from cancer, a few months after the Tony win.

But a few years before then Tandy was working endlessly. Her passionate energy neverceased. Her highlight year was in 1990. After decades of weaving in and out of minor film roles, Tandy appeared in a heartfelt drama called Driving Miss Daisy, opposite Morgan Freeman. In a business where youth was often celebrated, mature, elderly type female characters were few and far between.

Driving Miss Daisy is about the disparity between race, religion and social class in 1948 Atlanta Georgia. Tandy plays Daisy Werthan, a 72-year-old Jewish woman, who crashes her car and is hired as a chauffeur by her well off son so that this accident does not happen again for an elderly woman like herself. Daisy is bitter, mean and stubborn when Hoke Colburn is hired as her chauffeur, played by Morgan Freeman. Daisy is annoyed and nit-picky with Hoke's driving, only due to the fact that he is a black man. Hoke is friendly, open minded and talkative, yet Daisy just can't seem to let go of her prejudices and allow herself to remain at ease.

Jessica Tandy

As American society is in a transitory state due to the civil rights movement, so is Daisy. As she and Hoke begin to take trips around and out of town and with time Daisy warms up to Hoke. They share stories and life lessons and she realises that Hoke's dedication to working for her goes above and beyond, despite her snickers and rude comments at him. After a couple years Daisy is visited by Hoke at her retirement home due to her dementia and partial loss of sight. The two share a warm and quiet moment in each other's presence.

Driving Miss Daisy teaches us how important it is to treat people as an equal and with respect regardless of their race, ethnicity, religion, age or job. Tandy personifies the "old generation" —a woman who belongs to the older generation that is more close minded, prejudiced, inexperienced and uneducated on the diversity and inclusivity of the new age that continues to develop.

Tandy managed to not only lead a film about an elderly woman but win an Oscar for this role and become the oldest actress to win the Best Actress Oscar. Driving Miss Daisy eventually won 4 overall Oscars in 1990, out of 9 nominations. The Oscar win was the cherry on the cake for Tandy, as her talent and experience was finally rewarded for her work in film. A line-up of many minor roles culminated in this role that won more major awards on top of the Oscar.

Kathy Bates

The definition of a character actor is an actor who specialises in playing eccentric or unusual people, usually supporting characters. Kathy Bates is exactly that. Every single time Kathy Bates hits the screen she is someone else, someone enticing to follow, and convincingly unorthodox. In return Kathy Bates in real life as herself could not be more different to the characters she plays. Her love for acting started in high school but it took years since then to prove to everybody, including herself, that she could be a character actor and a leading lady at the same time. For this combination she won an Oscar.

Aware that her below average physical looks and southwestern accent were not up to par in the acting world to be cast as a glamorous heroine, Kathy still stuck to her desire to become an actress and moved to the bustling city of New York in 1970 at the age of 22. Having grown up in Memphis Tennessee and having attended university in Texas, Kathy's world expanded and she hustled her way in New York.

Kathy Bates was cast in her first film in 1971, in Milos Forman's comedy called Taking Off. It was Forman's first US produced film. In a matter of a few years his success as a filmmaker would skyrocket after the release of One Flew Over The Cuckoo's Nest, which actually brought Louise Fletcher an Oscar. She played a villain. In fact Kathy Bates would also win the Oscar for playing a villain in later years.

"The Oscar changed everything. Better salary, working with better people, better projects, more exposure, less privacy."

Kathy Bates

she found it difficult to secure more film roles. She said, "I'm not a stunning woman. I never was an ingénue; I've always just been a character actor. When I was younger it was a real problem, because I was never pretty enough for the roles that other young women were being cast in. The roles I was lucky enough to get were real stretches for me: usually a character who was older, or a little weird, or whatever. And it was hard, not just for the lack of work but because you have to face up to how people are looking at you. And you think, 'Well, y'know, I'm a real person.'"

Her second film role only happened in 1978 when she starred opposite Dustin Hoffman in Straight Time. Kathy worked mostly off Broadway in the late 1970s, like in Vanities, Crimes Of The Heart and Fifth Of July. However in the early 1980s things started to take off. When she appeared in the original Broadway version of Come Back to the 5 & Dime, Jimmy Dean, Jimmy Dean, Kathy was subsequently cast in the film version in 1982. She starred opposite Cher who was yet to win an Oscar herself. Bates simultaneously was fashioning a TV career too since the late 1970s. She started appearing in Doctors and All My Children, for example.

The 80s were more focused on stage success like in 'night Mother, Curse of the Starving Class and Frankie and Johnny in the Clair de Lune. She even got a Tony nomination for 'night Mother in 1983. Bates was building relationships in all spheres of entertainment; that made her name quite relevant throughout the 1980s and into the 1990s. By 1990 Bates managed to appear in films too like in The Morning After (opposite Jane Fonda), Arthur 2: On the Rocks (opposite Liza Minelli), Men Don't Leave (with Jessica Lange) and White Palace (with Susan Sarandon)— all Oscar winners by the way.

1990 was Kathy's breakthrough year. She starred in Stephen King's film adaptation of Misery. She played the psycho stalker Annie Wilkes opposite James Caan's character Paul Sheldon. Kathy Bates' performance on screen with those creepy closeups, lousy hair and clothes and haunting scenery made the film a cult classic.

Misery is a story about obsession. Wilkes holds Paul Sheldon, a successful writer, hostage because she is his biggest fan and will keep him hostage until he writes a final book to her favourite series of his. She goes through violent measures to forcefully keep Sheldon hostage; she breaks his legs, drugs him and forces him to write against his will. The character of Wilkes is multi-layered as her murdering past comes to attention.

Misery is a story about obsession. Wilkes holds Paul Sheldon, a successful writer, hostage because she is his biggest fan and will keep him hostage until he writes a final book to her favourite series of his. She goes through violent measures to forcefully keep Sheldon hostage; she breaks his legs, drugs him and forces him to write against his will. The character of Wilkes is multi-layered as her murdering past comes to attention.

Kathy Bates gives a masterful performance of a psycho killer. At times she is creepy and chilling and at times quite comical; she truly sucks in the audience in this exciting horror flick. It is a must see. And Bates' portrayal of a villain won her the Best Actress Oscar at the 1991 Oscar Ceremony. That same year Whoopi Goldberg became the second African American woman to win an Oscar (it was for Best Supporting Actress in Ghost).

Bates was now a bankable star. Her growing list of films and TV shows proved her versatility and maturity as an actress. Bates appeared in 1990s films like Fried Green Tomatoes (opposite Jessica Tandy, an acting veteran and Oscar winner too), Dolores Claiborne, Titanic (opposite Kate Winslet, another Oscar winner) and Primary Colours (for which she got nominated for a Best Supporting Actress Oscar). Bates has been nominated two more times for Best Supporting Actress: for the 2003 film About Schmidt and a 2020 film called Richard Jewel.

Discovering Kathy Bates filmography is a real treat because it's so colourful. Her diversity in characters and films, whether blockbusters like Titanic or quieter films like in Revolutionary Road, show the diverse talent she has. One minute you're laughing at her hilariously lewd scenes opposite Jack Nicholson in About Schmidt and in the next you're immersed in her depiction of multilingual Gertrude Stein in Midnight in Paris (with Marion Cotillard).

Of course Kathy Bates career has been with so many highs but she has certainly faced a series of lows. She has battled ovarian cancer and breast cancer. After a double mastectomy she has suffered lymphedema too. And has been a spokesperson on this condition. Kathy Bates to this day works on major Hollywood films (like in On The Basis Of Sex and The Highwaymen) as well as major TV shows like American Horror Story. Kathy Bates proves that it takes something other than looks, glamour and publicity to be an Oscar winning actress: it takes good taste, natural talent and hard work to win in Hollywood.

Emma Thompson

Along with being one of the most distinguished actors in Britain, Emma Thompson has been a spokesperson for the feminist movement from the early days of her career. Before the movement of modern feminism and female empowerment was relevant to society, particularly in the Hollywood world, Emma Thompson fashioned a career in entertainment in the early 1980s that proved that a woman can create on her own and stand her ground when it comes to her own business. To this day Emma Thompson's story is inspiring.

Born into a family of actors, it made sense as to what Emma would pursue for career-wise. Half English and half Scottish, Emma would spend her holidays in the Scottish countryside, making her feel more Scottish than English. Having grown up in a family that promoted creativity and education, the young Emma went on to study English Literature at the University of Cambridge. There she enrolled in a comedy troupe that consisted of fellow comedians who would be big names later on in English entertainment and ultimately worldwide, like Stephen Fry and Hugh Laurie. The Footlights Group it was called, and Emma (who was the first female performer) along with the all-male group would perform sketch comedy while studying at Cambridge in the late 1970s early 1980s. She ultimately became the first female vice president of the Footlights Group and co-directed the troupes' first all-female revue. Emma discovered the concept of feminism during her college years and she started dressing more grungy and tomboyish to not conform to what society wanted her to look like. After graduating from Cambridge in 1980, Thompson set out to appear in sketch comedy shows on TV, which she collaborated on with her fellow Footlights graduates. The connections that Thompson cultivated early on with Stephen Fry and Hugh Laurie clearly helped push her career forward. The idea of a female comedian was a novelty in English show business, particularly a college educated feminist comedienne. Her experience in TV got her work in a West End musical in 1985 called Me and My Girl.

"I don't have technique because I never learnt any."

This was Thompson's breakthrough. More successful appearances in TV followed like in Fortunes OF War and Tutti Frutti which garnered lots of attention. She also wrote and starred in her own TV comedy specials. Also at this time, in the late 1980s Thompson began collaborating with her boyfriend Kenneth Branagh, an actor and director. This union on and off screen advanced both of their careers. Emma's attachment to Branagh made her public image quite dependent on Branagh because of their extensive work together, particularly on stage, which focused on Shakespeare's plays directed by Branagh.

Emma's first film appearance was in 1989 in the film The Tall Guy. In 1991 she appeared opposite Judi Dench and Hugh Grant in Impromptu and in Dead Again directed and co-starred by Branagh.

Emma Thompson

1992 was yet another highlight year for Thompson who appeared opposite classic British stars like Anthony Hopkins, Vanessa Redgrave and Helena Bonham Carter in the adaptation of E. M. Forster's novel Howard's End. The Edwardian-themed film directed by James Ivory focused on the topics of class and gender. Thompson actively pursued the part of the forward-thinking, independent young woman Margaret Schlegel. Thompson won this role effortlessly and it became an important role because it helped her stray away from her association to Branagh. She could finally become more of an independent entity rather than the other half of a successful duo.

Howard's End follows the story of two sisters, Margaret and Helen Schlegel, played by Thompson and Bonham Carter respectively. Helen, the younger and more naive of the two, is love-obsessed, whereas Margaret is known as a spinster, for she has no husband or children. Their younger brother is graduating Oxford and the two sisters reside in London where it is evident that their parents are deceased and have left them a fortune. They meet a fellow wealthy family, the Wilcox's, with Hopkins and Redgrave as the husband and wife. When Margaret befriends Redgrave's character, the terminally ill Ruth Wilcox, she makes a strong impression of Ruth, which ultimately leads to Ruth making Margaret as the inheritor of her beloved estate called Howard's End, much to her husband's and children's' dismay. As the plot thickens the Schlegel and Wilcox families intertwine

even further and the presence of a third party, a young poverty London stricken couple, alleviate the conflicts and tensions among the families.

Emma Thompson's signature of playing sweet, well-mannered and open-minded women is evident in this role. Margaret, regardless of the difficulties she and her sister face, stays optimistic. She locks up her pain and only for a moment do we watch her cry quietly. Grace and empathy are what make the Schlegel sisters so giving and accepting to others.

Emma Thompson

Howard's End became an instant hit and got nominated for 9 Oscars at the 1993 ceremony. It won 3 which included Emma Thompson's win for Best Actress. Thompson became an overnight international success. Although Emma was now a big star independently, she still returned to the big screen with her husband two more times in Peter's Friends and Much Ado About Nothing. Thompson and Branagh's on-screen chemistry proved successful every single time. Why wouldn't they collaborate time and time again if the result was a success?

Thompson joined Anthony Hopkins once again in the 1993 film, The Remains Of The Day. It was nominated 8 times for Oscars and saw Thompson nominated for Best Actress in 1994. Furthermore Thompson was nominated for Best Supporting Actress at the same Oscars awards for her role in the movie In The Name Of The Father opposite Daniel Day Lewis.

Thompson, now a reputable star, appeared in a typical Hollywood film, Junior. But her true calling was in more romantic classic films like in Sense And Sensibility in 1995. Thompson adapted the Jane Austen novel into a script herself. She actually developed the script for five years until it came to the big screen. It was directed by Ang Lee and co-starred Thompson, Kate Winslet, Hugh Grant and Hugh Laurie.

Thompson was a big Jane Austen fan and proved her love for the writer in this film. Ultimately, Emma Thompson made history at the 1996 Oscars, when she won Best Adapted Screenplay for Sense and Sensibility. This win made Thompson the first and only person to have won a Best Actress and Best Adapted Screenplay at the Oscars. By 1995 Thompson and Branagh separated and during the filming of Sense and Sensibility Thompson started to date fellow actor and co-star Greg Wise who would eventually become her second husband.

More successful films followed like The Winter Guest, directed by fellow actor Alan Rickman and co-starring Emma's own mother Phyllida Law. In 1998, Thompson mesmerised audiences in Primary Colors. Kathy Bates (another Oscar winner) starred in the movie too. Although Thompson would weave in and out Hollywood and British cinema effortlessly, Hollywood executives kept trying to relocate her to LA and headline big Hollywood movies. But Thompson, who was always down to earth and true to her own set of integrities, refused to take on Hollywood fully. In fact, at the height of her career, she backed away from the industry as a whole in order to give birth to her daughter in 1999.

In the early 2000s Thompson naturally gravitated back to the spotlight in films like Maybe Baby and Wit. But her career truly rejuvenated in 2003 when she appeared in cult classic Love Actually alongside iconic British talent like Alan Rickman, Colin Firth, Liam Neeson, Keira Knightly and Hugh Grant. In 2005 she wrote the screenplay and acted in Nanny McPhee alongside Colin Firth. The filmography of Dame Emma Thompson is never-ending. To name a few more big titles, she has starred in Harry Potter, An Education, Brave, Burnt, Beauty and The Beast and also appeared in the live-action Disney film, Cruella.

Emma Thompson is loved by all generations of cinema goers. She is known for her portrayal of intelligent, sensible women with a strong moral compass but with a sense of humour and irony. She brings a down to earth and endearing essence to her characters. Her big moves as a scriptwriter and actress make her a big name in the entertainment industry and to this day she holds her own on the screen as a leading lady.

Emma Thompson

"Privacy is paradise."

Holly Hunter

Holly Hunter appeared in her most memorable role in a 1993 period drama called The Piano. The film's significance was in the unique storytelling from a psychologically mute woman's point of view during colonial New Zealand in the mid 19th century. But this film is even more significant when taken into consideration that it is a completely female-led. The Piano was directed, produced, written, edited by women, and its leading character was a woman. The film was nominated for 8 Oscars overall in 1994 and, proving the power of a women-run production, all 3 Oscars won for this film were awarded to women. This box office hit still has a lasting effect with its emotional story.

Holly Hunter, after completing her theatre studies at Carnegie Mellon University in Pittsburgh, moved to New York City to pursue acting. There she met another eventual best actress Oscar winner, Frances McDormand. Both would live together during their career beginnings in NYC. The two would reunite in 1987 in the film Raising Arizona. But Hunter moved to LA in the early 1980s after appearing on and off Broadway in the play called Crimes Of The Heart and The Miss Firecracker Contest both written by playwright Beth Henley. In 1981 Hunter made her film debut in The Burning, and subsequently appeared in Swing Shift and Blood Simple in 1984, the latter being her first collaboration with the Coen Brothers. Raising Arizona came after in 1987. That same year Broadcast News was released and garnered Hunter her first Oscar nomination for Best Actress.

Hunter, now a relevant star of the 1980s coming into the 1990s, appeared in the film adaptation of Beth Henley's play Miss Firecracker, and in Steven Spielberg's Always both in 1989. More major successes followed, like in Once Around and The Firm, for which she got nominated for Best Supporting Actress Oscar in 1994.

In the 1993 film The Piano by filmmaker Jane Campion, Holly Hunter transforms into Ada McGrath: a woman who doesn't speak, a mother, a wife, a lover. And, perhaps more than anything, she's a silent communicator of sincerity, sensitivity, power and love—through her piano.

Ada finds herself in a situation where she can't make decisions of her own. She marries a man she didn't choose and has to learn to inhabit an environment new and strange to her perceptions. Her eyes express vulnerable fragility that touch the viewer deeply. A special accent is put on her hair, skin, hands, fingers that are gentle and feminine, somewhat restrained, reflecting on a delicate interior self. Holly Hunter's

Holly Hunter

character was mute and therefore she had to exude and communicate through gestures, facial expressions, posture and silence. And, of course, the piano was her vocalisation.

Sometimes the sounds are melancholy. And sometimes the notes coming through Ada's fingers and soul are powerful. Holly Hunter insisted on playing the piano herself and alongside the graceful fragility came out true courage. The Piano's protagonist takes us, the spectators, on a journey as Ava evolves on her own path simultaneously. She learns to stand up for her desires. She has clear demands and dives into suffering and conflict, risking her current state of life. She is willing to sink into the deep sea in order to not separate her existence from her voice—the piano. This is nothing but a confirmation of her strong personality. A silent action speaking volumes of the power of womanhood in a patriarchal time.

As already mentioned, Hunter played the piano herself and shared that she fell in love with the musical pieces composed by Michael Nyman. This helped her connect emotionally to her character. And it shows. Some of the most effective moments in the film are linked to feelings of attraction, passion, eroticism and love, experienced between Ada and her lover, Baines. The Piano is about mystique and mystery, personal evolution and transformation, but also about the human ability to connect through desire. Desire something which Ada and Baines utilise to fulfil a profound longing. Here too, Holly Hunter's performance is subtle yet compelling, coming to life through her eyes and movements.

In the beginning of the story, Ada is an impenetrable character, who slowly lets us in; without words, but instead with sensibility, fragility, intensity, power and passion. It takes a skilful actor to deliver such a multifaceted performance. And it also takes an intelligible approach, an intimate look into language—or, rather, the many languages spoken by Ada—a task which Holly Hunter tackled with an undeniable grace.

Ultimately Hunter won the Best Actress Oscar for her work in The Piano. Anna Paquin, her co-star who played her daughter in the film, became the second youngest Oscar winner to win the Best Supporting actress Oscar, at the age of 11. In addition, Jane Campion, the writer and director of The Piano, won the Oscar for Best Original Screenplay too. That year of the Oscars remains to this day the only occasion where an actor was nominated for both the Best Actress and Best Supporting Actress category. Both Holly Hunter and Emma Thompson (the previous year's winner of best actress) got this distinction.

Holly Hunter

Jessica Lange

Most of us, probably the younger generation, are aware of Jessica Lange's recent work in collaboration with showrunner Ryan Murphy, like in American Horror Story and Feud for example. These projects brought her career a revival, because not many of us are aware of her elaborate film and TV achievements before her modern-day work. Jessica Lange is actually a two-time Oscar Winner: she has one for Best Supporting Actress and one for Best Actress. She is actually one of the most decorated stars to this day, even giving Meryl Streep a run for her money. In fact the two actresses have competed for roles ever since the 1970s, at the start of their careers. Jessica Lange is a star through and through, so let's see why.

After living a bohemian life on the road after dropping out of University of Minnesota, the young Jessica moved to Paris in the early 1970s. The aspiring actress roomed with Grace Jones and Jerry Hall during her free-spirited antics as a model in the French capital. She moved to New York soon after and signed with a modelling agency that introduced her to Dino De Laurentis—yes, exactly that Hollywood producer that told Meryl Streep that she was too ugly to play the title role in King Kong! But funnily enough, Lange secured this role. King Kong was her film debut in 1976. She even won the Golden Globe Award for New Star of the Year.

Lange, who was always involved with the arts like dancing, photography and mime, easily made connections with artists of every genre. She befriended Bob Fosse, by then a famous and well-established director and choreographer. He directed and choreographed major hits like Sweet Charity that headlined Oscar Winner Shirley MacLaine, as well as Cabaret which brought Liza Minnelli an Oscar. Fosse wrote a role especially for Lange in his musical film called All That Jazz in 1979.

"To stay interested in acting, I have to keep trying stuff I've never done before."

Lange began more successful collaborations with high fliers in the Hollywood scene. It was a quick rise to fame for Lange. In 1981 she appeared in The Postman Always Rings Twice opposite Jack Nicholson, directed by Bob Rafelson, one of the key figures in the New Hollywood Movement of the 1970s. He was one of the producers of Easy Rider in 1969 which was the definitive film of the New Hollywood Movement. That same year of 1981 Lange gave birth to a daughter with her partner and world-renown dancer and actor Mikhail Baryshnikov with whom she was with until 1982.

When I say fame came quickly for Lange, I mean it really made her a relevant star by 1983. Because she won her first Oscar that year, for her role in Tootsie. This rom-com

Lange starred in opposite Dustin Hoffman, Bill Murray and Geena Davis, directed by Sidney Pollack, garnered her the Best Supporting Actress Oscar at the 1983 Oscars. In fact Lange was also nominated for Best Actress that year too, which is a rarity in and of itself; this was for her role in 1982 film, Frances, a much more serious, historical drama film. Jessica Lange and Meryl Streep now faced competition once again, this time for the Best Actress Oscar. Streep of course won for her role in Sophie's Choice and Lange for Tootsie.

For many more years these two actresses would go head-to-head for awards and roles, like in Sweet Dreams in 1985. Meryl fought hard for the headlining role of Patsy Cline in this film, but Lange got it and was even nominated for Best Actress Oscar for this role.

Lange appeared in other Best Actress Nominated films like in 1984's Country, 1989's Music Box and 1994's Blue Sky.

1994's Blue Sky had a rocky release. The movie had been filmed in 1990 and completed in 1991, but its production studio, Orion Pictures, went bankrupt immediately after. Director Tony Richardson died of AIDS complications shortly after the film was completed. The movie seemed doomed to obscurity until it was finally released in 1994, and despite all the delays, it opened to critical acclaim. Jessica Lange, who plays Carly Marshall in the film, received many accolades for her performance—including winning Best Actress at the 1994 Academy Awards.

The film follows Carly (Lange) and her husband Major Hank Marshall (Tommy Lee Jones), who are having marital issues exacerbated by Carly's mental illness. Meanwhile, Hank is working as a nuclear engineer on an initiative named "Blue Sky" and needs to move his family from Hawaii to a base in Alabama in order to continue his work. Part of the reason he moves is because Carly has been frolicking on the beaches topless and was seen by Hank's co-workers. This upsets their kids and especially upsets Carly, who goes into a violent fit. Carly's issues cause Hank problems and embarrasses him, especially given all the strict military base restrictions.

While the tumultuous family relationships are key to the centre of the film, it also presents an interesting examination of military cover ups. The underground nuclear facility where Hank works serves to personify various Cold War anxieties (the film takes place in 1962), and the shady behaviours of the other officers and the ways they downplay the dangers of nuclear powers are reminiscent of films like 1983's Silkwood. The Cold War setting and the more conservative nature of the Alabama base also works to cause friction with Carly's more freewheeling nature. Of course, people were even less understanding of mental illness back then, so that causes issues with the ways Carly is perceived by those around her.

Carly is additionally obsessed with Hollywood stars like Brigitte Bardot: in fact, when called out for her topless beach excursions, she snaps that Bardot was celebrated for her topless performances. Carly is a bit deluded, as she herself had hoped to become an actress. Lange channels the energy of various Hollywood starlets into her performances in order to flesh out Carly's delusions and really bring her to life. Lange does so seemingly effortlessly, and it's hard to ignore just how incredibly layered and skilful her performance really is. Naturally, she steals every scene she's in.

Fun fact: the character of Carly is actually based on the mother of the screenwriter, Rama Stagner-Blum. Her parents had a similar relationship and her father also worked in the army. This was actually the only feature film Blum ever wrote.

The Los Angeles Times described Lange's character as "a sort of cross between a Tennessee Williams' hothouse violet—a deranged, damaged maiden—and a late '50s/early '60s glamorpuss in the Marilyn Monroe style." In fact, quite a few publications would compare Lange's portrayal to Marilyn Monroe, including The New York Times, Variety, and The Washington Post. The Tennessee Williams comparison is pretty spot-on, especially considering that Jessica Lange and Tommy Lee Jones had both previously been in a television adaptation of Cat On A Hot Tin Roof together back in 1984.

Jessica Lange

Lange won quite a few awards for her performance outside of the Academy Awards, as well. She won the Golden Globe for Best Actress in a Drama, Best Actress at the Los Angeles Film Critics Association Awards, and even snagged Best Foreign Actress at the Spanish Sant Jordi Awards. She was also nominated at the Chicago Film Critics Association Awards and the Screen Actors Guild Awards.

Indeed, Lange's performance in the role was worthy of all the praise it received. It's sexually charged and erratic, yet uniquely graceful. Lange truly made her star power known with this incredibly boisterous performance. While the film itself is a pretty solid family and military drama, it really is Lange's performance that makes it a must-watch. In fact, Best Actress was the only Oscar nomination the film received.

Other cast members include Anna Klemp in her film debut—the film earned her a nomination at the Young Artist Awards—and Annie Ross in her final film. Chris O'Donnell also appears in the film. He had previously been in the film Men Don't Leave alongside Jessica Lange. Later, he would appear in Batman Forever with Tommy Lee Jones.

Other than Oscar nominated films, Lange has appeared in other well received films like Crimes Of The Heart opposite other Oscar winners Diane Keaton and Sissy Spacek, Men Don't Leave with Kathy Bates and Cape Fear opposite Robert De Niro. She worked with De Niro again in Night And The City, Losing Isaiah with Halle Berry, A Thousand Acres with Michelle Pfeiffer and opposite Gwyneth Paltrow in Hush.

There have certainly been a few low profile and box office misses in Lange's career too. But she has also won audiences over with her performances on stage; most notably playing Blanch Du Bois in Streetcar Named Desire on Broadway and West End in the 1990s.

Lange appears sporadically on screen today but it is her TV career that has flourished in the last 10 years. In 2009 Lange appeared in Grey Gardens, a TV movie for which she won her first Emmy award. In 2011, Lange appeared in probably her most well-known modern project, American Horror Story. The show runner Ryan Murphy wrote a role in American Horror Story specifically for Lange. Murphy, a long-time admirer of Lange, stated that he chose her because he wanted to expose her work to a new generation of viewers. This sort of revival of Lange's career is like her third wave of fame: her first after her win for Tootsie, her second after her win for Blue Sky and her third after her AHS appearances. For her work on AHS, Lange has won two Emmys. She has collaborated with Murphy on other shows like Feud: Bette and Joan and The Politician. On top of her acting, Lange is also a Goodwill Ambassador for UNICEF.

It is Jessica Lange's enthusiasm towards acting that makes her irreplaceable. She is a powerful actress with a long-standing career. And for her varied roles on screen and on stage, she has had a fruitful career that goes strong to this day.

Susan Sarandon

Susan Sarandon has had a very eclectic career. Along with being a major Hollywood actress, her humanitarian and political engagements give her a solid reputation of an outspoken individual, and her beliefs and efforts to make the world a better place have given her even more credit and admiration from all generations. Her Oscar win in 1996 marked her mid-career, if you will, because she had multiple nominations under her belt already; she was a mature and serious actress by that point and her Oscar win cemented her as an influential woman in film.

The young and straight-out-of-college formerly Susan Tomalin took her first husband's name Sarandon, which is of Greek origin. Susan herself has Sicilian roots from her mother's side. She found herself cast in her first film, Joe, by chance, in 1970 when she accompanied her husband for his audition. But instead of him getting cast, Susan got cast instead. Thus was the beginning of Sarandon's film career. Five years later Sarandon appeared in one of her most well-known films, a cult classic, The Rocky Horror Picture Show. That same year she appeared in The Great Waldo Pepper.

"It's still not easy to find roles that offer more complex images of women."

In 1981 Susan was nominated her first time for the Best Actress Oscar for her role in Atlantic City. In 1980, Susan appeared opposite Oscar winner Shirley MacLaine in Loving Couples. In 1983 she starred in The Hunger opposite Catherine Denueve and David Bowie. In 1987 she appeared opposite Cher and Michele Pfeiffer in Witches of Eastwick. Later, Bull Durham, a commercial and critical success opposite Kevin Costner made Sarandon a household name. Sarandon was nominated for an Academy Award three more times in the 1990s, as Best Actress in Thelma & Louise (1991), Lorenzo's Oil (1992), and The Client (1994).

In 1995 she won the Best Actress Oscar for her role in Dead Man Walking. After such a diverse filmography Sarandon proved her dramatic skills in this film. She played a real-life nun named Sister Helen Prejean opposite Sean Penn in this crime drama film. The film was written, directed and produced by Susan's then boyfriend and fellow actor Tim Robbins whom she met on set of Bull Durham. Susan who was known for her outspokenness regarding topics of progressive and leftist political nature was told to withhold from speaking up on such causes in her Oscar acceptance speech.

Susan Sarandon

Dead Man Walking focuses on the relationship between Helen Prejean and Matthew Poncelet played by Penn. Poncelet, a man convicted of murder and rape of a young woman and murder of a young man, has been on death row for the past 6 years in Louisiana State Penitentiary. His death sentence, by method of lethal injection, is fast approaching. He requests for sister Helen to be his spiritual advisor. Having no experience with helping criminals, Helen takes on the case of Matthew regardless. She is incredibly empathetic, nurturing and down to earth. Regardless of Matthew's

racist, misogynistic and overtly white supremacist views on life, she acts as helping hand and ear to comfort Matthew during her visits to the prison. Although they try to appeal the death sentence, due to Matts claim that he did not commit the rape and murder because he only looked on as another man did the crime, his claim is ultimately proven false. Matt professes his regret for his heinous crime and asks for forgiveness to the families of the murdered. Helen looks on as Matt receives his dose of lethal injection. Through Sarandon's performance we are told the story of human cruelty, religion, human connection and morality.

Sarandon went on to star and produce Stepmom in 1998 opposite Julia Roberts. More films followed like Igby Goes Down, Shall We Dance, Enchanted and The Lovely Bones. Her filmography is ever-growing.

Moreover she has had a thriving TV career. Her appearances in shows like Friends, Malcolm in the Middle, Bernard and Doris, You Don't Know Jack and Feud: Bette and Joan (opposite Jessica Lange) have all garnered her Emmy nominations. Sarandon plays Bette Davis in Feud opposite Jessica Lange who plays Joan Crawford. A winning duo, both of whom have obviously won the Best Actress Oscar of course. In addition, Sarandon has excelled in narrating and hosting a line-up of documentaries ever since the 80s. She has presented almost 50 documentaries focused on social and political issues.

Susan Sarandon's humanitarian activism as well as her acting career is worthy of praise. In an industry that bases women's worth on their looks; Sarandon made it known that she is more than her looks. She has appeared in some very iconic films that hold up to this day. Susan Sarandon is one of a kind, that's for sure.

Frances McDormand

Frances McDormand is as fascinating in real life as she is on the screen. She is irreplaceable in Hollywood. Her performances are unforgettable in such iconic films. Her long standing success is a marriage between her acting and the Coen brothers writing and directing—literally a marriage. She has been married to Joel Coen since the start of her professional career and ever since McDormand has been unstoppable. Whatever Frances McDormand stars in will be a hit. That's why she is a three-time Oscar winner.

McDormand was adopted as a child. After graduating from the Yale School Of Drama in 1982 with an MFA, she then acted on stage briefly. During this time she roomed with Holly Hunter (a fellow Oscar winner and later co-star), Sam Raimi and with Joel and Ethan Coen in New York City. In a matter of two years after graduating from Yale, McDormand starred in her feature film debut which was written, edited, produced, and directed by the Coen Brothers, Blood Simple. That same year in 1984 when Blood Simple came out, Joel Coen and McDormand married. Ten years after that they would adopt their only son.

Her next two films were also Coen collaborations: Crimewave and Raising Arizona, the latter in which she co-starred with Holly Hunter. In 1989 she got a Best Supporting Actress Oscar nomination for her role in Mississippi Burning opposite Willem Dafoe and Gene Hackman. In 1990 she starred in Darkman, written and directed by Sam Raimi. McDormand has uncredited roles in more Coen Brother projects like in Miller's Crossing, Barton Fink and The Hudsucker Project.

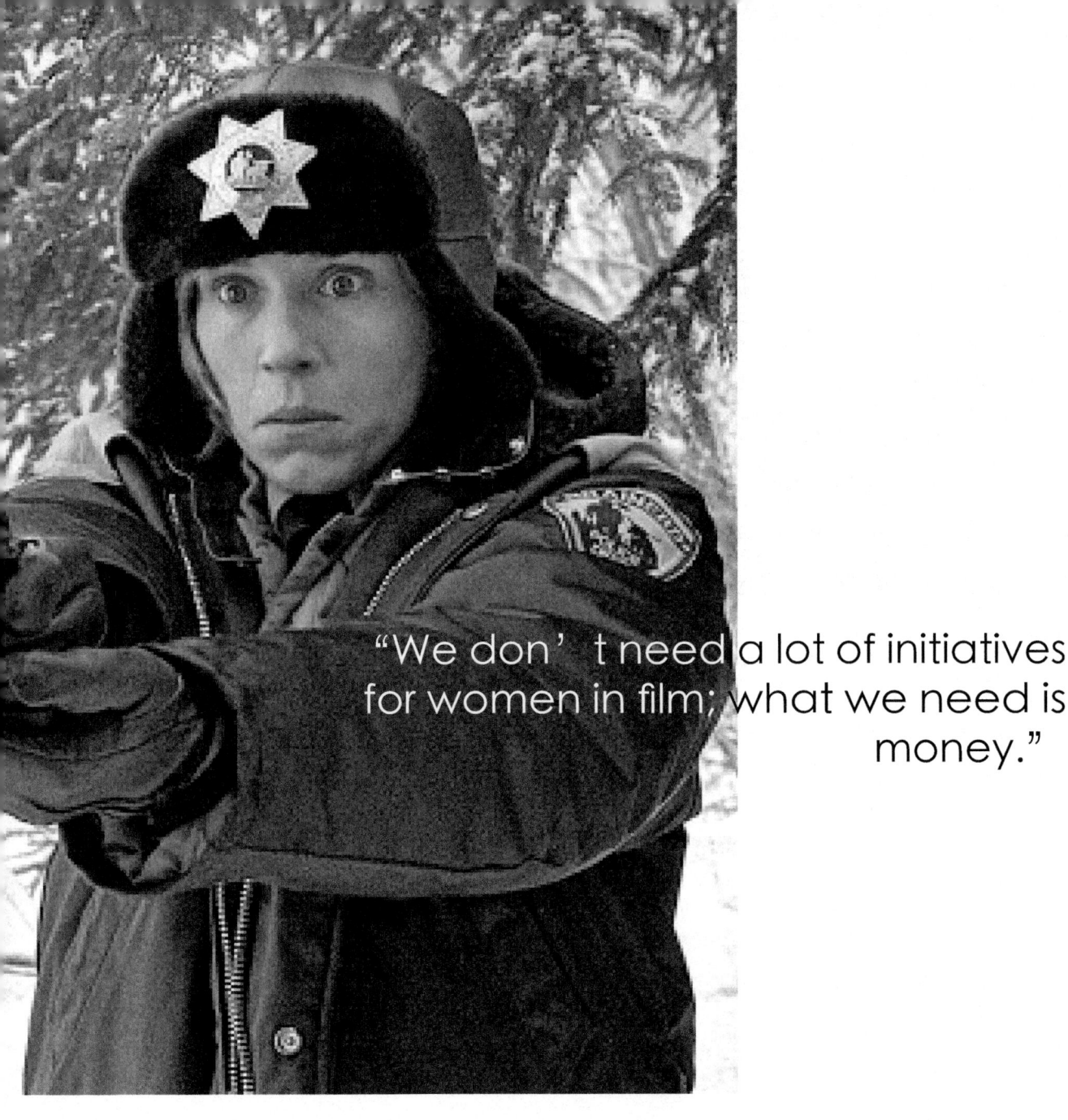

"We don't need a lot of initiatives for women in film; what we need is money."

She starred in other minor films during the 1990s. Her next Coen collaboration proved successful, though. The infamous Coen Brothers film Fargo was shot in 1995, came out the following year (1996) and in the 1997 Oscars was the winner of two Academy Awards: Best Screenplay Written Directly for the Screen (for Joel and Ethan Coen) and Best Actress (for Frances McDormand's portrayal of police chief Marge Gunderson). McDormand starred opposite William H Macy, Steve Buscemi and Peter Stormare. This film was a critical and commercial success. McDormand's delightful yet novel portrayal of a pregnant small-town Minnesota cop was unsurpassed. Fargo seems to be the Coen Brothers signature film that proved their auteurism, if you will. To this day people love this film and McDormand's "Minnesota Nice" accent and one-liners are often imitated.

But who is Marge and how did she become (and continues to be) a compelling and inspiring character? As a police chief, she is good at her job, capable and quite the talented detective. Within the film's plot she manages to follow the clues intelligently and ultimately resolves the mysteries presented by the unfolding story. It is not immediately obvious, but Marge's smart and consistent techniques lead her to success. As McDormand herself has said in interviews, she liked the character because she was able to surprise both the other protagonists and beyond that, Fargo's viewers.

Frances McDormand gave a performance that some may deem simplistic at first, but taking a closer look, it is clear the actress thrived in composing a multi-layered female lead. Marge is friendly, sweet, humble, loyal to her partner and to her colleagues. Moreover, she has a great sense of humour and memorable wit that audiences have found highly quotable since the film's release more than two decades ago. McDormand already had quality material in the script of the Coen Brothers, but she gave life to Marge in an impressive way. Adding to the aforementioned characteristics—being a rather wonderful, kind-hearted person and one of the few ones in Fargo with a moral compass—McDormand plays her role filling it with a symbiosis of sincerity and confidence. She is at the same time relatable, provoking sympathy within the viewer and acting with a goal, aware of her knowledge and skills as a police chief. Her motivations are clear and pure as she can't reasonably comprehend how certain degrees of evil are even possible.

Over the years it has been pointed out that it is not very common to see a female police chief or detective in feature Hollywood films. McDormand succeeded in creating a unique character that now has a near-cult status in the world of cinema. Another layer of her performance is how she tackled the more intimate aspects of Marge's personality beyond her professional vocation. For instance, the fact that she is pregnant yet this does not become central, turning her into a stereotypical mother-to-be heroine. And last but certainly not least, Frances McDormand enhances Marge with the warmth and affection she shares with her husband Norm. Their relationship contrasts other characters' communication by being honest, equal and harmonious.
Surrounded by the white snowy landscapes of Minnesota and North Dakota, Marge Gunderson navigates this harsh environment of cold and crime with a genuine heart and

undeniable detective competency brought into the light of the big screen by the fantastic (and Oscar-worthy!) performance of Frances McDormand. The film has been adapted into an FX anthology series of the same name. The Coen's have executive produced it.

In 1996, McDormand starred in another hit called Primal Fear. In the year 2000 she starred in Almost Famous for which she was nominated for Best Supporting Actress in 2001. Also in 2001 she starred in The Man Who Wasn't There, which was yet another Coen collaboration.

In 2005 McDormand banked another Best Supporting Actress Oscar nomination for her role in North Country, opposite fellow Best Actress Oscar winners Charlize Theron and Sissy Spacek. In 2008 Frances starred in Burn After Reading and in 2016, Hail Caesar!—both by the Coen Brothers. In between both of these highly successful films, Frances starred in films of a variety of genres: This Must Be The Place, Transformers, Moonrise Kingdom, Promised Land; she even did voice overs for Madagascar 3 and Good Dinosaur.

Frances McDormand

In 2012 McDormand won a Tony for her acting in a Broadway play called Good People. In 2014, HBO telecast a four-part mini-series called Olive Kitteridge, co-produced by and starring McDormand. The role won her the Primetime Emmy Award, thus making her the 12th actress to get the Triple Crown of Acting.

In 2018 McDormand struck gold yet again. She won her second Best Actress Oscar for her feisty, no-nonsense role in Three Billboards Outside Ebbing, Missouri. The crime drama with comedic touches was written, directed and produced by Martin McDonagh and co-starred Sam Rockwell and Woody Harrelson. McDormand went up to accept her second ever Oscar from a fellow two-time Best Actress Oscar winner, Jodie Foster, as well as Jennifer Lawrence, an Oscar winner too. McDormand got all of the female nominees to stand up in the audience for a round of applause. Pretty cool.

In 2018 McDormand voiced Wes Anderson's animation Isle of Dogs. Her third collaboration with Anderson was in The French Dispatch. She has also teamed up with her husband Joel once again to star in his film called The Tragedy Of Macbeth.

Frances McDormand has mentioned the representation of women in film on both occasions she went up to accept the Best Actress Oscar. She has starred in 7 films by female directors which is quite impressive. Her most recent being Nomadland directed by Chloe Zhao. McDormand also co-produced this film. She has an arresting presence on and off screen and for this work she received her third Best Actress Oscar in 2021.

"The Oscar sits on some shelf above my desk. If there was an earthquake, I could actually be killed by my own Academy Award."

Helen Hunt

Helen Hunt was perfectly set up for a fabulous acting career from the moment she was born. She was born into an artistic family: a photographer mother and an actor, director and acting coach father. Even her uncle was a director and grandmother a voice coach. Helen Hunt took advantage of this natural and trained talent and used it to start her acting career in TV when she was just a child. But that doesn't mean that she faced hardships securing serious film roles later in her life.

By the mid to late 80s Hunt was in her early 20s and had appeared in films like Rollercoaster and Girls Just Want To Have Fun. Her bigger break was in 1986 in Peggy Sue Got Married directed by Francis Ford Coppola which co-starred Kathleen Turner. Hunt was able to infuse film, TV and theatre work into a career throughout all these years. Even up until today she manages to work on all three mediums, which is something many major actresses have been able to succeed at, like Kathy Bates, Jessica Lange and Emma Thompson.

Hunt appeared in the stage production of Our Town in 1989 and Taming of The Shrew in 1990. In 1988 she starred in Stealing Beauty opposite Jodie Foster, in Next Of Kin the following year and in Twister in 1996, which was a hit. Meanwhile she scored many TV appearances, like in Mad About You which is her longest standing series role, and which eventually paid her $1 million per episode, and an appearance in Friends. This was all in the 90s when a multitude of sitcoms were at an all-time high in popularity. Thus, Helen being a series aficionado made people regard her as a TV star as opposed to a film star, even though she appeared in some popular films.

But her actual rise to Hollywood fame was in 1997. She starred in the romantic comedy opposite Jack Nicholson called As Good As It Gets. The 34-year-old actress was old enough to have an on-screen romance with the 60-year-old Nicholson without it being creepy, but young enough to keep Hollywood's status quo of having young actresses star opposite much older actors. Hollywood loves this dynamic. This box office hit

Disparate personalities writhe and collide in search of common ground in James L. Brooks' 1997 film As Good as It Gets. The inexplicable pull and push of love is the mystery at the centre of countless romantic comedies, but this particular story defines itself with the extremes of its' polarities. The love story which develops is one that on the surface has no right to exist, and the fun of the film is in seeing how it's extremely unusual circumstances force its protagonists to take on a painful and nearly

fruitless quest to understand each other. The film also has a little more to say than your average rom-com, and goes after a better-rounded look at relationships, beginning at the level of friendship. In fact, this film sets our characters off together on a note that doesn't even find common decency. Viewers who are familiar with the formulas of romantic comedies will find enough signposts here to think they know how everything is going to unfold, but the script sows doubts as the agonising awkwardness of the character's interaction may challenge their desire for the two leads to come together. Melvin Udall (Jack Nicholson) is a reclusive and neurotic romance novel writer who suffers from OCD, as well as an abrasive and ugly personality cultivated from years of lonely self-absorption. He freely hurls insults and disrespect at any person (or animal) that comes across his path. In our pre-credits introduction to him, he drops his neighbour's dog into a garbage chute. This makes it clear right away: he's no misunderstood introvert; this guy is a major jerk with serious issues. Naturally, he is a creature of habit, and one of his consistent routines is to drop in at his favourite New York City café for breakfast each morning. For someone so overtly misanthropic, it's a somewhat out of character indulgence. But without it, we have no movie, so we have to attribute it to the rapport he has with his regular waitress Carol (Helen Hunt). It's far from a warm and chummy one, but Carol is able to wrangle him, though he remains ever on the fine line of being banned for life for his verbal abuse of patrons and staff.

Helen Hunt

Carol is a complete inversion of Melvin. Whereas daily eating out and brutish behaviour is a luxury afforded him by the success of some 62 published novels, Carol is struggling to cover medical costs for her son, who is struggling from an unknown and poorly treated illness. When her difficulties mount and she begins to miss work, Melvin shows up at her apartment and makes the shockingly generous gesture of paying for her son's medical care, finally affording him the level of treatment he requires. Also thrown into the mix is Melvin's gay neighbour Simon (Greg Kinnear), who the two accompany on a road trip to ask his estranged parents for money after he is assaulted. The challenges of dealing with Melvin are far beyond what most people would be willing to suffer though. However, as Carol and Simon are compelled to embark on the trip with him out of necessity, they gradually uncover the compassion at Melvin's heart that he is unable to effectively express.

Kinnear's Simon is critical to the plot (and a cleverly placed narrative mediator between the two leads), and Nicholson's Melvin gets the funniest lines, but it's Hunt's Carol that holds the film together. As a hard-working single mother of a sick child, we see the incredible strain that is being put upon her, even before the constant presence of a crazy and obnoxious man. The vulnerability and weariness that she brings to the role gives the audience a genuine sense of concern and affection. She deserves better than Melvin, and we share in every cringe and disappointed look as he fails to give her the happiness that we want her to have.

Yet, the film ultimately submits to audience expectations, and we know that romance will spring up somehow. As Good as It Gets doesn't try to neatly tie up everything at the finish, but we end on a high note, seeing Carol happy and hoping Melvin can be the better man he aspires to be. We know he will not be cured overnight. There's certainly more friction to come, but things are on an upswing. The movie is playfully convenient in its plot devices (i.e. far-fetched), but it is still endearing because of the strength of its characters and what it has to say about the nuances of love and friendship.

Consequently Hunter appeared in more mainstream films like in Cast Away, What Women Want and Soul Surfer. In 2012 she regained prominence as an actress in the independent film called The Sessions for which she got nominated for Best Supporting Actress. Her most recent film is The Night Clerk.

Furthermore Hunt has won four Emmys for Outstanding Lead Actress in a Comedy Series for her work on Mad About You. In addition, she is a TV series director. She has directed episodes of Mad About You, Feud: Bette and Joan and The Politician to name a few. She has written, directed and starred in two films: Then She Found Me and Ride.

Not every actress is able to juggle so many hats and roles in a span of a lifetime like Helen Hunt.

"Women were real box office stars in the 40s, more so than men. People loved to see women's films. I think it was better then, except for the studio system."

Gwyneth Paltrow

Gwyneth Paltrow is an acting veteran at this point for she has been acting ever since her teenage years. She is an all-around Hollywood star, truly: not only a major high earning actress but an infamous businesswoman. She has been able to stay afloat even during controversial times due to her multi talent. Gwyneth Paltrow is the true definition of celebrity.

Much like Helen Hunt, Liza Minnelli and Jane Fonda, Gwyneth was born into an artistic family. She grew up on set with both her parents being industry professionals. Steven Spielberg is her godfather. Her film debut was in her father's TV film directorial called High in 1989 and her legitimate film debut was in Shout opposite John Travolta in 1990. In 1991 she appeared in Spielberg's Hook as the young Wendy Darling. She then starred in a line-up of Hollywood films opposite major stars. It wasn't until 1995 where she garnered critical acclaim. She starred opposite her then boyfriend Brad Pitt in Seven directed by David Fincher. The film was the 7th highest grossing film of 1995.

Gwyneth was unstoppable. She appeared in the Jane Austen adaptation called Emma in 1996 for which she won a Satellite Award for Best Actress. More leading roles followed like in Sliding Doors, Great Expectations, Hush (opposite Jessica Lange), A Perfect Murder and Shakespeare in Love.

Shakespeare In Love came out in 1998 with Gwyneth as the lead of this period romantic drama opposite major British talent. Gwyneth proved her marketable on-screen presence in this film. And for this she was rewarded very lavishly. She won the Best Actress Oscar for her role as Viola in Shakespeare in Love at the 1999 Oscars. Moreover, this film won a whopping extra 6 Oscars. It won The Best Picture Oscar and Judi Dench won the Best Supporting Actress Oscar. There was a lot of controversy over how that year's awards went about due to a very formidable individual being at the peak: Harvey Weinstein. He produced and distributed Shakespeare In Love and essentially bought his way to Oscar success. Miramax, his company, spent around $15 million to get this film promoted and force-fed to Hollywood execs, Academy Voters and beyond. The controversy this diabolical man accumulated is beyond this book's discussion and I don't want to focus on him, even though he was quite major to Gwyneth's success. However, Gwyneth

was indeed deeply affected by his predatory tactics to get her into bed, which she did not give in to. So, whether Paltrow deserved her Oscar or not is a controversy in and of itself. But that does not stop us from regarding her as a very iconic woman in film.

Shakespeare In Love is a fictional romantic period drama with a star-studded cast. The noble and sparkling Viola De Lesseps (Paltrow) begins a love affair with the talented and vibrant William Shakespeare (Joseph Fiennes) during the time he writes Romeo and Juliet, which is very much inspired by his love with Viola. Gwyneth Paltrow's Viola is a bohemian at heart, despite the pressure of being an upper-class young woman whose fate is already planned out. She is a rule-breaker by nature, a lover of arts and wears her heart on her sleeve. She finds freedom and knowledge through theatre and also through her relationship with Shakespeare. They are a foil to one another as she is the "rock", someone more grounded and realistic, and Shakespeare is the "kite" who soars to follow his passions without expectation of what the future will hold. Nonetheless, Viola is a wonderful example for young girls to follow their heart and to pursue what makes them happy as opposed to societal norms and parental pressure to fulfil their agenda.

Gwyneth Paltrow

We don't often see Oscar-winning actresses win for playing a soft natured and more overtly feminine character (which totally does not diminish her power in patriarchy); so Gwyneth's win was rather refreshing, especially considering the heavy movies this film ran against during the 1999 Academy Awards, like Elizabeth and Saving Private Ryan for example. The film as a whole transports you to another, long forgotten and rather mystical place, with the gorgeous costume design and splendid Shakespearean prose set in the Elizabethan Era.

As Leah Carlson-Downie writes so aptly on Screen Queens: "Viola was a revelation. She felt like a fully realised person in a way that many other female film characters didn't, in no small part thanks to Paltrow's performance. I saw myself in Viola's struggle to fulfil her emotional and sexual desires in a society that often dismisses such wants, when held by women, as unimportant."

Gwyneth starred in more major iconic films, like The Talented Mr Ripley, The Royal Tenenbaums and Bounce to name a few. She has a lot of film roles under her belt. While working on more major films like Iron Man, Country Strong (in which she sang in) and Contagion. Paltrow launched her internet lifestyle brand in 2008. At this point it is an institution, especially appealing to privileged white women. The Goop Company is estimated to be worth $250 million. Very impressive. Moreover, Paltrow has managed to keep high profile status as the face of major beauty and style brands and activist campaigns on top of being a mother.

Gwyneth Paltrow is like a wonder woman, she juggles many leadership hats. Her business ventures, mainly related to Goop seem to have overtaken her acting career success, but nonetheless she still remains a relevant star due to her work in such iconic films.

Hilary Swank

As we progress through this book we watch the rise to fame of all of these wonderful women, some who have had a not-so-privileged upbringing, proving that talent cannot be bought or inherited. Major Hollywood stars come from all walks of life, like Hilary Swank for example. And her troubled past certainly has poured into her troubled characters on screen. Hilary Swank's Oscar winning roles could not be more polarising to the previous year's winner Gwyneth Paltrow who won her Oscar: she won for playing a romantic character who comes from wealth and prominence; Swank's character went from rags to riches.

Swank, along with her troubled, jobless yet supportive mother, dropped out of high school and drove all the way to LA from Washington State, where they lived in a trailer in order to get Swank some auditions. The duo managed to get Swank a seemingly never-ending line-up of failed auditions while living out of their car or couch surfing. Swank finally secured her first film role in the 1992 film Buffy The Vampire Slayer and then the 1994 film The Next Karate Kid. Swank was always athletic and active so she was inclined for more physical roles. However, she always felt like an outsider; she was always bullied no matter where she lived. She felt that acting was her escape and therapy. Acting was also simply a meal ticket for her and her mother.

"I like to play women who blaze trails."

In a span of 7 years since Swank's film debut, she appeared in her most famous role ever: 1999's Boys Don't Cry, based on the true story of Brandon Teena. Swank played a young transgender man in crime infested Nebraska. With a $2 million budget, Swank got paid only $3000 overall. She did a full transformation to sound, look and act like Brandon Teena. Boys Don't Cry was directed by Kimberly Peirce, their feature film debut.

We follow the short and sad story of Brandon Teena who faces the hardships of living as a transgender man in rural Nebraska in 1993. The story is about prejudice, sexuality, human on human violence, love and self-acceptance. It's certainly a hard-hitting story that not many are brave enough to watch again for the ending for it is incredibly heart-breaking. The story of Brandon Teena is a story of the destruction caused by hate from humans placed onto other humans. Human cruelty is a horrendous thing, for it brings out the animal within us and the act of punishing another human for being different is a crime in and of itself.

Hilary Swank's dedication to give Teena the humanity, vulnerability, and softness he possessed is so potent in this performance that she was bound to be rewarded for it. Boys Don't Cry starred Peter Sarsgaard as the villain and Chloë Sevigny as the love interest, who too brought incredibly powerful performances.

The message of the movie is bigger than the performances and quality of production for it is a relevant message on violence against minorities, especially on violence against the LGBTQ community that is still surging today. The violent scenes towards Brandon are counteracted with scenes of tenderness and love between him and cisgender Lana Tisdel (Sevigny). It is a tragic love story, alongside being a story of survival.

Hilary Swank

I think this film was a catalyst for further LGBTQ films and stories to be told. In fact, the film was selected to be preserved in the United States Film Registry by the Library of Congress for its significance on American culture and history. The film was indeed a breakout LGBT film as well as Swank's breakout role. She won the Best Actress Oscar at the 2000 ceremony at the age of 25.

Once again Swank got physical for this role and played an aspiring trailer trash boxer. She also committed to another serious and heartfelt role. As in Boys Don't Cry, Swank gave a heart-wrenching performance with a tragic ending. And for this performance Swank triumphed at the 2005 Oscars with a Best Actress Oscar.

Swank then appeared in a variety of films like Black Dahlia, PS I Love You and The Resident. Furthermore, she has executive produced and starred in four films: Amelia, Conviction, You're Not You and What They Had.

Hilary Swank may not fit into every female lead mould, but the roles she has flourished deserve a round of applause. Only 13 other Actresses have the title of being a two-time Best Actress Oscar recipient. Hilary Swank's Oscars wins are truly so well deserved.

"I don't think I realised that the cost of fame is that it's open season on every moment of your life."

Julia Roberts

Julia Roberts is untouchable. With a rise to stardom so swift, her career beginnings prove that Hollywood was ready to accept her with open arms. With an already established much older actor brother, Julia entered the Hollywood sphere effortlessly at the age of 19. And since then, she has grown to become a cinematic icon. Nobody on film can laugh so vivaciously, argue so explosively and cry so earnestly than Julia Roberts.

Her first legitimate film role was in 1988's Satisfaction opposite Liam Neeson. That same year, another film came out that put her on the map: Mystic Pizza. A string of fantastically successful films followed like Steel Magnolias in 1989 (opposite Oscar winners Sally Field, Shirley MacLaine and Olympia Dukakis) and Pretty Woman in 1990. She received a Best Supporting Actress and Best Actress Oscar Nomination for each film respectively, all before the age of 24.

Roberts starred in more screen successes like Flatliners, Sleeping With The Enemy and Hook. In fact, almost every film Julia has starred in, to this day, has been a box office hit. Roberts starred in some iconic rom-coms during the 1990s like Notting Hill and My Best Friend's Wedding.

The 2000s were welcomed with more serious roles that secured Roberts superstar status. She starred in a drama biopic Erin Brockovich in the year 2000. This heartfelt film proved that Roberts was ready for an Oscar win. In case you haven't noticed a trend with these Best Actress Award winners, biopics are Oscar gold. Sissy Spacek, Anne Bancroft, and Charlize Theron are just a few of the actresses to win an Academy Award for portraying real-life people. Julia Roberts is also part of the biopic Best Actress group for her role as the titular character in 2000's Erin Brockovich.

Erin Brockovich is definitely one of her most iconic roles, right up there with Pretty Woman. The film tells the real-life story of Erin Brockovich, a single mother who worked to take down PG&E for contaminating water supplies. This dramatized version of Erin Brockovich is feisty yet distinctly down to Earth, and it's impressive that a household name like Julia Roberts could pull a character like that off and make it believable.

Shortly after portraying Erin Brockovich, Julia Roberts actually landed on The Hollywood Reporter's list of the 50 most influential women in show business. The fact that she became the first actress to make $20 million was

certainly a contributing factor.

Roberts' performance was met with great praise, with one critic, David Ansen, specifically praising the film for giving the talented actress a great script to work with. "Roberts has wasted her effervescence on many paltry projects," Ansen wrote, and unfortunately it's true—as much as I love Julia Roberts, I've definitely come away from a few of her films wishing she had turned it down (though I'm sure even her more trite films made her plenty of money, so who am I to complain!) Erin Brockovich not only lets her flex her dramatic acting skills, but it gives her a little bit of

Julia Roberts

romantic chemistry to play with and comedy to boot. Roberts does an excellent job showing both Brockovich's unwavering drive and the various ways her fight starts to grind her down. There's something unique about the way Roberts is able to play this supposedly average woman with such grace and gloss, without making her feel ungrounded. Roberts also delivers some pretty fantastic lines throughout the film. There is a lot of swearing in this film from her character, and the studio was actually initially worried that audiences would be turned off by the foul-mouthed lead.

Julia Roberts

Erin Brockovich has had a pretty huge cultural impact. It's one of those movies that everyone seems to know, even if they haven't seen it. There's also a famous monologue that Roberts delivers in the film about the "lame-ass offer". A portion of it goes as follows:

"So before you come back here with another lame ass offer, I want you to think real hard about what your spine is worth, Mr. Walker. Or what you might expect someone to pay you for your uterus, Ms. Sanchez. Then you take out your calculator and you multiply that number by a hundred. Anything less than that is a waste of our time!"

That monologue is still used in auditions and acting classes to this day. It's a pretty popular pick for a dramatic reading, which goes to show how much aspiring actors have been influenced by Roberts's performance in the film.

Notably, Julia Roberts received a pretty sizable check for her role in the film. She made $20 million as her salary for the film, making her the first female actress to ever earn that much for a role. Of course, the film did fantastically at the box-office, grossing over $256.3 million on a $52 million budget, so clearly paying for the extremely bankable actress was worth it.

The real Erin Brockovich and real-life lawyer Edward L. Masry were apparently impressed by the way Roberts portrayed Brockovich. In an interview with Vulture, Brockovich says she remembers her and Masry nudging one another and saying things like, "Oh my God, you did that ⋯" or "Oh my God, that's so you ⋯" in response to what their actor counterparts were doing on-screen. Originally, the real Brockovich had envisioned Goldie Hawn playing her and thought that Julia Roberts would never be picked to portray her on-screen, so the convincing performance came as quite a shock!

Famously, at the Oscars, Julia Roberts forgot to thank Erin Brockovich herself for the role.

"Shamefully, shamefully I forgot to thank Erin," Roberts had said at the post-Oscars press conference. "She is the centre of our universe for this movie!" It's funny, because Roberts had actually gone well over her acceptance speech time and still forgot to shout her out. When the Academy started to play her out, she said, "Everybody tried to shut me up—it didn't work with my parents and it won't work now, a gal's got to have her moment!"

In 2001, The Mexican, which starred Roberts opposite Brad Pitt was released as well as Ocean's Eleven. In 2004 she appeared in Closer opposite Oscar winner Natalie Portman. In 2010 she appeared in a film adaptation of Eat Pray Love, in Larry Crowne in 2011 and in 2013, August Osage County for which she was nominated for Best Supporting Actress Oscar. There are plenty of more successful films in between that show Julia's acting range. The list goes on and on.

Julia's latest film roles are in Wonder and Ben Is Back. She has been an executive producer for a handful of TV shows, like Queens Supreme, Homecoming and the American Girl TV films.

Julia Roberts' commanding star power proves that natural talent, especially one that is characteristic (like her infectious smile, tall stature and strong voice) brings instant attention. Julia Roberts runs a production company called Red Om Films as well being a UNICEF supporter. Her presence on and off screen will always be valued and rewarded.

"There have been so many people who have said to me, 'You can't do that,' but I've had an innate belief that they were wrong. Be unwavering and relentless in your approach."

Halle Berry

In 2002 Halle Berry made Oscar history. She became the first woman of colour to win the Best Actress Oscar. It took 73 years since the inaugural ceremony of the Oscars for a woman of colour, a black woman specifically, to win the Best Actress Oscar. Hollywood, the Academy and every entertainment industry for that matter has been infused with white supremacy. It runs deep. But Halle Berry has pushed hard from an early age to stick to her passions and become the icon that we know now. Halle Berry, along with being an incredibly beautiful woman, shows talent in playing diverse characters in all film genres. She exhibits vulnerability, femininity and strength from within that makes her one of the most successful leading ladies in Hollywood. Halle Berry was born to an African American father and Liverpool-born white mother in Ohio. Halle saw her father abuse her mother until they divorced when Halle was five years old. And ever since then she has lost all contact with her estranged father. While attending community college, Halle entered various beauty pageants, and went as far as winning Miss Teen All American in 1985 and Miss Ohio USA in 1986. In 1986 she was Miss USA first runner-up. Moreover Halle was the first African American Miss World entrant in 1986. Halle then moved to New York City to pursue a modelling career. She slept at a homeless shelter at one point, until she secured a few TV show appearances shortly in 1989. Halle was 23 years old and realised that her dreams to become a successful actress waited for her in Los Angeles, and so she moved there. Her film debut was in 1991 in Spike Lee's Jungle Fever, along with two other movies Strictly Business and The Last Boy Scout. During the 90s Halle carved her image of being a malleable and marketable actress. She appeared in successful films that proved just that in Boomerang, Queen: The Story of an American Family, Flintstones and Losing Isaiah (opposite Jessica Lange) as well as BAPS, Bulworth and Why Do Fools Fall In Love.

In 1999 Berry starred in an HBO biopic about Dorothy Dandridge, called Introducing Dorothy Dandridge. Dandridge was the very first African American actress in history to get nominated for the Best Actress Oscar, but lost to Grace Kelly in 1955. This film must have been a major experience for Berry as it was one that she fought hard for to be produced. She served as a co-producer on it. This film won multiple awards and Berry received a Golden Globe as well as an Emmy for Outstanding Lead Actress. This film truly opened a lot of doors for Berry who was about to hit her career pinnacle.

When the 2000s rolled in, Halle Berry starred in a number of memorable and mainstream films like in X-Men, Swordfish, Gothika, Catwoman, Die Another Day, and even did voiceover in Robots. But amid these high budget films, there was one particular one with a mere $4 million budget that allowed Berry to become the best actress: 2001's Monsters Ball.

Monster's Ball is a character study about two people on either side of a tense racial line who are brought together by tragedy. The film has a dark and violent narrative that is used to explore the ways in which its two main leads approach the soul-crushing challenges they are faced with. They are both presented with situations that upend their values and backgrounds, ones which are filled with complexity and pain. There are no easy answers available, and one of the major conflicts that the audience is faced with is trying to establish a sense of familiarity with them. As it is with human nature, much of what we see them say and do is a front for what they are struggling with internally, though they exhibit different degrees of transparency and empathy. It's a sometimes-uneven journey and doesn't always reveal the emotional truths that it aims for, but an exceptional cast keeps the audience invested in the troubled characters.

Halle Berry

Both of our leads are at a crossroad in their life as the film begins. Hank (Billy Bob Thornton) is a death row security guard, tasked with taking prisoners on their "final walk". His son Sonny (Heath Ledger) is attempting to follow in his father's footsteps, but lacks the cold veneer of indifference that the job requires. The first inmate who Sonny is tasked with accompanying is Lawrence (Sean "Diddy" Combs). He is husband to an exasperated, soon-to-be-single mother Leticia (Halle Berry), and father to a compulsively eating son Tyrell (Coronji Calhoun).

The event of Lawrence's execution proves to be a turning point for both Hank and Leticia. Sonny is disturbed by his role in Lawrence's death, and struggles as any healthy person would. He is more interested in trying to comfort Lawrence and freezes up when the fateful hour comes. This sends Lawrence into a rage, in which he blasts Sonny for being weak, pummelling him with blows that require the intervention of his fellow guards. The conflict spills over to their home, where Sonny pulls a gun on his father when he attempts to throw him out of the house. Hank tells his son that he doesn't love him, an exchange pre-empting his suicide. It's here we meet the actual root of Hank's rage and venom: his live-in father Buck. Buck is a widower who speaks in icy hateful terms about his wife, who also committed suicide, and spouts racism toward the black children in the neighbourhood who Sonny is friendly with.

On the night Lawrence dies, Leticia tries to distract herself with television and liquor. When she catches Tyrell alleviating his own anxieties with forbidden chocolate bars, she lambasts him for his weight and messy bedroom, losing her temper to the point of knocking him to the floor. In these two exchanges with their children, Hand and Leticia mirror their displaced rage. How the two cope and try to heal afterward is where we begin to see the dynamic that develops into a relationship. Hank is a highly guarded person, and we see the way in which his father is largely responsible for that. At his son's funeral, when Buck's only words at the graveside are "he was weak", Hank's quick directive to hurry up and get dirt on the box feels like more than just a literal instruction. He comes from a background where vulnerability is a character flaw, and he's learned to bury his truth. Leticia, on the other hand, seems to have already had her proverbial guts stomped by having a murderer husband and having had to prepare her son for a life without a father.

Another tragedy causes the two to cross paths when Tyrell is hit by a car and Hank happens to be the first passer-by. This plunges him directly into Leticia's life and incredible grief. It's a place of honesty and anguish that he's entirely unfamiliar with, particularly with a black woman. He struggles with the residual grip of his toxic upbringing to allow himself to experience love. Though the mounting escalation of horrible events is so overwhelming it stretches the limits of plausibility,

Halle Berry

Halle Berry's performance is so authentic that you can't help but be pulled in and feel a genuine exhaustion at the pain she's in. It's an especially interesting performance for Berry because of what a departure it was from her work up to that point. As a former Bond girl, she's had a number of roles where she played vibrant, skilfully seductive women. Though Monster's Ball contains what is undoubtedly her most explicit sex scene in any of her films, the world-weary Leticia takes the actress into new dramatic territory, and she thrives. It's really her performance that primes the audience for Monster's Balls' resolution. She eases us past the contrivances of the script with a remarkable performance.

The 2002 Academy Awards made big waves in race inclusivity because the two Best Acting Oscars went to two African Americans. Denzel Washington became the second ever black man to win the Best Actor Oscar for Training Day and Halle Berry became the first ever black woman to win the Best Actress Oscar. To this day, Halle's benchmark still stands.

Halle continued starring in the X-Men franchise, she starred in more science fiction and action films like Cloud Atlas, Kingsman: The Golden Circle and John Wick 3. She starred in a few thrillers on top like in Perfect Stranger, Dark Tide and The Call. Moreover she has co-produced a 2019 comedy series called Boomerang, starred and directed Bruised and starred and co-produced Kidnap.

Nicole Kidman

Nicole Kidman became the very first Australian actress to win the Best Actress Oscar in 2003. At 23 minutes and 30 seconds, Kidman's performance became the third shortest Best Actress winning performance of all time, after Louise Fletcher in One Flew Over the Cuckoo's Nest and Patricia Neal in Hud. Kidman, just as numerous Best Actress Oscar winners before her, won the Oscar for portraying a real-life person: the world-renowned author Virginia Woolf.

Kidman was born in Hawaii and grew up in Sydney, Australia. Having shown promise in acting since school, Kidman pursued exactly that early on. She attended multiple theatre schools in Australia. In 1983, at the age of 16, she made her Australian film debut in Bush Christmas and BMX Bandits. From that moment onward Nicole's acting career took off. She starred in more Australian films like Wind-rider, Emerald City and Dead Calm. The naturally curly redhead with porcelain skin and a 5'11 stature stood out and ventured into Hollywood at the onset of the 90s.

In 1990 she made her Hollywood debut in Days Of Thunder, a wildly successful film where Kidman starred alongside her then boyfriend and eventual husband Tom Cruise. Although Kidman was a newbie to the Hollywood scene, she was already a relevant award-winning star in Australia. She won the Australian Film Academy Award and a Logie Award in 1988 for her leading role in a miniseries called Vietnam and two more Logie Awards for her role in Bangkok Hilton series in 1990.

Kidman starred in more early 90s films like Flirting, Billy Bathgate and Far and Away opposite Tom Cruise. The 90s consisted of major Hollywood collaborations like Batman Forever, To Die For and The Portrait Of A Lady which was directed by Jane Campion, the same filmmaker that captured Holly Hunter in her Oscar-winning role. In the early 2000s Nicole appeared in Birth, Fur and Margot At The Wedding. More lower budget films. She also got paid a whopping $3.71 million for appearing in a four-minute Baz Luhrmann-directed Chanel No. 5 advert, making her the highest paid actress in a commercial at the time.

"I believe that as much as you take, you have to give back. It's important not to focus on yourself too much."

In the 1990s, Kidman, being the other half of a major Hollywood power couple with Tom Cruise, was always in the spotlight and that made her even more sought after. The couple appeared in their third and final film together in 1999 called Eyes Wide Shut directed by Stanley Kubrick. In 2001, news came out that the couple divorced. It is funny how Kidman, who towered over Cruise, barely wore heels during their relationship and on screen they made sure she appeared shorter to make their height difference less prominent. The moment they divorced Kidman threw those heels back on! Kidman realised that this was her moment to shine on film. She was no longer attached to her ex-husband but was now a single woman. He no longer defined her.

She starred in major films following the highly publicised and scrutinised divorce: Moulin Rouge!, Cold Mountain, Dogville and Stepford Wives. Kidman was nominated for the first time for the Best Actress Oscar for her singing, dancing and acting role in Moulin Rouge! By the way, she broke her rib on the set of the film and production was halted for her recovery.

Kidman said this: "Out of my divorce came work that was applauded so that was an interesting thing for me." And her most applauded role led her to become an Oscar winner. It was her brilliant acting in The Hours opposite Oscar winners Meryl Streep and Julianne Moore that solidified Kidman as an irreplaceable star. She portrayed the feminist writer Virginia Woolf. Kidman was unrecognisable in the role. She went through great lengths to fully immerse herself in playing a real-life figure, physically and vocally. Nicole, a left-handed person, practised using her right hand to write, since Woolf was right-handed. In 2003 she went up to accept her Best Actress Oscar, making her the first Australian actress to win a Best Actress Oscar.

In the 2002 film The Hours directed by Stephen Daldry, three stories of three women in three distinct decades intersect and overlap through the common emotional struggles and existential wonderings, haunting these main female characters.

Three powerhouse actresses portray three troubled women with charged inner worlds: Julianne Moore immerses herself in Laura Brown, Meryl Streep dives deep into Clarissa Vaughan, but our focus here will be the marvellous performance of Nicole Kidman who disappears into Virginia Woolf (whose life and art connect all three protagonists and narrative lines).

Kidman's work in The Hours was highly acclaimed and earned her the Academy Award for Best Actress. She is now known for her incredible talent to fully transform into a given character. Nicole Kidman approaches every role with insightful learning and intelligent exploration which then shines in her on-screen presence. The complex Virginia Woolf was no exception.

Nicole Kidman

When one watches the film, they might not even realise that this is Kidman as her facial features and expression are made very different through make-up and performance. First, let's discuss the exterior: besides make-up, Kidman had to also perform with a specially-customised, prosthetic nose which indeed changed her appearance. Critics and viewers were eager to investigate and make jokes about the prosthetic nose but this topic was always cut short as it was clear the actress had achieved much more than just "looking the part". She herself commented on how, when studying the many histories of Virginia Woolf as a woman, writer, wife, sister, she had to dissect the interior: more precisely, what was happening in the imagination of someone with brilliant talent and at the same time suffering with excruciating madness and depression.

Here is where Nicole Kidman's performance emerged as truly moving. With so much heart she became one of the most important writers of the 20th century. The actress captured a certain essence–the writer as an observer who constantly interprets the surrounding world to inspire their own literature. This was especially true of Woolf. And even more so— Nicole Kidman became Virginia Woolf at the end of her life, the Virginia Woolf who was intrigued by death and saw it as the only possible escape from the painful and agonising sadness of the world. Kidman spoke to the viewer through her eyes, movements, expressions, stillness and voice. The last words of the film vocalised by Kidman/Woolf echo and haunt with their beauty:

"Always the years between us. Always the years. Always the love. Always the hours."

The performance of Nicole Kidman is impressive because she understood and then presented through her skilful acting the heartbreaking search for happiness and impossibility to prolong the hours in which it can be experienced and lived, as they inevitably fade. Kidman's Virginia goes through a metamorphosis of struggles longing to be someone better and in the end of her path, finding peace within the river water. It's a masterful portrayal leaving its trace in the universe of the Seventh art.

Luhrmann and Kidman partnered again in 2008 epic adventure film called Australia co-starring Hugh Jackman. In 2011 Kidman garnered another Best Actress Oscar nomination for her role in Rabbit Hole. This indie drama with a $3 million budget was also co-produced by Kidman herself.

In 2014 Nicole had the opportunity to play yet another real-life figure and a fellow Oscar winner; Grace Kelly in the biopic called Grace Of Monaco. In 2017 Nicole got her one and only Best Supporting Actress Oscar nomination for her role in a biographical drama called Lion.

Nicole's aptitude to jump into physically transformative and risqué´ roles seems to bring her the most acclaim. She proved this fact in films like The Killing Of A Sacred Deer, The Beguiled, Destroyer, Bombshell and The Northman all are recent successes.

Although Kidman's TV career paused in the late 80s upon her Hollywood dream coming true, she has returned to giving brilliant TV performances in Big Little Lies (opposite major actresses and Oscar winners Meryl Streep, Reese Witherspoon and Laura Dern) as well as in the Undoing. Moreover, both HBO series were executive-produced by Kidman.

Nicole Kidman proves just how versatile she is. She brings a touch of sophistication and softness to complicated and intense female characters and can also bring out wrath and evil when needed too. Her transformations on screen are incredibly satisfying. All of the accolades presented to Nicole Kidman show her everlasting superiority but her Oscar win goes down in history as the most valuable.

Nicole Kidman

Charlize Theron

With the previous year's winner being the first ever Australian, Nicole Kidman, to win the best Actress Oscar, the next winner became the first South African to win the best actress Oscar. And that was Charlize Theron. Kidman and Nicole share similar traits: both are tall, blonde and feisty. They love playing real-life people and transforming physically for roles to a point of being unrecognisable. The two even starred alongside each other in Bombshell in 2019. It was a sudden rise to fame for Theron; she was at the right place at the right time. Her acting power is supreme and for that she always gets rewarded.

Charlize Theron was born to Afrikaans parents in South Africa. She grew up speaking Afrikaans, and learnt English by watching films and TV. Her mother fatally shot her father right in front of her when she was a child to defend herself since he was an abusive alcoholic. Therefore she grew up with only her mother. Their bond was strong and Charlize's mother was actually the one to buy her a one-way ticket to Los Angeles to take a chance at starting an acting career in Hollywood. The young Charlize moved to LA at the age of 19 and imminently was scouted by a talent agent. Funnily enough it was her explosive, hard headed attitude that made heads turn when she started arguing with a bank teller for refusing to cash her check sent from her mother. These antics got Charlize her first Hollywood connection as her future agent was watching the conflict unravel. The rest is history. She inherited an American accent straight away, attended acting classes and modelled on the side until she eventually went on auditions and secured her first film role.

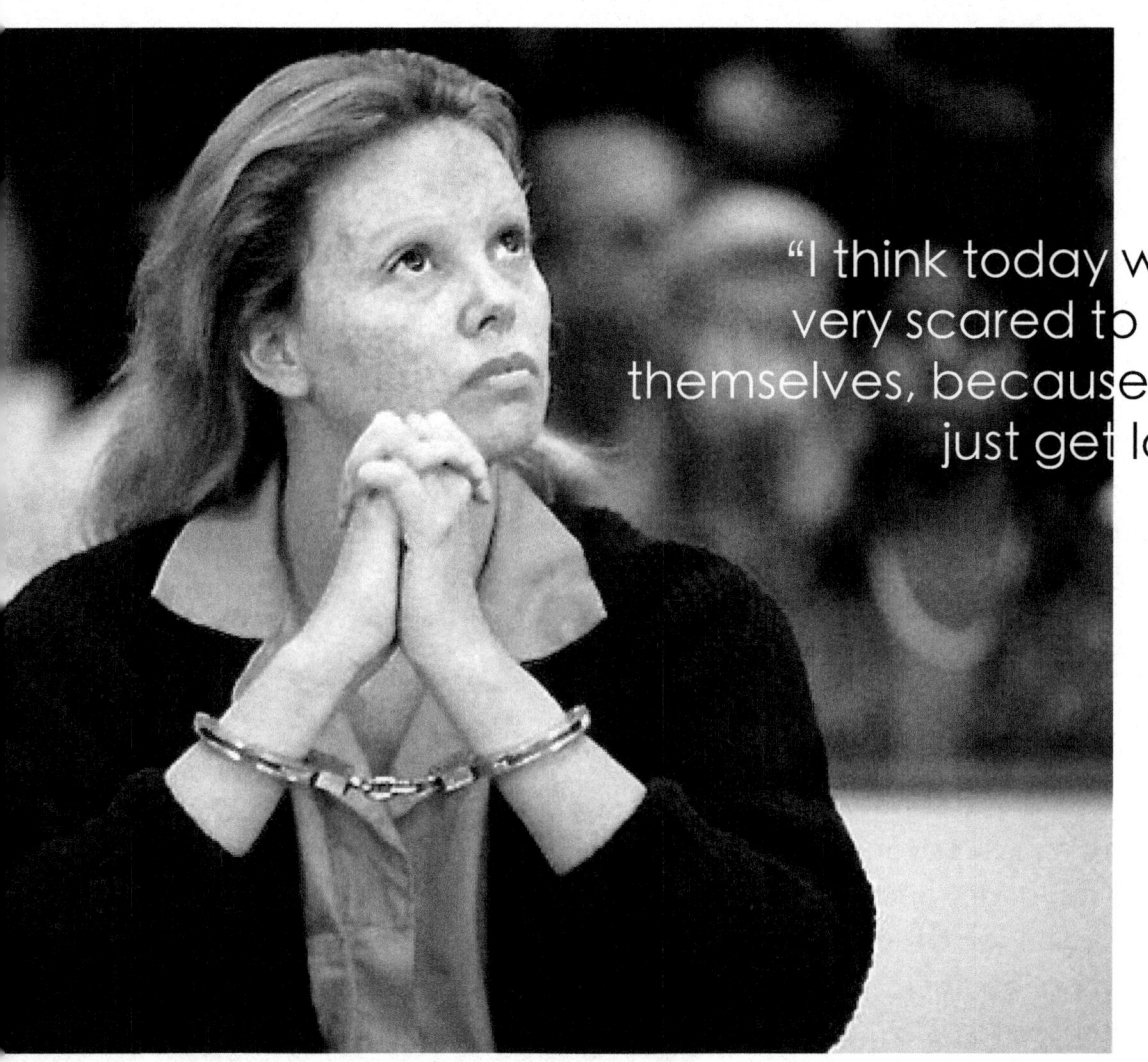

"I think today women are very scared to celebrate themselves, because then they just get labelled."

Charlize Theron

After a handful of minor roles Theron starred in her breakthrough role in 1997 at the age of 22, in a supernatural horror film called The Devil's Advocate opposite Keanu Reeves and Al Pacino.

She then starred in a mix of drama and crime films like Cider House Rules, Reindeer Games and The Italian Job. Theron proved that she could star opposite major Hollywood actors and hold her own in a scene.

But it was time for Theron to take the lead and provide a masterful performance as a leading lady. In 2003 this moment came. Charlize headlined in Monster, directed by Patty Jenkins and co-produced by Theron herself. Much like preceding Oscar winning actresses, Charlize took on the role of a real-life person: Aileen Wuornos, a mentally ill serial killer. Theron put on 30 pounds, shaved her eyebrows and completely immersed herself in the character. This role changed everything for Theron, she said, "I never got offered parts like that, never. And it took a woman, a first-time female director, to offer me that role." And Charlize, at the age of 29, got her first Oscar win at the 2004 Academy Awards. Monster became a box office hit worth $64.2 million from a $1.5 million budget.

Theron became exclusively the first and only South African to win the Best Actress Oscar. Her star status skyrocketed as well as her pay, making her one of the highest paid actresses. In 2006 Theron was nominated for the Oscar once again for her gritty role in North Country opposite fellow Oscar winner Frances McDormand and directed by Niki Caro and one more time in 2020 for Bombshell opposite Oscar winner Nicole Kidman.

Charlize, who has worked with various women film directors, said this: "I think the reason why female directors are so successful is because they're not just telling women stories. They might be telling stories that affect women but their studies on men are done so well so that they're universal directors. So I really believe this is a talent, and just understanding human conflict is so good that they can tell any genre, any kind of story, and that's why I think they're doing so well."
On top of producing Monster, Theron has produced and starred in other works like Dark Places, Atomic Blonde and Bombshell. Charlize has also starred in various incredibly dramatic, dark and off course physically demanding roles like in Road, Snow-White and The Huntsman, Mad Max Fury Road and Prometheus. On the set of Road, Charlize was so committed to her craft, that during the filming of a birthing scene, she screamed so hard that she damaged her vocal cords on set.

Other than work in film Theron has made big waves in activism focused on human rights in South Africa, African youth and women's rights. The Charlize Theron Africa Outreach Project (CTAOP) was created in 2007 by Theron a year before she was named a UN Messenger of Peace.

Charlize Theron

Theron's dedication to her work has resulted in some quite traumatic moments to her health during her career. She has torn her thumb ligaments, herniated a disc in her neck, broken teeth, caught a stomach virus, dislocated her jaw and, as mentioned before, injured her vocal cords during filming of various projects. Reckless or not, she clearly is incredibly resilient and committed.

There is a quote by Charlize that I think is brilliant: "We come on these junkets and it's like, 'So you don't play a glamorous role again.' Sometimes I just want to look at people and say, 'Have you really thought this through?' How many great stories can you tell in a Dior dress? Or is it because I've done a J'adore perfume ad that I can only be one type of woman? I don't think women are like that. We are many things. One day we wake up and we want to put on jeans and a T-shirt, and the next day we want to have our hair done. But that doesn't mean that I don't have access to raw emotion."

Charlize is unapologetically herself. She is riveting on screen and continues to prove that in order to stay a relevant star in Hollywood, one must be shrewd, adventurous and give it your all.

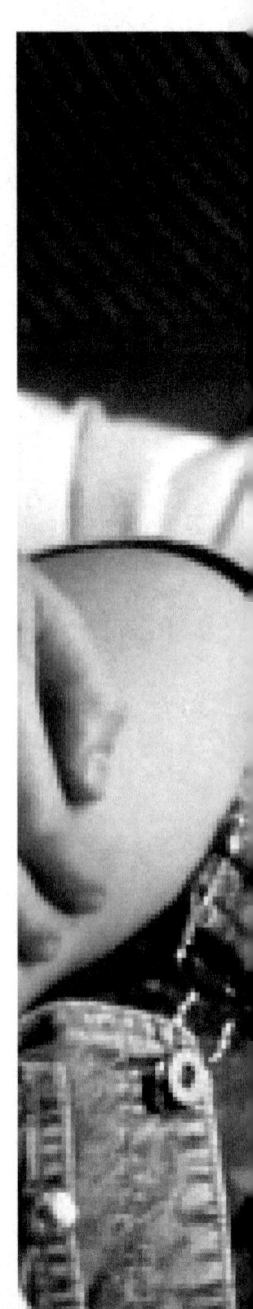

Reese Witherspoon

Reese Witherspoon has been a relevant star for decades. Her bubbly and well-balanced characters are an extension of who she is as a person and that makes her very likeable. With a wide range of film roles and genres, Reese has been able to transition from naive teen roles to those of a fearless young woman and now mature woman roles. It is thrilling to watch her career growth for she has been in incredible films playing unique characters that it would be hard to picture anybody else playing them. Having been brought up in a well-rounded family with both parents with medical backgrounds in the south, Reese was a true southern belle born in New Orleans and raised in Nashville. A straight-A student with an obsession to overachieve, the young Reese did not follow in her scholarly parents footsteps and started modelling, taking acting lessons and winning a talent fair by the age of 11.

In 1991 she made her film debut in The Man On The Moon at the age of 15. After graduating from high school Reese went on to study English Literature at Stanford University but dropped out a year later in order to pursue acting full time and starred in two major films Freeway and Fear. These films showed a more mature side to Witherspoon's acting. Both films came out in 1996. At the end of the 1990s she starred in a variety of cult favourite films like Pleasantville, Cruel Intentions and Election. In 2000 she had a minor role in American Psycho. She also appeared briefly in the series Friends. Witherspoon was already appreciated as a young starlet.

But it was in 2001 that made Reese Witherspoon a true Hollywood legend. Legally Blonde is probably her most recognized role. Every line of dialogue can be quoted, every outfit is an inspiration and every character is iconic. Legally Blonde was a cultural milestone for fashion, comedy and female-driven stories. This film has stood the test of time over 20 years later and Reese was at the forefront of playing charismatic and compassionate roles. Reese's salary skyrocketed after Legally Blonde and she got paid $2.5 million to $15 million for her further work.

"It's fun to do a comedy and hook people in and then hoodwink them into watching a serious movie. I like to lead in with the comedy and then hit them over the head with a drama."

The 2005 musical biopic Walk the Line followed Johnny Cash (Joaquin Phoenix) and his rise to country music stardom. It also followed his romance with June Carter, who was played by Reese Witherspoon. The role earned Witherspoon her first (and so far, only) Academy Award for Best Actress.

Witherspoon truly did a phenomenal job as June Carter Cash, as she brought a specific charm and energy to the film. Her performance was praised by critics for her charisma. Sight and Sound wrote that "Witherspoon, who has perhaps the tougher task of lending depth and darkness to the role of June, whose frighteningly chipper stage act—a musical-comedy hybrid—constantly courts (but never marries) mockery." In fact, critics just about unanimously agreed that the part was the best Witherspoon performance of her career thus far.

The chemistry between Witherspoon and Phoenix was incredible, as well, and the two worked fantastically with one another. Their romance was wholeheartedly believable, and the sexual tension between the two characters was practically palpable. At its core, Walk the Line is a romance story between June and Johnny, so the ways Phoenix and Witherspoon played off of one another is what truly makes the film work. Director James Mangold reported that Phoenix and Witherspoon had grown incredibly close over the course of filming, to the point where they had made tactical agreements not to finish the film should the other one drop out.

However, even with that being said, their initial relationship had actually been quite fraught. They were both incredibly nervous about having to sing for the movie, and apparently that anxiety bled into their on-set relationship early on. They admitted in interviews that they frequently argued during their six month stretch of singing lessons, and they weren't really able to connect and befriend one another until filming had actually started.

Witherspoon swept awards season across the board for Walk The Line. In addition to her Oscar, she also won the BAFTA Award for Best Actress in a Leading Role, a Golden Globe Award for Best Actress – Motion Picture Comedy or Musical, a BFCA Critics' Choice Award for Best Actress, a National Society of Film Critics Award for Best Actress, an Online Film Critics Society Award for Best Actress, a Satellite Award for Best Actress – Motion Picture, and a Screen Actors Guild Award for Outstanding Performance by a Female Actor in a Leading Role.

Reese Witherspoon

June Carter Cash herself approved of Reese Witherspoon's portrayal and casting in the film. Unfortunately, June Carter Cash died shortly before production began. Witherspoon was permitted to search through her closet in order to further research for her role. Witherspoon had carefully studied videos of June Carter and listened to her sing and talk in order to mimic the singer's voice. In fact, Witherspoon performed all the songs in the movie herself, which really helped sell her performance. Witherspoon even learned to play the autoharp so that she could adequately play enactments of stage performances. Her dedication to the role and the fact that she also sang definitely contributed to her Oscar nomination. Compare this to Sissy Spacek's performance in the film Coal Miner's Daughter, where Spacek's singing was considered to be an element that won her the Oscar.

While June Carter Cash and Johnny Cash themselves approved of the casting choices, their kids were far more critical of the film. Katy Cash, who was Johnny's second oldest daughter with his first wife, Vivian (who was portrayed by Ginnifer Goodwin in the film), felt that while the performances were "Oscar-worthy" the film treated her parents too harshly. She felt that it made her mother look bad and was disappointed with how little it showed Johnny Cash interacting with his children. Meanwhile, Roseanne Cash, the eldest daughter of Johnny and Vivian, was even more critical. She called the movie "painful" and similarly felt that it demeaned her mother. "My mom was basically a nonentity in the entire film except for the mad little psycho who hated his career. That's not true. She loved his career and was proud of him until he started taking drugs and stopped coming home," Kathy Cash said. John Carter Cash, June and Johnny's only son, acknowledged that both of his half-siblings' complaints were merited. However, he was more happy with the film's end result and actually served as executive producer for the film.

Reese was the second actress to win the Best Actress Oscar for portraying a female singer in a biography: the first was Sissy Spacek for Coal Miner's Daughter. Witherspoon would later go on to be nominated for Best Actress again in 2015 for her performance in the movie Wild, which saw her playing another biographical role, this time as Cheryl Strayed. Strayed had written a memoir about her 1,100-mile hiking trip that was adapted into a film by Nick Hornby. Witherspoon ended up losing to Julianne Moore in Still Alice.

Further effective and diverse acting work by Reese can be seen in films like Water For Elephants, Devil's Knot and Wild. And other than acting credits, Reese has a generous amount of producing credits. She executive produced and reprised her role of Elle Woods in Legally Blonde 2. She also produced and starred in Penelope, Hot Pursuit, Gone Girl starring Rosamund Pike and Lucy In The Sky starring Natalie Portman.

Furthermore she has starred and executive produced HBO series Big Little Lies opposite Hollywood legends Meryl Streep, Nicole Kidman and Laura Dern. She starred and produced further series like the Morning Show opposite Jennifer Aniston and Little Fires Everywhere with Kerry Washington.

She said, "The battles that we face in this business aren't financial, but they are moral. And I certainly think that the longer you can keep your values, and your morality intact, and keep your head on your shoulders about what is important at the end of the day, you can get the most out of this business and really emerge with something wonderful." These words are quite telling of Reese Witherspoon's intelligence.

Reese's level-headedness in show business has led her to become a well-rounded woman who juggles family, creative work and other business ventures like Hello Sunshine a media company founded by her in 2016 and Pacific Standard the subsidiary production company in 2012. She is like Hollywood's golden child for she has basically grown up on screen and in the public eye. Reese Witherspoon is loved by many and continues to show diverse female driven stories on film and TV.

Helen Mirren

As one of the most prominent and established British actors, Helen Mirren must have lots of stories to tell ever since her career began in the late 60s. And of course she is not simply Helen Mirren, she is Dame Helen Mirren. A regality, a poise and sensibility is attached to Helen Mirren and a lot of other older British actress for that matter, like Emma Thompson and Judi Dench. So in return, of course Helen Mirren won the Best Actress Oscar for a role that gave her an opportunity to showcase these qualities for a role none other than play Queen Elizabeth the second.

Helen was born to a working-class English mother and Russian father. In fact, he changed their original last name, Mironov, to a more anglicised Mirren when Helen was 10 years old. Helen was actually raised anti-monarchist, but clearly this sentiment was let go, considering that her most awarded film role would be for playing Queen Elizabeth.

The young Helen started acting in school productions and eventually auditioned to join the National Youth Theatre in London, which she got into. Much like many British actresses before her, Helen started her acting career on stage. It's really like a rite of passage for British talent to stem from theatre or some sort of legitimate training. Thus at the age of 20, Helen debuted as Cleopatra in the stage production of Antony And Cleopatra in 1965. Her film career simultaneously started to take off in the late 1960s too. Her film debut was as an uncredited role in a British film called Press For Time, but a more solid role was in a film rendition of Shakespeare's Midsummer Night's Dream in 1968 opposite Judi Dench and Ian Holm. Mirren's stage success was imminent and led to her securing an agent and joining the Royal Shakespeare Company.

"I resent having witnessed the survival of some very mediocre male actors and the professional demise of the very brilliant female ones."

A seemingly never-ending list of theatre productions helped Mirren become a relevant British actress in the UK scene. But that did not erase the fact that she was constantly objectified for her womanly figure and questioned as to whether her success stemmed from her attractiveness or her talent. Well, she certainly pushed back the sexists and proved them wrong.

Her rapid collection of film acting credits, as well as TV credits, showed her versatility: like in Caligula an erotic historical drama in 1979 and The Long Good Friday a British gangster film, which became Mirren's breakthrough role in 1980 and helped her secure a major role in Excalibur in 1981. Excalibur was a mediaeval fantasy film based on the legend

of King Arthur and it featured a number of British talents that were soon to be household names like Liam Neesan, Patrick Stewart, Gabriel Byrne and Ciaran Hinds. Liam Neesan and Helen Mirren actually started dating while shooting this film. This film was obviously a success and helped Mirren secure more substantial roles like one in Cal in 1984, an Irish drama that won Mirren the Best Actress award at the Cannes Film Festival.

In 1989 Mirren appeared in The Cook, the Thief, His Wife & Her Lover, quite a controversial film for its nude scenes and violence. She starred in more star-studded films like In The Comfort Of Strangers, The Passion of Ayn Rand a TV film for which she won an Emmy for Best Actress and The Roman Spring of Mrs. Stone that co-starred Oscar winner Anne Bancroft.

In 1995 Mirren starred as the lead role in the Madness Of King George as Queen Charlotte. For this role Mirren was nominated for an Oscar for the very first time in the Best Supporting Actress Category. In 2002 she would be nominated again for Best Supporting Actress for her role in Gosford Park opposite Oscar winner Maggie Smith.

In 2006 Mirren starred in her most rewarded and notable role amid her incredible catalogue of film, TV and stage work. She starred as Queen Elizabeth II in the film titled The Queen. She appeared opposite Michael Sheen as Tony Blair and James Cromwell as Prince Phillip. The film was a huge commercial success.

The film is told from the personal perspective of the Queen during the time of Princess Diana's death. The role of playing Queen Elizabeth II is not an easy feat, but Mirren gave a multi-layered performance that painted the Queen as neither a woman of virtue nor vice. She is cold, distant and initially exceptionally aloof to the death of Princess Diana. This film is an intimate glimpse into the life of the royal family during the media phenomenon surrounding the death of Diana and how they dealt with the circumstances. Mirren as Elizabeth shows no glimmer of remorse or weakness as she handles her duties; yet we see her actually shed a tear when she is alone, by a riverbed, with no-one to witness her moment of vulnerability. We as an audience finally

are proven that she is in fact a human with feelings. The closeup of Mirren's face during the film evokes all of the secrets, feelings and thoughts inside the head of the Queen. For this role Mirren got nominated for the first time for the Best Actress Oscar and won in 2007.

In 2010 was got nominated one more time for Best Actress for her role in The Last Station. Mirren furthered her presence on screen in Hollywood films like Hitchcock where she played scriptwriter Alma Reville, Hitchcock's wife, Trumbo in which she plays the infamous Hedda Hopper, Eye In The Sky as a UK military officer and in Winchester a horror film.

Helen Mirren's Oscar win was long awaited since by that point she had been a very seasoned star. Her contribution to the history of theatre, film and TV is incredibly potent. She really is the poster woman for British theatre trained brilliance.

Helen Mirren

"My parents always told me that if you want something, you can do whatever you have to do to get it. As long as it's not against someone else."

Marion Cotillard

Marion Cotillard's consistency in bringing touching roles in French and English-speaking cinema has made her one of the most distinctive actresses of our time. Her remarkable French accent, slightly croaky voice and soft glamour has helped her stand out as a typical femme fatale type character. A femme fatale is known to bring distress and demise to the male counterpart; she is a mysterious woman, a seductress who captures the attention of many through her feminine charm. We could argue that Marion Cotillard's Oscar win in 2008 for her role of playing the French musical idol Edith Piaf in La Vie En Rose was a story of a femme fatale.

Marion began her acting journey very young. Her introduction to film began through her parents who too were actors and drama teachers. After finishing drama school in 1994, at the age of 19, Marion started appearing in French films like The Story of a Boy Who Wanted to Be Kissed, La Belle Verte and the Taxi comedy films which were her most popular works at that time in the late 90s.

Marion Cotillard

Big Fish, a 2003 Tim Burton film, was Marion's first American and first English language film. In 2007, little known in Hollywood, Marion starred in a drama biopic about French singer Edith Piaf. Marion would lip sync the highly complex songs by Piaf and also underwent a full transformation to look and sound close to Piaf. Edith Piaf could be considered a femme fatale, even though we might not instantly deduce so. A femme fatale literally means a "disastrous woman" in French.

And Piaf was certainly that, for she brought a lot of destruction to her and other people's lives. The men she encountered along the way of finding her worldwide success eventually suffered (two of whom in the film would even suddenly die shortly after meeting her). Edith was a femme fatale without even being aware of it. That is something clearly conveyed in the journey of Marion's performance. She showed the unusual physicality, the larger-than-life personality and the enigmatic charm that

Piaf possessed. This proved that a femme fatale does not have to be a typical beauty with over glamorised style. It is not looks that has the world falling to her feet. It's really about her energy and the inexplicably intoxicating power she has over people. The film was directed by Olivier Dahan, co-starring Gerard Depardieu, Emmanuelle Seigner and Catherine Allegret (who is actually Simone Signoret's daughter).

The 2008 Oscar ceremony was the second time in Oscar history (the first being in 1964) that all of the four acting Oscars were awarded to non-Americans. It was a celebration of European talent as Marion's Best Actress win represented France, Tilda Swinton's and Daniel Day Lewis's the UK and Javier Bardem's Spain. Marion became the second actress to win the Best Actress Oscar for an exclusively non-English speaking role (after Sophia Loren for Two Women). Furthermore the movie won an Oscar for Best Makeup. Marion had her eyebrows and hairline shaved, and wore various wigs and heavy makeup to personify Edith at various stages of her life. This film and this win solidified Marion as a now bankable star, not just in Europe but also in Hollywood. Marion's work with major Hollywood stars and directors made her a household name and established her as not simply a French actress but a Hollywood actress. As her career has progressed, she has shown how she manages to combine work in French-speaking and English-speaking roles. She has starred in a line-up of major films with ensemble casts of relevant and Oscars winning stars like in Public Enemies directed by Michael Mann opposite Johnny Depp and Christian Bale, Inception opposite Leonardo DiCaprio and Dark Knight Rises (which was her second Christopher Nolan collaboration after Inception), Midnight In Paris directed by Woody Allen, Contagion with Kate Winslet and Gwyneth Paltrow directed by Stephen Soderbergh, The Immigrant opposite Joaquin Phoenix directed by James Gray and Allied opposite Brad Pitt directed by Robert Zemeckis.

Marion Cotillard

A variety of dramatic European films show Cotillard's versatility, like Rust and Bone, Ismael's Bones, It's Only the End of the World and Macbeth. Furthermore Marion has worked alongside her actor and filmmaker husband Guillaume Canet in a number of French films like The Last Flight, Little White Lies and Blood Ties. In 2014 Cotillard starred in Two Days, One Night, a low budget Belgian/French film. The film premiered at the 2014 Cannes Film Festival. She was nominated for the Best Actress Oscar in 2015 too, but lost to Julianne Moore.

Other than acting Cotillard is an established singer and musician. She has performed songs for a variety of film soundtracks and adverts, particularly Dior campaigns and a Chanel No. 5 advert.
Marion's deep work in philanthropy and environmental activism also is impressive. She has been a Greenpeace ambassador since 2001 and has been a member of various organisations focused on saving the forests and helping endangered species. Marion continues to be in amazing films and proves her versatility and elegance on and off screen.

Kate Winslet

Kate Winslet is known as a powerhouse of an actress for her risqué, troubled and often physically demanding roles. Off screen she is down-to-earth, ambitious and a true English rose. She is lauded as one of the most influential actresses of her generation. Her extensive list of non-commercial work overpowers her more typical Hollywood films, showing that what is most important to her is a depth of character which is less exposed in Hollywood films. A number of films she has been in since the beginning of her career have not been the most commercially successful but her performances have always been praised. There's a star quality that she possesses that brings colour and humanity to a story.

Kate's childhood was not easy as she grew up in a low-income household in England. However her parents always nurtured her dream of acting and so she pursued it since school. Her weight, often an obstacle to her getting cast as a minor role in school plays, did not discourage her belief in herself. After leaving school at 16 she worked at a delicatessen while going to acting school and she also got herself an agent. At the age of 17 she got her hands on a script that would change her life. After auditioning for this role she received a call while working on her shift, making a sandwich for a customer. The moment she found out she had got the part, out of 175 potential girls who had auditioned for the role, Kate dropped all her work responsibilities and set off to New Zealand to shoot Peter Jackson's psychological drama called Heavenly Creatures which came out in 1994.

This instant hit made Kate the object of praise by audiences and film critics and a great candidate for further amazing roles that pushed her further into deep character research and performance. Kate consequently caught the eye of fellow thespian and Oscar winner Emma Thompson who cast her in her adaptation of Jane Austen's novel Sense and Sensibility. This 1995 film gave the fresh-faced Kate another moment to shine. This role actually brought Kate her first Oscar nomination for Best Supporting Actress.

"Ultimately, you just have one life. You never know unless you try. And you never get anywhere unless you

Two more British period pieces followed: Jude and Hamlet. But it was in 1997, when Kate was merely 22 years old, when she became a recognized worldwide star for her unforgettable role in Titanic. This film was written, produced and directed by James Cameron and offered equally brilliant performances by Leonardo DiCaprio, Kathy Bates and Billy Zane. Kate plunged (no pun intended!) into this role of playing Rose opposite DiCaprio's Jack. It goes without saying that this movie changed both Kate's and Leo's life. But although nominated for the first time for the Best Actress Oscar for her role in this film she did not win. Instead of following the route of appearing in more big budget Hollywood movies, which Kate could have easily done at that point after Titanic, she followed her desire to

star in lower budget movies, like Hideous Kinky and Holy Smoke! which was written, produced and directed by Jane Campion, who actually led Holly Hunter to win the Best Actress Oscar for The Piano. Quills, Enigma and Iris followed. Kate was nominated for Best Supporting Actress once again for her role in Iris.

Kate grew to be and act mature well beyond her years, and she played roles that were intense, complex and typically in historical settings. She had never really had the opportunity to play somebody contemporary and unconventional. But the opportunity to play the stereotypically "Manic Pixie Dream Girl" of Clementine fell into Winslet's hands. This role in this science fiction romance drama opposite Jim Carrey helped Kate escape the typical British rose film trope while still bringing elaborate and troubled women protagonists to the screen. It was Kate's ticket to exploring even more diverse types of leading ladies. For her role in Eternal Sunshine of the Spotless Mind, Kate was nominated for a Best Actress Oscar.

Kate, now in her early 30s, starred in a variety of projects like Finding Neverland, All The King's Men, Little Children, The Holiday and voicing Flushed Away. These movies were a mixture of box office hits and misses but Kate was always shining on the screen for her masterful performances. Thus, she got nominated once again for Best Actress for her role in Little Children.

Kate's reputation of being a bare-it-all actress, so to speak, has led her to speaking openly about female nudity; that it should not feel shameful, that it is not inappropriate or outrageous for a woman well in her 40s, who has had children, to go nude. She's clear that having a healthy body image is important. She said: "I don't look in the mirror and go, 'Oh, I look fantastic!' Of course I don't. Nobody is perfect. I just don't believe in perfection. But I do believe in saying, 'This is who I am and look at me not being perfect!' I'm proud of that."

This leads me to her most critically rewarded role: The Reader, based on Bernhard Schlink's novel of the same name. Kate played Hanna Schmitz, a far older woman who starts a romance with a 15-year-old school boy Michael Berg (Davis Kross; later played by Ralph Fiennes) in 1958 Germany. The drama was directed by Stephen Daldry who also directed The Hours that starred Nicole Kidman who won the Best Actress Oscar for her role in the film. Kate Winslet's Oscar win was long overdue.

And in 2009 she finally won it. The presentation of her award was quite special as it was essentially presented to her not by one person but by 5 previous Oscar winners on the stage. And it followed with a glorious Oscar acceptance speech.

The Reader is really a story of redemption, coming of age, hauntings of the past and justice. Kate Winslet show superb acting in this film. Every emotion and inner turmoil of Hanna Schmitz is nuanced through Kate Winslet's masterful performance. She was totally tense, pained and in deep worry throughout the film.

The film has largely been criticised for its romanticization of the Holocaust, for the story is set in post Holocaust Germany (between 1958 and 1995), by softening the impact of Nazi aggression toward Jewish people in the plotline. The plot and character focus (especially of Hanna, who we come to find out later in the plot was a concentration camp guard who committed war crimes) were criticised, especially as there is sympathy for Hanna. The pity we feel for Hanna is only supported by the backstory of her relationship with Michael, in which we find a life-changing clue that could potentially save her from being imprisoned for life. But Hanna's personal problems are not an excuse for her heinous crimes.

According to Richard Propes from The Independent Critic: "Were it solely for the performance of Kate Winslet, The Reader would be worth seeing. While it is a film that does not itself measure up to the greatness of Winslet's performance, The Reader is likely to play most successfully to those who accept it solely as a film about Michael and Hanna and who are able to allow its Holocaust themes to reside largely as background exposition."

Kate, after the Oscar win, reconnected with Leonardo DiCaprio and Kathy Bates in Sam Mendes's Revolutionary Road. Actually Winslet and Mendes were married at that time. She was also in Contagion with fellow Best Actress Oscar winner's Marion Cotillard and Gwyneth Paltrow and in Steve Jobs for which she received her most recent Best Supporting Actress Oscar nom.

There is a much more extensive succession of films with Winslet's talent (Ammonite and Avatar 2 to name a couple) but her Oscar history is certainly one for the books. At age 33, she surpassed her own record as the youngest performer to receive six Oscar nominations. Her seventh of course became her most fruitful. Kate Winslet is a driving force in all of her works, without a doubt. She is exploratory and fearless when it comes to her work. Her passion, dedication and innate talent will always be celebrated.

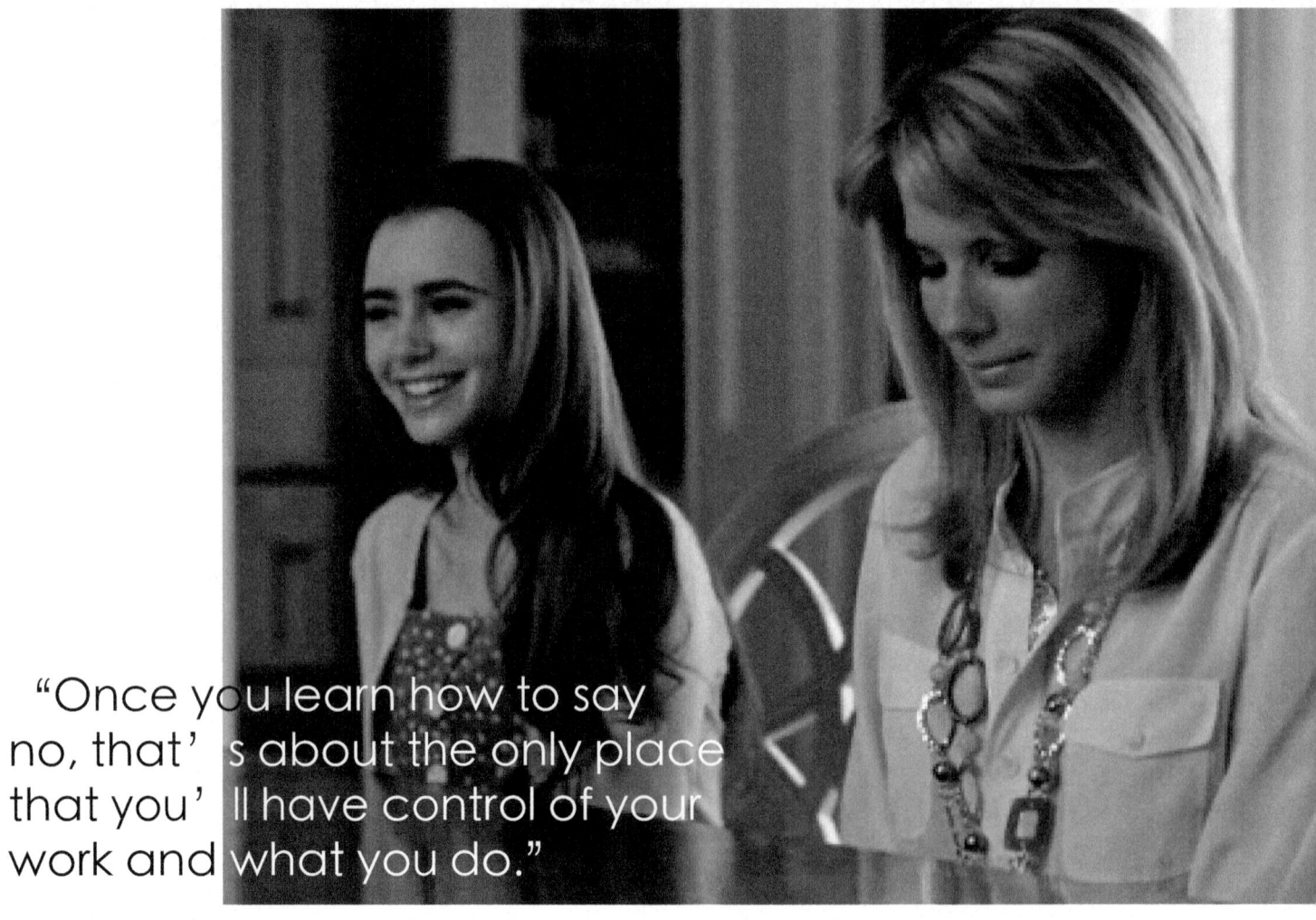

"Once you learn how to say no, that's about the only place that you'll have control of your work and what you do."

Sandra Bullock

Typically a comedic actress, Sandra Bullock freed herself from getting typecast in female-driven comedies when she appeared in The Blind Side. Appearances in string of comedic films since the 90s gave Sandra the impression that she was not made to be an Oscar winner, but she proved herself wrong. Although The Blind Side's content has problematic aspects, Sandra's performance was appreciated by many.

After graduating from East Carolina University with a BFA in Drama in 1982, Bullock moved to New York City to conquer the acting world. While working odd jobs in Manhattan, Sandra took acting lessons with Sanford Meisner and consequently secured minor roles in TV and in student films. After appearing in a string of movies and even starring opposite Shirley MacLaine in Randa Haines Wrestling Ernest Hemingway, Bullock had her Hollywood breakthrough after appearing in Speed opposite Keanu Reeves in 1994. This movie helped Bullock establish her image as a leading lady in rom-coms.

She then appeared in While You Were Sleeping, Two If By The Sea, Practical Magic (opposite fellow Oscar winner Nicole Kidman), Forces Of Nature and Gun Shy. Coming into the 2000s Bullock starred in arguably her most notable roles: in Miss Congeniality and The Proposal. But there was more to Sandra than meets the eye; she's more than just a beautiful, stylish and effortlessly funny woman. She's fluent German (since her mother is German and her growing up in Germany until age 12) and she is a well-versed film producer who has produced many of her films since the 90s. Her acting range also goes much further than rom-coms.

Thus, in 2009 Sandra after much deliberation (three times turning down this role in fact) took on the role of playing real life woman Leigh Anne Tuohy in The Blind Side. Sandra, unsure of whether she had the ability to leverage this role since she was so different from Leigh, ultimately made the right decision. The Blind Side was directed by John Lee Hancock and co-starred Quinton Aaron who played the real-life Michael Oher, aka Big Mike. Although the film focused on the journey of Michael Oher through the eyes of Leigh, the two actors truly carried this film hand in hand.

Sandra Bullock

The story follows Leigh Anne, a feisty interior designer, mother of two and wife of a wealthy businessman who meets Michael, a lost, poor and foster care boy. The two accidentally befriend one another and start a journey to help Michael live a better life than that of his trash-picking, couch-surfing past in Tennessee. She helps him find his purpose which ultimately leads him to play professional football in the NFL. An unexpected match for sure, but this story proves exactly the fact that two people from complete polar opposite walks of life can help one another and bring meaning to each other's existence.

Bullock became an ultimate blonde bombshell, God-fearing, stiletto-stomping power woman, which was very different to what she was used to depict in her previous comedies. Sandra truly evoked the meaning of this film—that we should not take privilege for granted. However, the film has been criticised for the "white saviour narrative" and Uncle Tom and racial stereotypes evoked in the story.

The Blind Side, with a $29 million budget, made a whopping $309.2 million in the box office. Bullock's performance was said to be "convincing enough as an energetic, multitasking woman of the New South, who knows her own mind and usually gets her own way" by the New York Times.

Turns out Sandra's doubts about taking on this role were uncalled for. She was a natural in this film. And for her performance in The Blind Side she received her first Oscar nomination and ultimately won it for Best Actress at the 2010 ceremony. After two decades of working in the film industry, Sandra hit her winning streak. Sandra wore a shimmering champagne-hued Marchesa gown. A classic smooth silhouette paired with asymmetric lace beaded embroidery on the top half and sequined bottom evoked an element of old Hollywood glamour, especially with her side-slicked hair and red lip.

Bullock managed to get nominated one more time in 2014 for Best Actress for her role as Dr. Ryan Stone in the survival space movie Gravity. This two-hander with George Clooney directed by Alfonso Cuaron continued to show the versatility and leading lady energy that Bullock possesses on screen. Bullock has starred in further well received works like in Our Brand Is Crisis, Oceans 8 and Bird Box: all remarkable female driven films.

Sandra's career has been ever evolving for the better. She proves that real talent and intelligent career moves don't get you typecast, they get you further than that. Her down to earth and warm attitude as well as her impeccable style makes her a classic that will always be admired.

Sandra Bullock

Natalie Portman

As the saying goes, "You are the product of your own environment". Natalie Portman, since the age of 12, has worked with some of the biggest names in cinema and consequently became one herself very quickly. The professional, fast paced and adult environment she grew up in moulded Natalie into a powerhouse of an actress, as well as an activist and beauty icon.

The Israeli-American got her big break in acting at the age of 12, when she was cast in Luc Besson's action-drama Leon: The Professional opposite Jean Reno and Gary Oldman. The film catapulted the mature and ambitious-beyond-her-years Natalie to stardom. She then starred in major films like Mars Attacks and the Star Wars franchise during her teenage years.

By her early 20s, not only did Natalie graduate from Harvard with a bachelor's degree in Psychology, but after studying she returned to acting and decided to transition to more adult characters like those in Closer, V for Vendetta and Goya's Ghosts. Natalie's superior choice in diverse, bankable and to this day popular films proved her versatility. She also starred in The Other Boleyn Girl and Brothers.

However after almost 20 years of starring in ensemble casts, Natalie finally had the spotlight only on her. Her moment to shine was in 2010, when she starred in Black Swan, opposite Vincent Cassel and Mila Kunis, directed by Darren Aranofsky. Natalie inhabited the role of ballet dancer Nina Sayers in this psychological horror film. The story is a spiral into insanity from the perspective of career, image and perfection-obsessed Nina.

Natalie said this about her role: "There were some nights that I thought I literally was going to die. It was the first time I understood how you could get so wrapped up in a role that it could sort of take you down."

"I tend to lean toward strong female stories. I want to make things that don't already exist out there."

Darren Aronofky's Black Swan is an incredible psychological thriller about a tortured, insecure ballet dancer trying to secure a role in a production of Swan Lake. The main character, Nina Sayers, finds herself competing with a rival ballerina, Lily, for the main role. Nina is a perfect fit for one half of the role, the pure and fragile White Swan, but she's not quite sultry and fierce enough to play the Black Swan. Nina begins to lose her tenuous grip on reality as she fights to embody this complicated character.

Now, just reading that plot summary, it's pretty clear that it takes an immensely talented actress to swap back and forth between the White Swan and the Black Swan, right? Well, that is exactly what Natalie Portman pulls off in her role as Nina. Her performance snagged her a well-earned Academy

Award for Best Actress. Nina Sayers is an intensely demanding role, and Portman rose to the occasion and absolutely nailed it.

Portman's performance is downright iconic. The line, "I'm the swan queen, you're the one who never left the corp" is intensely quotable, and it's partially thanks to Portman's feverish delivery. She plays the role with passion throughout. Portman is able to skilfully oscillate between Nina's more subdued behaviours and the wilder mannerisms that she adopts as her sanity slips.

Amazingly, Portman told the media that she didn't actually relate to any of the deeply held insecurities of Nina. In the film, the character is plagued by feelings of ineptitude and is tormented by her overprotective mother. Portman's performance was so convincing that people began to wonder whether or not her career was affected in similar ways.

"You always have to understand your character," Portman told Vanity Fair, "but you don't necessarily have to have felt the same thing yourself. You just have to imagine what it might be like."

Mila Kunis gave an excellent performance too. While she did not win Best Supporting Actress that year, she was nominated. Like Portman, Kunis also underwent rigorous training in the art of ballet. Lily's character truly embodies the essence of the Black Swan, and Kunis plays the role with an astoundingly frightening sultriness. Portman had actually recommended Kunis to Aronofsky for the role.

Winona Ryder also pulls out a small but stunning performance as Beth, an ageing ballerina. In 2010, it had been quite some time since Ryder had been given a chance to shine on screen. I was incredibly thankful to see her again in such a fantastic and fitting role. Beth snaps at Nina in one particularly chilling scene, and while it's a short sequence, it's uniquely memorable.

Natalie Portman

Interestingly enough, there was a bit of controversy about Portman's performance. This focused particularly on her dancing. Dancer Sarah Lane did serve as a dance double for Portman, as Portman's intensive training still didn't quite sell her as a master ballerina. That's not a criticism of Portman, of course: her performance and dedication is still incredible, but no one can become a fully trained dancer in a year's time. Dance Magazine's Wendy Perron pointed out that many falsely believed that Portman did all of her own dancing, which led to the film's choreographer, Benjamin Milliepied, to defend Portman. While Portman and Kunis were both impressive, it's important to give credit to their "dance doubles": Sarah Lane and Maria Riccetto.

That being said, Portman still had to put in quite a bit of training. Aronofsky is known to really put his actors through the ringer, as his films put a heavy emphasis on performance. Portman recounted that "it was great but also physically hard" to do the final climactic scene where Nina fights with herself in the mirror. Portman also discusses how her dance double did a great deal of the actual dancing, but she still had to do quite a bit of it herself. "With all this broken fake glass and fighting and jujitsu—it was kind of insane." Portman said. "That was the only time I got injured. I mean, I got ballet injuries, but that was the day I got a non-ballet injury, I hit my head and had to get an M.R.I."

Black Swan was a divisive film upon its release. Not everyone was into its horror-tinged melodrama. In fact, Entertainment Weekly called it "one of the year's most love-it-or-hate-it movies". Still, even the critics who hated it couldn't help but pile on praise for Portman's fantastic performance. Even if the psychological aspects of the film aren't quite your thing, Portman's performance is engrossing. It's easy to get swept up in the world of Nina Sayers thanks to Portman's highly in-tune performance. Fun fact: Natalie met her husband Benjamin Milliepied on the set of Black Swan; he served as choreographer and dancer in the film.

At the Oscars, the pregnant Natalie wore a draped aubergine purple dress by Rodarte to accept her award. The chiffon flow with a shorter front gave some leg action for Natalie. Her soft side-swept waves and tousled earrings were a perfect addition to the jewel toned elegant look for the Oscars.

After this highlight of Portman's career, she starred in a variety of commercial and indie type films like Thor, Knight Of Cups and Planetarium. For her role of playing the real-life figure Jackie Kennedy in Jackie, a biopic focusing on Jackie's life during her times of being a First Lady, Portman received her second Best Actress Oscar nomination in 2017. Song To Song in 2017 was Portman's second collaboration with director Terrence Mallick after Knight Of Cups. Both actually feature fellow Oscar winner Cate Blanchett. Whatever role it may be, Natalie brings it with truth and intelligence like in Annihilation or Lucy In The Sky.

Natalie Portman is known to be the most well rounded, thoughtful and intelligent actress today. Her classic look works in all films and her hunger to grow and adapt in film and in life makes her exciting to follow.

Jennifer Lawrence

Jennifer Lawrence, ever since getting scouted by a modelling agent, has impressed casting agents instead with her mature and effortless acting talent. Her decision to pursue an acting career as opposed to modelling helped her secure important roles opposite Hollywood actors early on.

Her first acting role was in Garden Party in 2008. That same year she was in The Burning Plain that co-starred Charlize Theron who played the older version of Lawrence's character. In 2010 Lawrence had a breakthrough in her career after getting cast in Winter's Bone, a mystery drama set in rural Ozarks in Missouri. Lawrence, still a teenager during filming, took on the role of a mother figure to her poverty-stricken family when her mother suffers from debilitating mental health and father goes suddenly missing. Lawrence plays the 17-year-old Ree Dolly who starts to clash with her crime- and drug-infested family and locals in order to secure financial stability and find out about her missing father. Lawrence's performance gained her first Oscar nomination for Best Actress at the 2011 Oscars. Thus was the beginning of her reputation of being labelled a promising young actress.

Lawrence, now a great audience attraction, especially due to her a marketable personality since she is known for her self-deprecating and unrestrained energy, made her very likeable. She was cast in two major projects: X-Men: First Class where she played a new version of Mystique and Katniss Everdeen in the wildly successful Hunger Games film series. After the legendary success of these films, Lawrence caught the eye of David O'Russell, who was looking for an actress to play Tiffany in Silver Linings Playbook.

"Even as far back as when I started acting at 14, I know I've never considered failure."

Who is this highly flawed but charmingly likeable woman named Tiffany Maxwell? Performed with honesty by young talented actress Jennifer Lawrence, provoking engagement and empathy, Tiffany, self-described as "sloppy and dirty", is a woman in search of her own happiness dealing with internal trouble, trauma and darkness. In 2012's Silver Linings Playbook, directed by David O. Russell, starring Bradley Cooper and Robert De Niro among other great

Jennifer Lawrence

Hollywood actors, Tiffany mediates between her self-discovery and improvement and her on-screen partner Pat's journey through his disrupted mental health.

For her portrayal, Lawrence was awarded with an Oscar for Best Actress at the 2013 Academy Awards ceremony. Many viewers and critics saw that she was capable of a consistent performance that combined wonderful dialogue with other characters and a strong ability to create a memorable female lead.

Jennifer Lawrence infuses in her role both the mediator and the individually-standing female protagonist. As she goes through a self-destructive stage at first and evolving to a caring and aware person, what really comes out in the performance is this promising potential for development. On the one hand, she supports Pat in coping with his bipolar disorder and on the other, Tiffany preserves her uniqueness and accomplishes visible growth that ultimately leads her to a more joyful life. She stays true to her direct way of communicating: she is brutally honest, speaking her mind. This is the cause of many inadequate conversations and situations within the film that contribute to its comedic, light and hopeful tone. Tiffany is promiscuous but she's also hurt; she follows her drive and desire, igniting the connection between her and Pat. A lovely chemistry develops between Cooper and Lawrence which is another skill admired by many in the young actress.

Jennifer Lawrence

One of the impressive instruments she uses in her acting is the ability to sharply switch between moods, tones and expressions. From calm, quiet, hidden behind her black hair that covers her face and eyes to an erupting volcano of emotion, anger, passion and enthusiasm. This is seen, for instance, in the memorable dinner scene with Pat as well as towards the film's end and the emblematic dance competition. Like Pat and the movie itself, as the dance sequence, Lawrence plays a chaotic yet attractive Tiffany who connects with the audience on an emotional level. She belongs to the film's world and manages to stand out in it with her wit, strength and particular personality.

Silver Lining Playbook is about improvement, about being the best possible self a person can be despite the many challenges of life and in this plot's case: mental illness. And even more so, as this cinematic story is about humanity. Jennifer Lawrence creates a very human character, a highly flawed but charmingly likeable woman, imperfect and inspiring, problematic and uplifting—all in one enriching, winning performance!

David O Russell said this of Lawrence: "You showed up as a raw talent with no neurosis and no self-consciousness. She was completely fearless. She has a certain energy that hasn't been in movies in a while. Young and old and loose and powerful and focused. You walk in 20 minutes into the movie and you take over the movie. I remember feeling, when we shot your intro, there was an awareness that we we're introducing a new talent and a new energy that felt very special. It was like, 'Who's this person?' You owned this space."

Richard Coliss from Time magazine said that: " Lawrence is that rare young actress who plays, who is, grown-up. Sullen and sultry, she lends a mature intelligence to any role, whether as the one sane person in Winter's Bone or as Raven (Mystique) in X-Men: First Class. Her Tiffany at first seems more dangerous than Pat Jr."

Silver Linings Playbook ultimately made $236.4 million at the box office against a $21 million budget. Jennifer's performance in this hit made her the second youngest Best Actress Oscar winner ever. At the 2013 ceremony, Jennifer wore a pale pink strapless dress by Christian Dior Couture. She managed to trip up the stairs on her way up to accept the golden statuette.

After the success of Silver Lining Playbook, Jennifer teamed up with David O' Russel again for two more entertaining films: American Hustle and Joy. In 2016 and 2017 Lawrence starred in her most risqué roles to date: Passengers and Mother!.
Jennifer Lawrence's consistency of bringing leading lady characters has made her one of the highest paid actress in Hollywood, and one of most sought after too.

"I believe that a creative career is only as good as the risks that you take with it."

Cate Blanchett

Woody Allen sure can bring incredible films to the forefront of Academy success. He directed Diane Keaton in her Oscar-winning performance in Annie Hall. He did so once again with Cate Blanchett for her arresting performance in Blue Jasmine. Cate's Oscar win was legendary because she had taken her time ever since the 90s to design her reputation of a powerful film actress. After an amalgamation of substantial and critically acclaimed roles, Blue Jasmine was the shining star atop of the pyramid of earlier successes.

After breaking into film acting in 1996, Cate would get her first Best Actress Oscar nomination after only 3 years in 1999 for her role as Queen Elizabeth I in Shekhar Kapur's Elizabeth. In 2005 she won the Best Supporting Actress Oscar for depicting the iconic Katharine Hepburn (who had won a total of 4 Oscars herself) in The Aviator directed by Martin Scorsese. Cate would get two more Best Supporting Oscar nominations for Notes On Scandal and I'm Not There, plus another Best Actress Oscar nom for her reprisal of Elizabeth in Elizabeth: The Golden Age. Cate's consistent Oscar-nominated films would also be infused with more memorable performances like in The Lord Of The Rings Trilogy, The Curious Case Of Benjamin Button and Hanna.

In 2013, Cate starred in Blue Jasmine written and directed by Woody Allen. Blue Jasmine upon further investigation is rather reminiscent of an earlier drama: A Streetcar Named Desire. A woman entering a new, unfamiliar and rather uncomfortable environment, filled with uncomfortable situations and people, while she slowly submerges into a dark mental state, sounds like a timeless story. And Woody Allen's modern take is even more thought-provoking as it applies to modern relationships and modern society. The film is truly meaningful through and through. Even down to the choice of names of the characters. Cate Blanchett as Jasmine: symbolic of the modesty, sensuality and purity that the character effortlessly represents, but also love and motherhood, two aspects of herself that she does not truly get to experience properly. This brings her a lot of pain. Blanchett takes us on an emotional experience that leaves us speechless till the very last second. We feel sorry for Jasmine yet are judgmental of her at the same time.

Furthermore, the quality of the secondary and antagonistic characters in the film, like Hal (played by Alec Baldwin) is excellent. Jasmine's crook of a husband, Hal, perfectly reminds us of the antagonist Hal 9000 from 2001:Space Odyssey. His secretive and sleazy ways ultimately ruin Jasmine's hypergamous and lavish lifestyle. Or what about Ginger, Jasmine's estranged, lower class adoptive sister, played by Sally Hawkins and Chilli, Ginger's ignorant and pushy boyfriend, played by Bobby Cannavale? They are a perfect combination that allows Jasmine to creep further into her mental illness. Their suffocating spice leaves the audience with a bitter taste in their mouths.

In the wide array of legendary cinema Allen has created, Blue Jasmine may be his best work yet. The visuals and scenery are crisp and refreshing, yet the message is dark and heavy. This is a combination that only Cate Blanchett can help bring to the forefront. A woman who is draped in a Chanel dress, a Birkin bag and Cartier watch living off of her husband's money and living a luxury life in Manhattan, could make a viewer not at all sympathetic to her. But she suffers from bipolar disorder that she has kept under wraps since her tumultuous childhood. This woman is hated by the audience yet she evokes sympathy for her past is brought to the surface as the film moves forward. We finally realise that there is no one out there who cares for Jasmine, who worries for her, who is willing to help her; she is left abandoned and blue.

The 2014 Oscars were incredibly competitive for the Best Actress category. Cate went head-to-head with Amy Adams for her role in American Hustle, Sandra Bullock for Gravity, Judi Dench for Philomena and of course the ever-present Meryl Streep for August: Osage County. After years of consistent nominations Cate became the sixth actress to win both a Best Supporting and Best Actress Oscar. She became the second ever Australian to win the Best Actress Oscar, the first being Nicole Kidman. Blue Jasmine made $99.1 million at the box office with an $18 million budget.

Cate Blanchett

At the ceremony, Cate wore an Armani Prive gown that was worth $100,000 and her Chopard jewellery including earrings with 62 opals, plus a 49-carat diamond bracelet and ring cost approximately $18 million. Pure timeless elegance.

In 2016 Cate was nominated for Best Actress Oscar once more for Carol. She teamed up with a female-led cast in Oceans 8 in 2018. Cate continues to appear regularly in great quality productions. Our eyes are always peeled for work starring her. Comparing Cate's fragile and insecure Jasmine to who she is in real life, a confident, self-assured and bold woman proves her talent no end, and for that she is considered one of the greats.

"If you're reading IMDB, half of it's made up. You can't trust it or Wikipedia, which is just lies, lies!"

Julianne Moore

Julianne Moore has the ability to portray complex female characters who face hardships but with a soft and vulnerable edge. A strong female character is not supposed to be perfect; she is flawed and realistic. Julianne Moore brings inner anguish to her characters that makes us truly feel compassionate when circumstances give her suffering. That is why she won the Best Actress Oscar in 2015 for her career-defining role in Still Alice.

Julianne was born to an American father and Scottish immigrant mother. Julianne, her two younger siblings and her parents would live in various parts of the US due to her father's job of being a military judge. The constant moving around, changing schools and homes made Julianne an insecure and shy child who had difficulty making friends. Nonetheless this on-the-go lifestyle gave Julianne a wide outlook on life as well as an ability to be a chameleon in terms of behaviour. This reinvention of character helped her acting career. But acting was certainly not in Julianne's interest growing up. A good girl by nature and straight-A student, becoming a doctor was the plan of action, but after appearing in school plays, one of her teachers encouraged her to pursue acting. The sensible Julianne turned to her parents who too would approve of this aspiration to act but insisted on her getting a BFA in Theatre at Boston University first.

In 1983 she graduated and moved to NYC where she worked as a waitress and eventually got her start in Off-Broadway and small TV roles. Before turning to film, Julianne actually thrived on TV. She won a Daytime Emmy Award for Outstanding Ingenue in a Drama Series in 1988 for her role in a TV series called As the World Turns.

In 1990 Moore made her film debut in Tales from the Darkside: The Movie. Her TV and film experiences were integral to her moving forward in giving diverse performances on screen. She also starred in The Hand That Rocks the Cradle, The Gun in Betty Lou's Handbag and Body Of Evidence. These were mostly supporting roles but nonetheless Julianne appeared in multiple movies a year in the 90s that accumulated to her eventually securing major roles. In 1993 she starred in an ensemble cast film called Short Cuts directed by Robert Altman who actually cast Julianne himself after seeing her in a production of Chekhov's production of Uncle Vanya. Julianne worked on this stage production for four years before her film debut actually. This role in Short Cuts was Julianne's career breakthrough.

This breakthrough followed more breakthrough roles that helped make Julianne a relevant and popular actress, like in Vanya on 42nd Street which was a film version of the Uncle Vanya play that Julianne did in the late 80s, and Safe in 1995.

The rest of the 90s consisted of diverse roles like those in Nine Months, The Lost World: Jurassic Park and Boogie Nights. She received her first Oscar nomination for Best Supporting Actress for her role in Boogie Nights, playing a troubled adult film actress trying to gain custody of her son during the late 70s and early 80s.

In the year 2000 Julianne got her first Best Leading Actress Oscar nomination for her role in The End Of The Affair a romance drama opposite Ralph Fiennes. 2003 was Julianne's highlight year because she became the 9th performer to receive two Oscar nominations in one year. She was nominated for best supporting actress for her role in The Hours (opposite Meryl Streep and Nicole Kidman) and for Best Actress for her role in Far From Heaven.

Julianne's filmography is so extensive and diverse. Furthermore she has a record of 5 movie releases in one year, in 2014. This was also her most rewarding year. All 5 films were once again as diverse as ever. But one truly showed Moore's mastery of acting: Still Alice. This film was directed by Richard Glatzer and Wash Westmoreland and was based on Lisa Genova's bestselling 2007 novel of the same name.

Julianne Moore

Julianne plays Alice, a 50-year-old Columbia University Linguistics professor, who suddenly begins to experience memory loss, which quickly leads her to being diagnosed with early onset Alzheimer's disease. Of course, Alice's world comes crashing down and her family. The seemingly perfect, well rounded, educated, financially steady family with lots of memories and love is hit by this sudden shock. Alec Baldwin plays her husband, John, and Kristen Stewart, Kate Bosworth and Hunter Parrish play their children.

Alice's disease is sudden and develops quickly for the worse. Through the eyes of Alice we watch her forget small things at first. Her mind is hazy as if she is underwater or lost in a thick fog. She can't remember where she is located during her run around Columbia's campus, then forgets the syllabus for her lecture and then her dinner plans. Her relationships with her family, especially her husband, become rocky. She is apologetic and they sympathise with her, but this condition is unfixable. It only gets worse. Alice eventually leaves her job after telling the dean about her condition and this makes her even more lost and helpless. After all, her work, her career was always her pride and joy.

She begins to rapidly decline. Alice begins to forget words, her children's names and eventually that her children even are her children. The whole family is so busy and Alec's character is not willing to be by his wife's side as support and help due to his own work ambitions. With Alice's memory quickly abandoning her, Kristen Stewart's character comes back home from working in LA to take care of her mom. Alice says, "I used to be someone who knew a lot. No one asks for my opinion or advice anymore. I miss that. I used to be curious and independent and confident. I miss being sure of things. There's no peace in being unsure of everything all the time. I miss doing everything easily. I miss being a part of what's happening. I miss feeling wanted. I miss my life and my family." These words bring forward the essence of Alice and what is most important to her: to simply feel adequate and in control.

Moore's incredibly touching and tear-jerking performance about a woman losing herself was lauded as her finest work yet. According to the LA Times, "Moore is especially good at the wordless elements of this transformation, allowing us to see through the changing contours of her face what it is like when your mind empties out." The 2015 Oscars were not a disappointment either because Moore also won the Best Actress Oscar.

Moore has graced the screen many more times in commercial and indie favourites like Hunger Games: Mockingjay Part 1, Kingsman: The Golden Circle and The Woman In The Window. Julianne Moore is not afraid of exposing the inner turmoil of a woman, that's what she does best. Even in silence, no dialogue, her characters expose a lot. She said, "I'm looking for the truth. The audience doesn't come to see you, they come to see themselves." Julianne can adapt to many genres and characters whether they are protagonists or antagonists. They all resonate.

Brie Larson

From teen star in young adult flicks to serious mature actress in drama and action films, Brie Larson's on-screen presence in diverse female roles makes her a successful actress and activist through and through. At the age of 26 she won the Best Actress Oscar in one of the most unique, exhilarating and meaningful films: Room.

Brie, along with her mother and sister, moved to Los Angeles to fulfil her dream of acting right before her 9th birthday. This led to Brie getting cast in late-90s TV shows as a child actress. In 2004, at the age of 14, Brie made her film debut in 13 Going On 30, which followed with more light-hearted films like Sleepover, Hoot and Greenberg. In 2010 she starred in a more antagonistic role in cult favourite Scott Pilgrim vs The World. Coming into her early 20s Brie starred in even more relevant and entertaining films but in supporting roles like in 21 Jump Street, Don Jon and Spectacular Now.

She had reputation of playing uncomplicated, angsty and mean characters; the mean and popular girl trope. This typecast Larson. However there was more to Larson than playing girly mean girls. After he watched her in the movie Short Term 12, Larson was cast by director Lenny Abrahamson in his film called Room based on Emma Donohue's novel of the same name in 2010. This 2015 film showed Larson in a completely different light.

"Women are such strong, powerful leaders, and a lot of the time, we play it silent."

She plays 24-year-old Joy Newsome, a young mother to 5-year-old Jack who refers to her as Ma. They live in a tiny box of a shed which they refer to as Room. The two are trapped in this room, with only a skylight as their light source, and minimal furniture and food. Jack, having been born and bred in this room, has never seen the outside world. Joy and Jack are held hostage by Old Nick, who we find out is Joy's abductor who impregnated her after abducting her when she was 17. And ever since Joy has not been exposed to the world and has been a prisoner to Old Nick. After all these years of being missing, Joy sets up a plan with Jack who is old enough to follow along, to escape from Room.

Brie Larson

This heartfelt drama about freedom, the mother and child bond and the transition from child to adult is a nail-biter to say the least. The details help paint the big picture, which makes it a masterpiece. Brie Larson and co-star Jacob Tremblay bring a real mother son relationship to the screen. The push and pull relationship is authentic between Joy and Jack. Joy's depression and anguish for freedom is counteracted with Jack's naivety and imagination. They are like a team who saves one another throughout the whole story.

Empire wrote: "Larson has been threatening for years to truly break out, and Room should be the film to make it happen. She's so raw as to verge on unwatchable, the pain she conveys is just too upsetting to sit with." Brie's earnest performance made her the Best Actress Oscar winner in 2016. At the same ceremony, Alicia Vikander won Best Supporting Actress for The Danish Girl.

Larson wore a royal blue spaghetti strap Gucci gown to the ceremony. It had ruffled panels down to the floor and minimal pearl earrings and wreath hair clip. Her raspberry lip colour matched the extravagant jewelled brooch belt which made the look more glamorous.

Brie Larson

Although her career has been seemingly smooth sailing, especially for someone who has been acting since childhood, she brought to light her struggle maintaining her work in the industry. She mentioned in the Hollywood Reporter Actress Roundtable that she actually tried to quit acting all together many times due to the anxieties surrounding constant casting rejections.

After the monumental success of Room, Brie went on to star in further major ensemble works like in Free Fire and Kong: Skull Island that were both set in the 1970s. She also appeared in a more heartfelt drama like The Glass Castle, which gave yet another taste of her dramatic chops. Larson also first directed and produced Unicorn Store, a fantasy comedy drama in 2017. The film is described by the Independent as: "A feminine spin on the many, many films we've seen about men who refuse to grow up. And it's a worthy entry, with plenty of unexpected laughs that play on the universal misery of adult life. Larson approaches Unicorn Store with such earnest emotion—both in her performance and the film's direction—that the film quickly becomes something much more."

Then came Captain Marvel in 2019, yet another Marvel superhero film but with a woman as the lead superhero. This was Larson's and Samuel L. Jackson third collaboration on screen after Kong and Unicorn Store.

Brie Larson is nothing short of versatile and multitalented. There is a fire from within in all of her roles. It is good that she decided not to quit acting because we are sure to see much more amazing work from her. Brie always gives it her all.

"Comedy was my sport. It taught me how to roll with the punches. Failure is the exact same as success when it comes to comedy because it just keeps coming. It never stops."

Emma Stone

Emma Stone's trademark red hair and husky voice, paired with an approachable, sarcastic and girl next door type of charisma, makes her one of the most fun to watch actresses these days. She mixes high profile films with more experimental works that showcase her versatility. But her underlying sense of humour and lightness is always present. Emma Stone is incredibly charming on and off screen.

She dropped out of school and moved to Los Angeles with her mother at the age of 15 to pursue an acting career, much like Brie Larson and Hilary Swank who also dropped out of school and moved to LA with their mothers. "Project Hollywood" was underway for Stone upon the big move: this was the title of her PowerPoint pitch to her parents in order to get them on board with her plan to succeed in Hollywood as an actress.

After appearing in a number of small TV roles, Emma secured her first feature role in Superbad. Emma's natural talent in comedy boosted her as a comedic actress in further work like in The House Bunny and Zombieland. Easy A (2010) was her breakthrough when she assumed the title character of high schooler Olive Pendergast in this comedy drama. Stone, now in her early 20s, decided to stray away from getting typecast as the quirky, girl next door type to more mature but nonetheless lively characters like in the rom-com Crazy, Stupid, Love and historical drama The Help, both in 2011. Both roles were very different and showed Stone's versatility.

Amazing Spiderman, Croods and Gangster Squad followed, making Emma a household name. In 2014 she was nominated for Best Supporting Actress for her role in Birdman. But her moment of true star power happened in 2016.

La La Land (2016), a romantic musical film directed by Damien Chazelle, starred Emma Stone and Ryan Gosling. It was Stone's and Gosling's third collaboration together. This on-screen union was powerful. La La Land takes us on an emotional rollercoaster with Stone playing Mia and Gosling playing Sebastian, chasing their Hollywood dreams of becoming an actress and musician respectively. The story is about never giving up on your dreams, taking risks, sheer luck, the hardships of struggling artists and of course love. There is a lot that you can do cinematically with such wonderful themes, and Damien Chazelle did not hold back with making it as magical as possible. The story is human because it is relatable to all of us but the theatrical choreography, catchy musical numbers and dreamy tone under the premise of idyllic Californian landscapes, tranquil lighting, vibrant costumes and set design felt like stepping

into Hollywood in the 50s. Chazelle told the Hollywood Reporter: "There is something very poetic about the city I think, about a city that is built by people with these unrealistic dreams and people who kind of just put it all on the line for that. Now more than ever we need hope and romance on the screen, and I think there's something about musicals that just gets at something that only movies can do."

Emma Stone's peak in this film was her performance of the song "Audition (The Fools Who Dream)". This moment in the film singlehandedly truly made Stone worth winning an Oscar. She stands under a single spotlight and nothing more, yet this is the most powerful moment. Vox described Stone's role of playing Mia as "brittle and brave, fervent and fantastic, a little goofy and extremely skilled. It's a nuanced, wonderful performance. She uses every square inch of her expressive face, letting even the smallest of twitches tell an entire interior story."

Stone glows with enthusiasm, ambition and enchantment in the film—she dives into singing and dancing even though she isn't professionally trained beforehand. At the same time, she portrays desperation within the artist's creative process and frustration inside her romantic relationship to Gosling's character Sebastian. Thus, the nuanced performance of Emma Stone will live on forever as she managed to beautifully personify notions of aspiration, hope and zeal.

Perhaps, most of all, La La Land is about dreaming, about not giving up on one's most important dreams even if that means compromising another essential aspect of life. As viewers, critics and film-lovers have pointed out, Emma Stone's character Mia starts out full of colour, which is reflected in her clothes, for instance. She looks for opportunities for acting jobs and then falls in love—a wonderful adventurous affair performed by Stone and Gosling with true chemistry and lovable attraction. It is then that both characters realise that making it big will mean sacrificing time, and putting in the effort and to truly explore what their dreams mean.

Emma Stone's character realises that she should be more confident in her skills and ideas. She begins to write on her own which turns her into the artist she has always aspired to be. Then, her colours become less and less bright, more serious until in the very last scene Mia wears a black dress, having achieved her professional dream but also having rejected the dream of passionate love. Emma Stone approaches her protagonist with wit, care, sensitivity and vulnerability alongside much performative charisma in a nostalgic love letter to the musical film. This makes her work memorable in the eyes of spectators and a layered portrayal deserving of many revisits, in-depth analyses, interpretations and explorations.

The film grossed $446 million worldwide against a production budget of $30 million. The 28-year-old Stone made $26 million from this film alone, making her the highest paid actress in 2017 according to Forbes.

At the 2017 Academy Awards La La Land got 14 nominations, making it the third film to receive that many. It won 6 of them, including Chazelle winning Best Director (La La Land was his third ever feature film), which made as him the youngest winner of Best Director at the age of 32. Stone went head-to-head with Isabelle Huppert, Ruth Negga, Natalie Portman and Meryl Streep for Best Leading Actress. And she won!

She wore a 1920s flapper-inspired gown by Givenchy to accept the matching golden trophy. This golden figure-hugging beaded wonder took 1,700 hours and a team of 11 to create. It is one of the most exquisite dresses on the red carpet because it gives a nod to old Hollywood's classic glamour.

Viola Davis won for Best Supporting Actress for her role in Fences. Actually 3 out of the 5 Best Supporting Actress

nominees were black that year. Viola's win made her the first African-American to achieve the Triple Crown of Acting.

Stone's win may have been slightly overshadowed by that year's awkward Best Picture scramble when La La Land was falsely named as that year's winner and Moonlight came out as reigning supreme. To this day, this moment's cringe factor is remembered.

Nonetheless Emma Stone's title of leading lady carried on to further work like Battle of the Sexes, a biographical sports film about Billie Jean King. The Favourite, a period black comedy set in 18th century England starred Stone,

Olivia Colman

A fairly new actress to the Hollywood scene, Olivia Colman, is a true English Rose: down to earth, self-deprecating and unpretentious. She often plays royalty and so it's fitting she won the Best Actress Oscar for exactly such a role. But she didn't play royalty in the classic sense; but someone more bizarre and ridiculous, not in the least bit noble minded. This is somebody only Olivia Colman would succeed in embodying.

The privately-educated Colman has been immersed in acting since school. At age 16 she played Jean Brodie in a school production of The Prime of Miss Jean Brodie. Maggie Smith actually won her Best Actress Oscar for the same role in the film adaptation. Colman briefly attended Cambridge University, where she starred in a Footlights production. The very same Footlights group that Emma Thompson started her acting journey on.

At the age of 26 Colman made her professional acting debut in a BBC comedy sketch show Bruiser. More TV shows followed suit, particularly comedies. Her TV profile is way more elaborate than her film one, actually. But Colman started starring in minor roles in comedy films in the early 2000s like in Confetti, Hot Fuzz and Grow Your Own. She also voiced a number of animations. In 2011 Colman played Carol Thatcher in Iron Lady opposite Meryl Streep. Behind those prosthetics you would hardly know it's her.

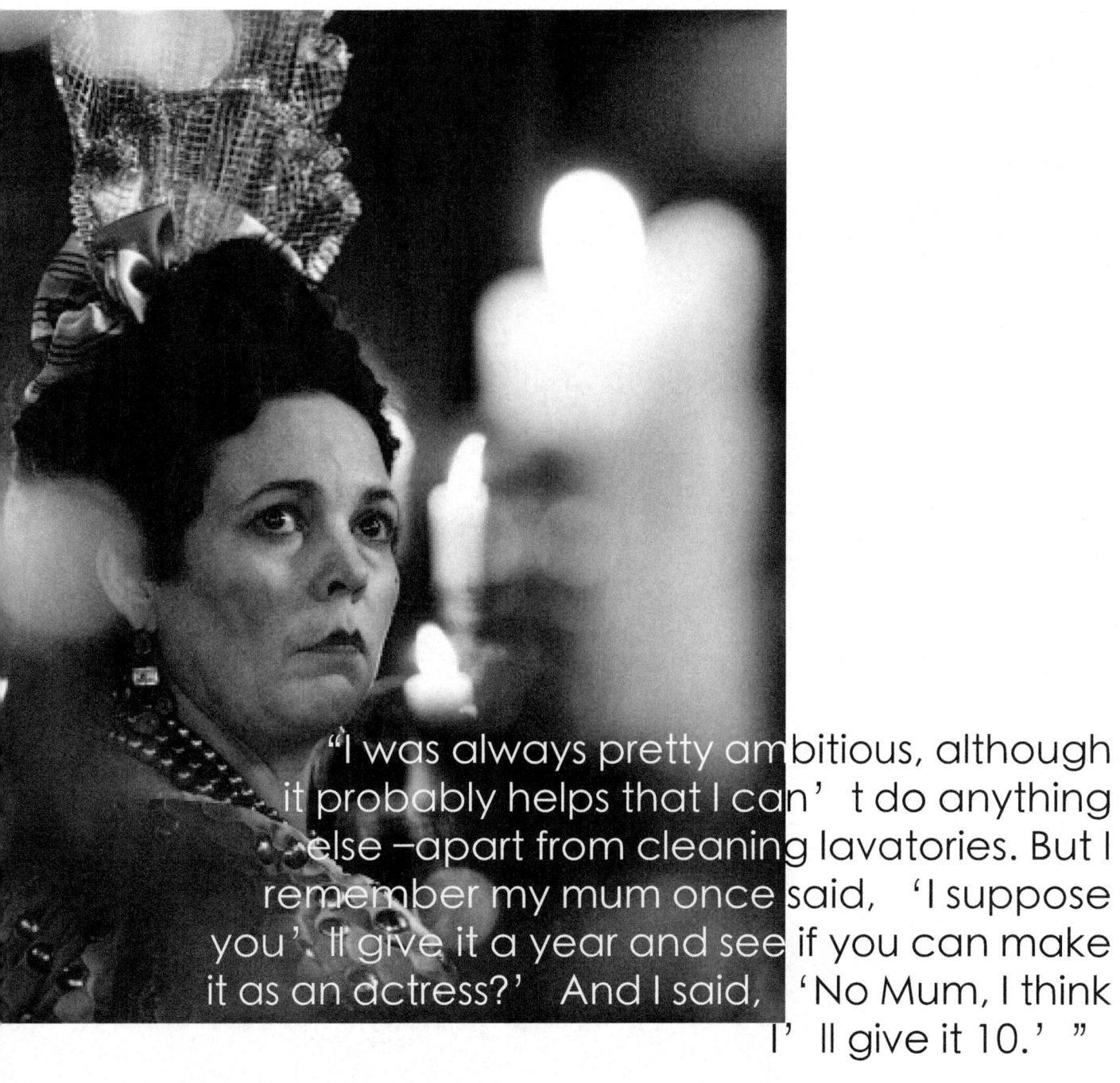

"I was always pretty ambitious, although it probably helps that I can't do anything else —apart from cleaning lavatories. But I remember my mum once said, 'I suppose you'll give it a year and see if you can make it as an actress?' And I said, 'No Mum, I think I'll give it 10.' "

Colman's film career was a slow burn. She was not really Hollywood material, because she was not as young and not as relevant as other actresses, and she was incredibly British. This was very niche. Her as a leading lady

was not in the books, especially in the Hollywood scene. However this changed in 2019 when she was the first and only choice to star in The Favourite.

The Favourite is a rare find. It was directed by Yorgos Lanthimos, famous

for his offbeat, dark comedy films, that make him an auteur. It has three female leads that are in a battle with one another and it showcases major star-studded acting talent in a non-glamorised, commercial way. The film, with a $15 million budget, made $96 million, proving further that female-driven films are tremendously profitable. The Favourite was actually Colman's second collaboration with Lanthimos, after The Lobster (2015).

Olivia Colman and Rachel Weisz as a powerful trifecta. Stone was nominated for Best Supporting Actress for The Favourite in 2019. Colman won the Best Actress Oscar that year. Following, in 2021, Stone appeared in the Disney origin story as the titular role of Cruella De Vil in Cruella, directed by Craig Gillespie, opposite Emma Thompson. In 2024 Stone won her second Oscar for her titular role of Bella Baxter in Yorgos Lanthimos directorial; Poor Things. Ultimately Stone's "Project Hollywood" came out to be a success! Emma Stone loves to challenge herself by taking on diverse female leads; inspiring ones that make us dream a little bigger.

The Favourite follows three women: Sarah, Duchess of Marlborough played by Rachel Wiesz, Baroness Abigail Masham played by Emma Stone and Queen Anne played by Olivia Colman. Two cousins, Stone and Weisz characters, compete to be the Queen's favourite. They take whatever ridiculous measures are needed to earn that title of being the favourite. Queen Anne, played by Colman, is equally, if not more, volatile, unhinged and problematic. The Favourite is about jealousy, the toxicity of power and female sexuality.

Olivia Colman is explosive, complicated and completely in her element in this film. The Guardian states: "Colman is simply superb as the miscast monarch, combining childish pathos with queenie cantankerousness, and a palpable sense of pain. For all Colman's perfectly timed comedy, it's these moments of Anne's existential angst that really strike home."

The 2019 Best Actress Oscar contenders were diverse and very competitive: they included Yalitza Aparicio in Roma, Glenn Close in The Wife, Lady Gaga in A Star Is Born and Melissa McCarthy in Can You Ever Forgive Me? Olivia Colman beat all of these women and won the award. A genuinely shocked and shaky Colman gave one of the most comedic speeches through her tear-filled eyes, as her co-stars and director watched her in tears too.

Following the success of The Favourite, Colman was nominated for an Academy Award for Best Supporting Actress for her role in 2020's The Father and in 2021 she served as executive producer of The Lost Daughter, for which she was nominated for the Oscar for Best Actress.

Colman is arguably more prolific in television. Her work in Broadchurch, Fleabag and The Crown are among her most memorable. And these performances further prove that she can be funny and dramatic on screen.

Colman's career unravelling is unique. But so are her characters. Her skill and talent on film and TV is ever-evolving. The projects get bigger and bigger and more recognized. It is exciting to see what else she might bring to the screen.

Olivia Colman

"Being horrible in a big film is a quicker nosedive than doing an obscure film and making no money."

Renee Zellweger

The multi-talented Renee Zellweger met her second wave of Oscar success in 2020 by winning the Best Actress Oscar for her role in Judy where she plays the iconic Judy Garland. The 2020 Oscars were looking promising for Zellweger who was the oldest Best Actress nominee. With the previous two years winners being Frances McDormand, then 61, and Olivia Colman, then 45, Renee Zellweger, aged 51, amplified the power of older, mature actresses over the age of 40, winning the title of Best Actress among a sea of fresh-faced actresses.

The Texas-native Renee, of Norwegian and Swiss descent, caught the acting bug during her English studies at the University of Texas. She began to star in pretty relevant films in the early 90s that have become cult favourites at this point like Dazed and Confused, Reality Bites and Empire Records. After these romantic coming of age films Renee had her breakthrough in 1996 after appearing in Jerry McGuire as the lead role opposite Tom Cruise. This film was a box office hit and made Renee a relevant name in romantic comedies.

This led her to getting cast in her most famous role as Bridget Jones in Bridget Jones's Diary in 2001. She would reprise this iconic role two more times. This romantic comedy film directed by Sharon Maguire, based on Helen Fielding's 1996 novel of the same name, starred Colin Firth and Hugh Grant as well as a handful of other English classical actors and comics. It tells the story of the 30-something, single, love-starved and eternally-in-an-existential-crisis Bridget. Renee truly disappeared in this role; she was no longer the deep-thinking, heavy-accented Texan. She was now the British-accented, unpretentious, pudgy-faced, chain-smoking Bridget, with mousy hair who always found herself the butt of the joke. Renee truly brought one of the most memorable and original female characters on film, on the same level as Reese Witherspoon with Elle Woods in Legally Blonde. The film was an obvious box office hit and Zellweger was nominated for the Best Actress Oscar in 2002.

Another Best Actress Oscar nomination followed in 2003 when she starred in another completely different and much more epic project: Chicago, a musical film set in the 1920s opposite Catherine Zeta-Jones and Richard Gere, directed by Rob Marshall. Renee's character, a husband-killer who dreams of becoming a vaudevillian, gets sent to jail and meets a conglomerate of other husband-killers including Zeta-Jones. Although Zellweger did not win the Best Actress Oscar for this dazzling singing and dancing role for herself, Catherine Zeta-Jones did win the Best Supporting Actress Oscar. Chicago goes down in history as one of the most successful film musicals with 12 overall Oscar nominations and 6 wins.

2004 was an even more fruitful year for Renee who won the Best Supporting Actress Oscar for her role in Cold Mountain, an epic war drama based on the bestselling 1997 novel of the same name by Charles Frazier. Cold Mountain co-starred Nicole Kidman and Jude Law opposite Renee who played Ruby Thewes. All three are on a journey for survival during the American Civil War. Ruby becomes the right-hand woman and aid to Nicole Kidman's lead character of Ada. The two women try surviving the hardships of living in Cold Mountain, a Confederate territory.

After a number of successful productions like Shark Tale, Bee Movie, Case 39 and Cinderella Man, Renee took 6 years off from work. At the height of her career, a superstar stepped down from her throne. You would think that she was never coming back to the spotlight. She talked about her conscious decision to go on hiatus to Vanity Fair: "I was fatigued and wasn't taking the time I needed to recover between projects, and it caught up with me. I got sick of the sound of my own voice: it was time to go away and grow up a bit. I found anonymity, so I could have exchanges with people on a human level and be seen and heard, not be defined by this image that precedes me when I walk into a room. You cannot be a good storyteller if you don't have life experiences, and you can't relate to people."

After 6 years of not appearing on screen at all, it was 2016 and it would seem that the younger film going generation would have no clue as to who Zellweger was, or those who did had long forgot about her. So when she came back to the big screen in 2016, it was with a box office failure in The Whole Truth. Her relevancy was no more—or so it seemed.

But there was one tried and true successful cinematic formula: Bridget Jones. As the original Bridget Jones fans grew up, so did Renee. It was time for a comeback. In 2016 Zellweger made her third and most recent reprisal of the now pregnant and older Bridget Jones in Bridget Jones's Baby, which reminded us of Zellweger's status as a major movie star. This was her comeback to the spotlight.

Only 3 years later, in 2019, she starred in Judy, a biopic. Directed by Rupert Gold, it is an adaptation of the Olivier- and Tony-nominated West End and Broadway play End of the Rainbow by Peter Quilter. Renee played the role of Judy Garland in the final year of her life as her health deteriorates on stage in Britain. The film is infused with flashbacks of Garland's career during her teenage years, especially her filming of The Wizard Of Oz. Judy showed the complicated history of Garland from childhood as a teen star to now, when her personal life is in shambles, and her health is reaching a boiling point after decades of substance abuse and overworking.

Renee Zellweger

Renee embodies Garland and gives humanity to the iconic star as well as performing all of Garland's most popular songs by herself without making it a caricature. This film once again serves as a reminder of Renee's skill and passion for full immersion into a character: mind,

body and spirit. And this performance resonated stronger than ever with audiences and the Academy. it made Renee a 2-time Oscar winner, but now, she won Best Actress in 2020.

Sify describes her performance as such: "She sinks into the character with amazing realism, recreating the mannerisms, posture, facial expressions and vocal cadences of the legend. She excels remarkably in portraying Judy Garland to perfection, including singing her dozen songs with a few of them hitting the right notes, to sway you into loving the legend despite her shortcomings."

The 2020 was one of the most dazzling years for film. 1917, Parasite, The Irishman, Once Upon A Time In Hollywood, Little Women, Marriage Story, Jojo Rabbit and Joker were a few of many cinematic triumphs made by Hollywood newcomers like Greta Gerwig and Bong Joon Ho and also veterans like Martin Scorsese and Quentin Tarantino. Renee among 4 other incredible actresses was the veteran and her Oscar win was well deserving for her transformative performance of embracing Judy Garland.

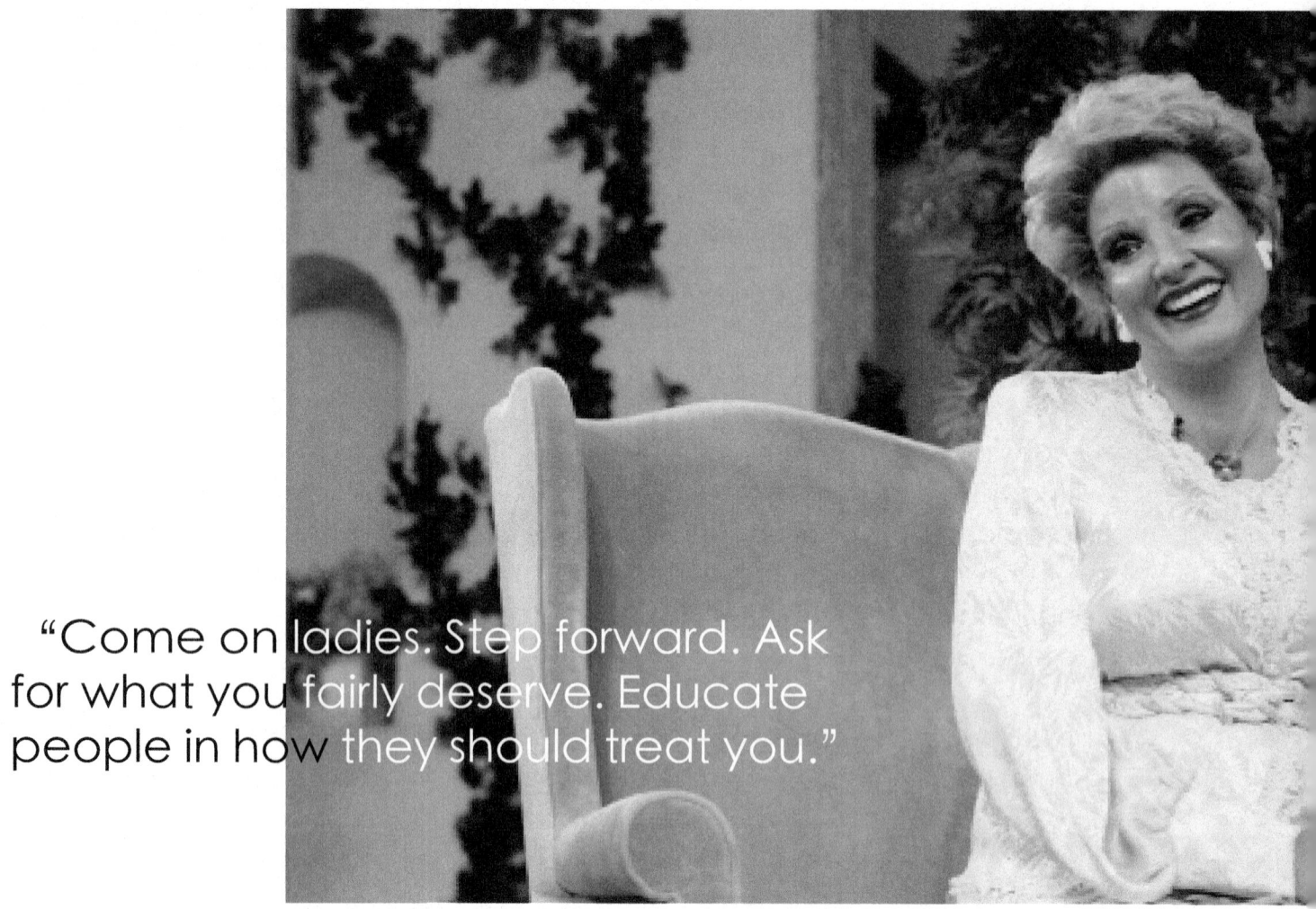

"Come on ladies. Step forward. Ask for what you fairly deserve. Educate people in how they should treat you."

Jessica Chastain

In 2008, at the age of 31, Jessica Chastain made her film debut in Jolene. After tirelessly designing a reputation of a promising young actress since her teens, she found it hard to secure roles due to her unconventional redhead looks. Nonetheless, the Sacramento-born-and-raised starlet followed her passion for performance on stage and TV at first, and then transitioned to film.

Although Chastain starred in more low-profile films after Jolene premiered, it was not until 2011 that she had a career breakthrough. She was on audiences' and film execs' radars due to appearing in 6 film releases in 2011 alone: the most prominent being in Terrence Mallick's The Tree Of Life and Tate Taylor's The Help. The former won the Palme d'Or at the 2011 Cannes Film Festival and the latter garnered multiple award nominations for Jessica's acting, including the Best Supporting Actress award at the Academy Awards. With the star-studded cast in The Help and its poignant historical narrative, Jessica proved that she can hold her own in a Hollywood feature.

In combination with film acting, Chastain still continued stage acting, a passion that she had since childhood after reading Shakespeare at school. Lawless, Madagascar 3, Zero Dark Thirty and Mama were further films that Chastain starred in that won critical and financial acclaim. These diverse genre choices helped Chastain showcase her versatility and not be typecast as the token redhead she often was afraid of being depicted as.

In hindsight, it must feel very rewarding and more deliciously enjoyable to receive your first Best Actress Oscar after designing a long-list of fabulous filmography as opposed to receiving it early in your career. Jessica Chastain's filmography up until her Oscar win consists of major motion pictures like Interstellar, A Most Violent Year, The Martian, Crimson Peak, Miss Sloane, Molly's Game and Ava, to name only a few of the more well-known ones.

In 2022 Jessica Chastain deservedly received her Best Actress Oscar for her role in 2021 biographical drama, The Eyes of Tammy Faye directed by Michael Showalter and co-starring Andrew Garfield. In the film, we follow the life of Tammy Faye who falls in love with Jim Bakker (Garfield) in college during a Christian class. The two partner up

Jessica Chastain

romantically but also professionally to become, over time and well into the 1990s, a huge televangelical business. As the couple become very popular show presenters, Jim's sleazy ways and secret business deals lead to their downfall.

We watch the monumental rise of Tammy from an ambitious yet sweet natured Christian girl to a drugged-up and washed-up televangelist fighting for her sanity. Unfortunately so, and early on, we notice the conniving and manipulative ways Jim has power over poor Tammy, who simply, because of her good nature, wanted to bring love and peace to the Christian community. But Jim had ulterior motives to rip off people's money. The Eyes of Tammy Faye is essentially a movie about broken marriages, deceit, religion as a base for business, liberalism in a bigoted society and sexuality.

Jessica Chastain, as did many other Best Actress Oscar winners, made a full transformation to look and sound like Tammy Faye Bakker. Charlize Theron did it for Monster, Nicole Kidman for The Hours and Marion Cotillard for La Vie En Rose. Transforming physically in fact makes it easier to get into character and inhibit their true mannerisms and voice. The delicate and feminine features of Chastain morphed into a wider-jawed, overlined-lipped and busty Tammy Faye with exaggerated drawn-on eyebrows and gaudy nails. Not only did Chastain spend 4 to 7 hours in the makeup chair but she recorded an applicable soundtrack to the movie with her real vocals that were used in the film during performances on the Christian show.

Chastain's performance is full of sorrow, rage, desire and helplessness that make us root for Tammy and pity the shameful circumstances she finds herself in. Chastain's integrity to give Tammy the sympathy and respect she deserves is evident and Garfield's Jim as a foil to Jessica's Tammy is also a good addition to this film, but at time's Garfield seems miscast for he does not quite reach the convincing corrupt sliminess we want him to portray.

I think the essence of Tammy is best highlighted in her words to Jim, early on in their relationship: "I'm a very practical person. And what you see is all there is of me. You know, I don't pretend to be something I'm not, because what you see is all you get. And I love people. I have a genuine, genuine love for people. And I hurt when people hurt, and probably a little more dramatic than people would like me to be. But I enjoy that. That's just who I am."

To the Oscar ceremony Jessica wore a gaudy, yet graceful, custom Gucci ball gown in metallic, peach and lilac hues. The ruffled hem and metallic thread and sequin give a 1970s touch, very much stemming from Alessandro Michele's signature vision but also as a nod to The Eyes Of Tammy Faye, as a section of the film is set during the 1970s. The dress was beautiful; in fact Jessica always looks phenomenal on the red carpet.

What is even more admirable about Jessica are her views and advocacy for feminism and gender equality in the workplace, better wages for female actors and giving women a platform to speak up on sexual harassment. She's about female empowerment and support.

From very humble beginnings of being a deeply shy theatre kid coming from a low-income family, with a mother as her only parent and a young sister who had committed suicide early in her life, it is truly commendable to see the incredible success and happiness of Jessica Chastain. Her Oscar win is the cherry on the cake of her achievements, for it took her many years of hard work and determination of doing what she loves to earn it. Watching Jessica Chastain in any work she does is a treat and her efforts for gender equality and support for women's rights remain inspiring.

Michelle Yeoh

Malay born Chinese actress, Michelle Yeoh, has been working in the film industry since the early 80s. Her rise to fame happened in the early 90s with her reputation of being a multitalented actress and stunt woman that garnered her lots of success in Hong Kong action films. Since then her rise to worldwide fame became imminent and by the early 2000s she situated herself as a marketable and very successful asian actress in Hollywood. It took over almost 40 years for Michelle Yeoh to become revered as the best actress in the world, when she won the Best Actress Oscar in 2023 for a role that totally changed her life.

When Jessica Chastain and Halle Berry, both previous Best Actress Oscar winners, announced the nominees of the Best Actress Oscar Award on stage on the night of the 2023 Academy Awards there was an obvious cheer from the crowd when the name Michelle Yeoh was uttered, more resounding than when the other nominees were announced; Andrea Riseborough, Ana De Armas, Michelle Williams and Cate Blanchett.

It took 21 years, since Halle Berry's legendary Best Actress Oscar win in 2002 for her role in Monsters Ball, for another woman of colour to receive the prestigious accolade. The crowd roared and cheered for Michelle Yeoh when her name was uttered as the winner; the second woman of colour and first asian woman to win the Best Actress Oscar.

When it came to Yeoh accepting her prize, a pinnacle of acting success, she wore a white Dior Haute Couture gown to accept the Best Actress in a Leading Role Oscar in the May 2023 ceremony. She looked ethereal and graceful in the timeless dress and with her hair swept to the side with silver accessories to compliment her look, she looked glamorous with the feathery fringe embellishments but in a classy way, which is the best way to represent yourself at such a prestigious event.

Everything Everywhere All At Once, is the movie that Michelle appeared as the lead in and won the Oscar for. It is a blend of genres you could think off; but typically considered an absurdist-action-fantasy-comedy family drama co-starring more iconic actors; Ke Huy Quan, Stephanie Hsu, Jamie Lee Curtis and James Hong. Directed by Daniel Kwan and Daniel Scheinhert, two fellow Emerson College Graduates, with a budget of less than $25 Million the film became a box office hit, garnering $141.2 Million and a plethora of media attention. Along with Yeoh's Oscar win, the movie received a further 6 Oscars: Best Picture,Best Supporting Actor for Quan, Best Supporting Actress for Curtis, Best Director and Best Original Screenplay for Kwan and Scheinert, and Best Film Editing. Everything Everywhere All At Once is currently estimated to be the most awarded film of all time.

In Everything Everywhere All At Once we follow the rocky relationships of Evelyn Quan Wang (Yeoh) with her husband Waymond Wang (Quan) and daughter Joy Wang (Hsu). The Chinese-American immigrant family is faced with problems with the IRS for not following tax rules and as a result are taken on an audit case by IRS inspector Deirdre Beaubeirdre (Curtis). The movie takes us on an instant visual journey when Evelyn is faced with the challenge to save the parallel universes she exists in from being destroyed by an evil being (who turns out to be the evil version of her daughter in another universe). Evelyn switches from one universe to another in the multiverse and fights opposing forces and along the way follows a journey of self discovery and creating strong bonds with her husband, daughter and with life itself. It is a story of coming to terms with her past as an immigrant in America, finding comfort in not being a perfect family but sharing unconditional love for each other and also ironically understanding that life has no meaning.

Michelle Yeoh allows herself to explore and showcase all sides of her talent; including her stunt skills.

Despite this legendary success of Michelle, she has a rich history before this that cannot be left unnoticed. Having come from a well off Chinese-Malasian family, Michelle sought to build a career of her own from a early age. Her love and involvement in dance, particularly ballet pushed her to enrol in London's Royal Academy of Dance. Just like fellow Oscar winner Halle Berry, Michelle was a pageant queen too; repressing Malaysia in 1983's Miss World and even winning the title of Miss Moomba International in 1984.

Soon after Yeoh pursued her love for martial arts and acting by being an action star in Hong Kong action movies. She starred alongside Jackie Chan in films like Police Story and My Lucky Stars in 1985.

Michelle Yeoh

Yeoh's big break in Hollywood was her big action debut in 1997's Tomorrow Never Dies, playing a "female Jame Bond," opposite Pierce Brosnan. Further major work followed; making Yeoh a Hollywood staple in predominantly Asian focused storylines like 2000s Crouching Tiger, Hidden Dragon and 2005s Memoirs Of A Geisha. 2007 Sci-fi movie Sunshine, opposite a star studded cast, made Michelle a signature actress in Hollywood movies.
Her more recent major projects are Crazy Rich Asians, Shang-Chi and the Legend of the Ten Rings and the upcoming Avatar movies.

Despite the media previously minimising her importance on the film scene as an asian actress, over time Michelle Yeoh has proven she is above the judgmental voices and has become a fabulous actress full of energy and class who proves that women can have it all regardless of their race and age. She truly can be and do "everything everywhere all at once," unapologetically.
With the ever-changing landscape of filmmaking, we can look forward to more women of colour not only leading major motion pictures but also winning Oscars; particularly in the Leading Actress category. It is a pleasure to see diverse ethnic and racial representation of people from all backgrounds on film.

Printed in Great Britain
by Amazon